EMILY DICKINSON AND THE
RELIGIOUS IMAGINATION

Dickinson knew the Bible well. She was profoundly aware of Christian theology and she was writing at a time when comparative religion was extremely popular. This book is the first to consider Dickinson's religious imagery outside the dynamic of her personal faith and doubt. It argues that religious myths and symbols, from the sun-god to the open tomb, are essential to understanding the similetic movement of Dickinson's poetry – the reach for a comparable, though not identical, experience in the struggles and wrongs of Abraham, Jacob and Moses, and the life, death and resurrection of Christ.

Linda Freedman situates the poet within the context of American typology, interprets her alongside contemporary and modern theology and makes important connections to Shakespeare and the British Romantics. Dickinson emerges as a deeply troubled thinker who needs to be understood within both religious and Romantic traditions.

LINDA FREEDMAN is the Keasbey Research Fellow in American Studies, Selwyn College, Cambridge.

EMILY DICKINSON AND THE RELIGIOUS IMAGINATION

LINDA FREEDMAN

CAMBRIDGE
UNIVERSITY PRESS

CAMBRIDGE
UNIVERSITY PRESS

University Printing House, Cambridge CB2 8BS, United Kingdom

Cambridge University Press is part of the University of Cambridge.

It furthers the University's mission by disseminating knowledge in the pursuit of education, learning and research at the highest international levels of excellence.

www.cambridge.org
Information on this title: www.cambridge.org/9781107006171

First published 2011

A catalogue record for this publication is available from the British Library

Library of Congress Cataloguing in Publication data
Freedman, Linda, 1980–
Emily Dickinson and the religious imagination / Linda Freedman.
p. cm.
Includes bibliographical references and index.
ISBN 978-1-107-00617-1
1. Dickinson, Emily, 1830–1886–Religion. 2. Dickinson, Emily, 1830–1886–
Knowledge–Theology. 3. Dickinson, Emily, 1830–1886–Symbolism.
4. Typology (Theology) in literature. 5. Theology–United States–History. I. Title.
PS1541.Z5F74 2011
811'.4–dc22
2011026301

ISBN 978-1-107-00617-1 Hardback

To Sam

Contents

Acknowledgments

The idea for this book grew out of a doctoral thesis that was funded by the Arts and Humanities Research Council and supervised by Dr Alan Marshall at King's College London. I am extremely grateful to the Council and to Alan for all the help I received. I would also like to thank Clive Bush and Janet Floyd for the support and guidance they provided, and the British Library, the Houghton Library, Amherst College Archives and the Jones Library in Amherst, for access to all research materials.

The book has been finished with the help of a great many people. I am indebted to Susan Manning and Fiona Green for the valuable advice they offered on making the transition from thesis to book. I am grateful to Selwyn College and the Cambridge English Faculty for giving me a fellowship and providing an intellectually stimulating environment in which to complete this project, and to Ray Ryan and Maartje Scheltens for bringing it to press.

My greatest thanks must go to my family. My parents have always encouraged and supported me. My father-in-law, Lawrence, read every word of the manuscript and offered extremely constructive advice. My husband, Sam, introduced me to Dickinson and has helped this project grow from a casual chat in a bookshop cafe to what it is today. Most importantly, my children, Ava and Oscar, have made this the best year of my life and have been beautifully behaved while I finished the manuscript.

A note on texts

It is a tribute to the recent work by scholars such as Virginia Jackson, Martha Nell Smith, Sharon Cameron and Marta Werner that what constitutes a 'Dickinson poem' remains an open question for students of her work. Together with the publication of Franklin's *Manuscript Books*, Smith's development of the online Dickinson archive has made available for view a number of Dickinson's manuscripts, exposed the incongruities of her handwriting and punctuation and begun a discussion, in which there is surely still much work to be done, about the forms in which Dickinson's 'poems' come. My use of quotation marks here is an acknowledgment of Jackson's argument that theories of lyric reading have governed Dickinson's edition and reception. She states a fundamental problem: versions of lyric reading took many of Dickinson's lines out of their contingent relations in letters to family and friends and so made everything that was not a lyric disappear. Dickinson, too, was party to her own reception, copying lines from her letters onto bifolium sheets and either binding them into fascicles or leaving them unbound and dispatching poems in letters or letter-poems to chosen readers. It is certainly true that, reprinted in the editions of Johnson or Franklin, these lines appear to us as lyrics and in our eagerness to read them as such we have lost much of the historical contingency of the letter. But it may also be true that some of the qualities associated with lyric reading can be applied to Dickinson's letters, many of which are thoroughly performative, governed by personae we find in the fascicles and sets, or signed with literary and biblical pseudonyms. In this area, Marietta Messmer's *A Vice for Voices* is an invaluable resource.

In the wake of this scholarship, then, I continue to refer to poems and letters because these words still seem to me to be the best we have to express Dickinson's writing, although letter-poem and epigrammatic verse become increasingly appropriate in her last years. I do not refer to them as lyrics because the lyric carries a narrower set of assumptions about form and purpose. Unless otherwise stated, the poems are reproduced and dated according to Franklin's Varorium edition, but the numbering of Johnson's 1955 edition is also given. I adopt Johnson's terms 'variant' and 'dash' in order to refer to Dickinson's use of alternate (or perhaps consonant) words and the gestural marks that have been variously interpreted as punctuation by her editors. I do this for ease of communication but in the awareness that the graphic fixity suggested by 'variant' and 'dash' is somewhat at odds with the appearance of Dickinson's manuscripts. I discuss the variants or the appearance of poems as/in letters and fragments when it seems directly relevant to my argument about Dickinson's religious imagination. But I would advise students to make full use of the archival scholarship and the *Manuscript Books* to take their interest in Dickinson further. I also refer to Dickinson's 'poetic purpose' or 'vocation', by which I mean to express the drive, intensity, artistry and eagerness of her verbal expressions. I think it entirely possible, and indeed necessary, for letters and fragments to be considered as part of this vocation. Dickinson was sometimes slight or silly, but she was rarely thoughtless when putting pen or pencil to paper.

Introduction: Dickinson and religion

In 1862 Emily Dickinson was at the peak of her creative power. This was the time when many of her most interesting poems with broadly religious themes emerged, including her famous description in a letter to Thomas Wentworth Higginson of God as an 'eclipse' that her family worshipped each morning.[1] Dickinson's well-known 'eclipse' is a small example of her ambivalent feelings about religion and faith. An eclipse has a curious and dominating presence. In the early world, eclipses were worshipped because they inspired fear. Even today, on the rare occasions when an eclipse appears, it draws our curiosity and our wonder. This poet's eclipse is both sarcastic and appreciative. Her sarcasm no doubt stemmed from a disregard for unquestioning faith. But her disregard was combined with a more equivocal appreciation of religion. That appreciation is the subject of this book.

The animating absence of Dickinson's 'eclipse' gave James McIntosh the subject for his book *Nimble Believing: Dickinson and the Unknown*. This book is an important precursor to my work in several ways. I am in complete accord with his claim that 'the unknown is not so much a subject she takes up as a condition of her poetic existence she perpetually comes up against'.[2] This seems to me to be a wonderful way of expressing the vitality of Dickinson's poetic texture and the paradox of her epistemic reaching enabled and halted by its own limitations. His emphasis on the variety of Dickinson's religious tones and the influences of Puritan and liberal thought has also helped my study of her religious imagination. But McIntosh, like many excellent critics before him, returns in the end to the question of whether Dickinson really believed in God.[3] Through her poetry he ascribes Dickinson a personal faith which encompasses (and partly relies upon) doubt, concluding that, for her, the unknown was the ground upon which one truly encountered God. So, his study assesses Dickinson's poetry as an expression of faith.

I

This is not another answer to that question, but a departure. I am advancing a way of reading the allusive complexity of Dickinson's work that recognises we do not need to decide whether or not she believed in God to understand the way in which religion fed her imagination and her sense of poetic purpose. I aim to show how Dickinson's Puritan heritage, as it mixed with the liberal Christianity growing up in Boston, and fused with classical mythology, was a source of poetic enrichment and not a barrier to creativity that she simply reacted against.[4] In a complementary but rather different approach which takes in a number of other writers, Elisa New has argued that the Puritan theology of Jonathan Edwards and Edward Taylor was carried on in poetry in the years after Emerson's 'Divinity School Address' (1838) called for a new age of 'poet-priest[s]'.[5] She suggests that growing up beside the mainstream tradition known as Emersonian was another tradition that was, in effect, anti-Emersonian because it found poetic language structurally resistant to the very idea of transcendence and Ralph Waldo Emerson's tenet of deferral incompatible with the realisation of the poem. For New, Emerson's reinvention of religion as a species of poetry was tested and found wanting by the very poetic innovators to whom he addressed himself.[6]

Like New, I do not think that poetry became Dickinson's secular way of being religious or that poetry replaced religion in Dickinson's thought. I will draw some preliminary distinctions between religion, theology and faith as they are used in this book. Religion, I take to be a more inclusive term, encompassing doctrine and dogma as well as tales, temperament and tone. Theology is the study and rationalisation of God, which relates philosophically to epistemic absence and aesthetically to the representation of a notional absolute or 'slant' truth-telling (Fr1263). Faith is both a matter of disposition and part of an epistemic framework of uncertainty which necessarily includes doubt. Dickinson may be sarcastic, subversive and witty but she also has a deep investment in the poetic thinking through of theological problems and she is fascinated by the structures of faith. The relationship between Dickinson's ironic distance and her philosophical or empathic investment in religion is often difficult to negotiate and the collision is frequently important to the quality of her verse. To provide a generalised explanation risks making Dickinson seem schematic, which she certainly was not. But to assume that the relationship is incidental or simply contradictory misses a lot. It helps to notice that Dickinson's undercutting of religious attitudes is frequently greater than her undercutting of religious objects. It is also important that Dickinson's masterful ironies often relate to poetic as well as religious enthusiasm.

If Emerson forged a connection between religious and poetic office, Dickinson more commonly explored the relationship between religious and poetic difficulty.

The argument is this: there is a vital relationship between Dickinson's ideas about poetry and her ideas about religion which encourages a critical flexibility between literature and theology. This reciprocally informing relationship has high stakes for both disciplines. Theology lends poetry a rich vocabulary for understanding the difficulties of poetic expression and vocation which so often appeared to Dickinson to be shrouded in the same kind of epistemological darkness as God. In return, Dickinson's poetry allows for a particular structuring of thought which can help us negotiate theological problems. Some of the most pertinent examples of this reciprocity are found in Dickinson's meditations on sacrifice and resurrection where the form of the verse actually helps clarify some of the theological complexities surrounding loss and return even as those complexities inflect Dickinson's understanding of the permanence or impermanence of her own poetic self.

But it is important not to claim Dickinson too absolutely for a long dark night of the soul or to declare an eternal truce between art and religion. Literature and theology have much to lose from this reciprocal relationship if their differences are not preserved. There is anguish in Dickinson's religious imagination, but there is also humour and wit. This is part of the relationship I explore. Poetry makes a place for irreverence in theology and it is also able to challenge it and probe its meanings and doctrines. The province of the two is different, and Dickinson is profoundly interested in province, place and boundary so it would be wrong to think she is not aware of this and even more wrong to think she does not exploit it. The relationship between embodiment and incarnation, representation and revelation in the first chapter is one example of the tension, as well as the debt, that exists between art and religion and such tension illustrates the advantage of addressing theological issues poetically rather than from a position of faith.

Dickinson's poems are able to illuminate religious and theological difficulties even as those difficulties often seem intensely relevant to her own poetic identity and quest and this is because she understood poetics to be engaged in a similar kind of epistemological enterprise as religious modes of thinking.[7] This is why her poetry is sometimes able to structure theological problems as well as render the many tones and emotions contained within religious narratives and practice. Her best poems test the reach of human experience and knowledge, exposing the uncertainties

and gaps at the heart of her poetic endeavour through their engagement
with religious themes. Religion is more than a context in which to read
Dickinson; it gave her the conceptual and emotional vocabulary with
which to stage and explore the epistemic problems at the core of her own
aesthetic.

IMAGINING THE 'BEYOND'

Dickinson's very specific knowledge of particular Puritan and liberal theologies together with her interest in comparative religion make her religious imagination poetically distinct and intellectually interesting. But
it is important to first understand the more basic drive that led her to
hold poetry and religion in an imaginative analogous relationship and
that lay beneath her intelligent probing of inherited and contemporary
ideas. Four poems from 1862 help provide a general introduction to the
dynamic exchange Dickinson creates between artistic and religious forms
of imagining the 'beyond'. The first, 'I found the words to every thought',
suggests that she turned to religion as an artist who understood the animating power of the unspeakable and who felt herself to be simultaneously
subject to, and representative of, an overwhelming force. It conceives of
the problem of inspiration as Platonic illumination – an apprehension of
an absolute which her experiential verse cannot render in comprehensible
'words'.

From the second, 'This World is not Conclusion', we get a sense of
Dickinson's ambivalent feelings about faith and her deep preoccupation
with different attitudes towards the unknown. The third and fourth poems
illustrate the connection between that preoccupation and Dickinson's
sense of poetic purpose. 'I dwell in Possibility' has often been regarded as
a kind of Dickinsonian manifesto precisely because of the way it portrays
openness to the beyond as the necessary condition of poetic endeavour.
But there can be little doubt that it shows Dickinson in one of her more
optimistic moods which is why I have juxtaposed it with 'From Blank
to Blank' which indicates the difficulties she saw in poetic and religious
journeying.

Dickinson wrote 'I found the words' in the same year that she commented to Higginson on her family's worship of an 'eclipse' and it is not
hard to spot a relationship between her 'eclipse' and the blaze of the noon
sun in this poem:

> I found the words to every thought
> I ever had – but One –

> And that – defies me –
> As a Hand did try to chalk the Sun
>
> To Races – nurtured in the Dark –
> How would your Own – begin?
> Can Blaze be shown in Cochineal –
> Or Noon – in Mazarin?
>
> (Fr436; J581)

As an archetypal figure of divinity, the sun's value for Dickinson was very similar to its value for early mythology. It strikes her as a principle of absolute light and the speaker's problem is in telling the story of this light – making the compromise necessary to accommodate the absolute in relative terms. Her move from language to picture is an impulse towards understanding the age of the problem – the way in which it preoccupied primitive man. The problem is rooted in the difference between direct and indirect experience; the difference between feeling or intimation and second-hand rendition.

Like the inhabitants of Plato's cave, 'nurtured in the Dark', these 'Races' see flickering shadows of the reality they cannot fully comprehend. To have a thought is equivalent to knowing the sun; to hear about it is only comparable to seeing a rough and primitive drawing, or a flickering shadow thrown upon the cave's wall.[8] The clumsiness of representation is emphasised by the disembodied 'hand', which seems as detached from its human owner as the sign from its referent; a referent which functions as both the intersection and vanishing point of all meaning. Noticeably, though, this clumsy 'try' is all we know of her thought. Like an eclipse, the subject of this poem is constituted by its seeming absence.

However, seeming absence is a very different thing to absence. The subject fails to appear but that does not mean that it fails to attend. It 'defies' the speaker, choosing to exert an agency and power greater than hers, but remaining shrouded in a mystery which can only be expressed by analogy to the paradoxically life-giving and destructive power of the noon sun. It is no accident that she finds her analogy, here, in the difficulty of narrating divine power or that she refers back to primitive forms of religious narrative (the chalked image of the sun) in order to emphasise that generations have endured the same problem.

'I found the words' begins to map the common ground Dickinson identified between poetic and religious narratives and sources. 'This World is not Conclusion' brings an important qualification to this Platonic theme as it illustrates the antagonism that set her half against the blind credo of faith and half in favour of the leap she understood by analogy to artistic vision:

> This World is not Conclusion –
> A Species stands beyond –
> Invisible, as Music –
> But positive, as Sound –
> It beckons, and it baffles –
> Philosophy, don't know –
> And through a Riddle, at the last –
> Sagacity, must go –
> To guess it, puzzles scholars –
> To gain it, Men have borne
> Contempt of Generations
> And Crucifixion, shown –
> Faith slips – and laughs, and rallies –
> Blushes, if any see –
> Plucks at a twig of Evidence –
> And asks a Vane, the way –
> Much Gesture, from the Pulpit –
> Strong Hallelujahs roll –
> Narcotics cannot still the Tooth
> That nibbles at the soul –
>
> (Fr373; J501)

Initially describing the beyond in the scientific term of a 'species', Dickinson renders the notion of otherworldliness doubtful even as she upholds its existence in her mind. As a creature we would like to categorise in known terms, this 'species' eludes us. A tangible absence, 'Invisible as Music – / But positive as Sound –', and a poetic figure not unlike Dickinson's 'eclipse', it fails to appear but it does not fail to attend the speaker's imagination. The poet's domestication of the 'beyond' through the language of science is partly scathing of the mind that would categorise the unknown in known terms and partly in sympathy with that need. Dickinson's 'species' becomes a comic figure, the beckoning and baffling object of desire that undermines every effort of human reaching with its trickster habits, forcing 'sagacity' to perform a humiliating jump through the hoop of 'riddle'. But if the beyond has a kind of trickster quality in this poem, it is also deeply and movingly beautiful. Dickinson's musical similes bear testimony to the profoundly affecting quality of a tangible otherworldly absence.

Like so many of Dickinson's religious poems, this is as much about how we understand a paradox as the paradox itself. 'Faith', here personified as a young, foolish but quite likeable girl, is a question of response.

Jovially tripping and steadying herself, embarrassed at her slip and blushing as might any New England eighteen-year-old stumbling at her first ball, she looks to the flimsy support of natural theology's 'Evidence' and asks directions in vain. Dickinson's pun on 'Vane' casts a gently ironic eye on the well-meaning but pointless efforts of the happy faithful. She reserves her greatest sarcasm for the habits of the Revivalist church that, for all its boisterous assertiveness, cannot hide the empty gestures and mechanical movements that underpin its own doctrinal surety.

The triumphant sounding of its own emptiness is the 'Narcotic' of the Revivalist church. But it is powerless, Dickinson suggests, to still the movement of the questing mind or soul. Her musical similes imply that this journey is analogous to her own artistic quest and the motivation is clearly one of internal torture, a desire that reduces the soul as much as stimulates it.[9] Dickinson's understanding of the beyond in this poem begins from negation, 'This World is not Conclusion', and it ends on a similar note. We are left to wonder how much remains of the soul that is gradually eroded by the gnawing pangs of faith and doubt. Both the poetic and the religious leap end as a hobble, but that is preferable to the misguided skipping of 'Faith' or the foolish stridency of the church.

Dickinson's unsettled poetic questing is reflected, among other things, in the open-endedness of her written forms. Her variants imply a reluctance to make definitive choices about the way in which any poem should be read. She has a tendency, especially towards the end of her life, to break quite suddenly into (what seems to be) consciously lineated verse form in the middle of a prose letter. And she regularly curtails her verbal expressions with a refusal to admit of finite ending. In doing so, she leaves room for optimistic interpretations of poetic possibility in terms of a more welcoming 'beyond'. Such possibility has long been considered part of Dickinson's aesthetic and finds its most well-known expression in the following poem:

> I dwell in Possibility –
> A fairer House than Prose –
> More numerous of Windows –
> Superior – for Doors –
>
> Of Chambers as the Cedars –
> Impregnable of eye –
> And for an everlasting Roof
> The Gambrels of the Sky –
>
> Of Visitors – the fairest –
> For Occupation – This –

> The spreading wide my narrow Hands
> To gather Paradise –
> (Fr466; J657)

The juxtaposition of 'Possibility' with 'Prose' has led many critics to see the former as poetry, its attributes grand and exciting and a contrast to the prosaic nature of everyday reality.[10] This interpretation is supported by readings from across Dickinson's oeuvre. Eleanor Heginbotham's evaluation of fascicle 21, in which 'They shut me up in Prose' is displayed on the opposite page to 'This was a Poet', argues that Dickinson's arrangement is a witty joke in which prose visually confronts poetry – the preferred terrain of the 'little girl' closeted in the wardrobe.[11] In 'I dwell in Possibility', Dickinson defines her 'Occupation' through the paradox of a phenomenological poetic that exploits the tension between an impossible space of absolute being and a possible place of relative habitation. The poem carries the conceit of the house right through to the final stanza where it is reconfigured in terms of the speaker's own body, the 'narrow Hands' that are both the enabling condition for poetic agency and the comical limitation to its aims.[12] The speaker dwells in a place that is still in the process of being made and gestures beyond itself to a fuller and freer space.

'I dwell in Possibility' is relatively hopeful, making the place of possibility, defined by the conditions and constraints of mortal existence, a partial rendering of poetic 'Paradise' and straining towards its greater achievement. 'From Blank to Blank' describes a similar thrust into the infinite in far less enthusiastic terms:

> From Blank to Blank
> A Threadless Way
> I pushed Mechanic feet –
> To stop – or perish – or advance –
> Alike indifferent –
>
> If end I gained
> It ends beyond
> Indefinite disclosed –
> I shut my eyes – and groped as well
> 'Twas lighter – to be Blind –
> (Fr484; J761)

As Elisa New argues in her reading of this poem, the link between the poetic and spiritual project is forged in the pun on 'blank' and 'mechanic feet' which refer both to prosodic bewilderment and hard spiritual journey. In New's reading, the poet carries out an absurd quest as a faithful wanderer. So, the theological or poetic journey towards a God of known terms is 'blanked out'.[13] By the logic of New's argument, Dickinson's irony is directed against the gathering of Paradise. Yet in the midst of the night-journey and the blindness that forms part of the conversion narrative, comes only a semi-ironic moment of divine illumination. Dickinson puns on 'lighter', suggesting both the bliss of blind ignorance in the face of the 'Indefinite' and the blinding light of an encounter with God or the power of Tiresius, the blind seer.

The blindness is somehow enabling. The 'threadless way' of her journey follows no known path, so it has no discernible 'thread'. But Dickinson's vocabulary also suggests the fate of many sewing-machine workers who went blind as they worked the 'mechanic feet' of their factory appliances.[14] Having gone blind, Dickinson's speaker suggests she is better able for the task at hand. The industrial allusion implies that a 'threadless way' is productive. The conditional 'if' that opens the second stanza leaves fulfilment a supposition, its boundaries 'beyond' the compass of consciousness. And that same sense of 'beyond' enters the darkness of the last line in the pun on 'lighter' – a half-acknowledged, half-realised sense of the multiple 'ends' of poetic achievement.

'Indefinite disclosed' mirrors revelation in aesthetic terms. What is 'indefinite' is the verbal rendering of the infinite – that which cannot be fixed, itemised or definitively understood. Dickinson's poetics render the animating principle of their being indefinite – in terms of her variants, dashes, similes and the grammatical constructions of conditional meaning that lend her poems their characteristic opacity. Her refusal to admit of finite ending in her poetry, her frequently displayed desire to push past the end of the poem with a dash and/or an incomplete meaning, is part of this gestural movement which hinges on an experiential chasm between humanity and divinity, time and eternity, the corruptible and incorruptible, this side and the beyond. It is important that Dickinson cannot help making the moment of religious arrival ironic; she struggles to have faith in poetic arrival as well. Instead, it is the negative space that interests her and the interim experiences of possibility and blindness.

These poems give a sense of the variety of tone to be found in the lively discussion that Dickinson encourages between religious and aesthetic forms of imagining. They illuminate the dynamic interplay Dickinson engenders between poetic and religious enterprise as they start to map the common ground in terms of an animating absence of knowledge and sense of non-arrival. But they also show the reserve which her enthusiastic descriptions of 'possibility' cannot belie. She may have used irony to attack the foolish or dogmatic faith that irritated her but she also used it to defend against the more difficult leap of faith that seemed profoundly relevant to her own poetic quest to negotiate the meaning of the beyond.

THE NARRATIVE

It is not easy to decide which story to follow in this book as there are many narratives to be found in Dickinson's writings. As Sharon Cameron and Eleanor Heginbotham have shown, there are stories to be found among the variants and within the fascicles and sets.[15] Aliki Barnstone has recently argued that there is also a story to be told about Dickinson's poetic development that is keenly engaged with the changing cultural and political scene around her.[16] Barnstone, in particular, has issued a challenge to those critics who would see Dickinson's poetry as unchanging and timeless, and confer upon it the mythic status that has often characterised depictions of her life.

I pursue lateral rather than linear interpretations of Dickinson's religious imagination, but this is not to say that there are no empirically traceable changes. Her early education undoubtedly enabled much of her later experiment as she made use of her wide reading and exploited the tensions of natural theology.[17] I remain nervous about making de facto judgments about Dickinson's poetic development, partly because the judgments formed in response to Johnson's earlier dating of the poems frequently now seem erroneous or at least dated. However, on the assumption that Franklin's dating is correct, it seems tempting to observe that, while Dickinson was always imaginatively engaged with religion and returned to treat the same themes in comparable ways throughout her life, there was a real flourishing of this interest at the moment when she seemed to be most poetically productive. A great number of her most interesting theological poems emerge in the period of 1861–3, but this study deliberately treats poems from across her oeuvre in order to illustrate the enduring relevance and nuanced interplay of its themes.

This is not intended to reinforce the 'Myth of Amherst'. There are occasions when a particular death or event provokes a peculiarly theological response. Two examples that I discuss in detail are the shooting of Mrs Vanderbilt (explored as part of a resurrection trope in 'To this World she Returned') and the death of Margaret Cowan (which led to a meditation on 1 Cor. 15.35). There are other times when Dickinson's age or the inclusion of a poem, or version of a poem, as part of a letter has a direct effect on the way its religious themes can be read. So while my discussion is thematic rather than chronological, I try to strike a balance between an awareness of Dickinson's worldly engagement and an awareness of the poet's enduring preoccupations.[18]

In the tradition which Dickinson's New England upbringing inherited, the incarnation of God in Christ was the lens through which other religious narratives gained meaning and the archetypal example of human–divine communication. The Gospel story was the axial point in the poet's mythic world and a life which, imaginatively interpreted, is forever at the forefront of her understanding of poetry. For this reason, scenes from the life of Christ provide a very basic framework for my discussion of her religious imagination. Dickinson's life of Christ begins with the incarnation which undergoes a complex reconfiguration in her embodied poetic. The relation between incarnation and embodiment remains a key theme as she shows a particular interest in moments of Christological extremity – instances of process, suffering and change and the scenes of Baptism, transfiguration, Gethsemane, crucifixion and resurrection – which draw particular attention to the mediatory nature of incarnation. But the chapters in this book discuss ideas that are only partly satisfied by the relevant moment in the Christian story. From Baptism, I explore Dickinson's extended interest in naming; from transfiguration I extrapolate to encounters with light; Gethsemane locates the quest narrative; crucifixion leads to sacrifice; and resurrection is a more complex imaginative stimulus than that allowed by Christ's return. From the paradox of the incarnate God and from religious stories of naming, light, quest, sacrifice and resurrection emerge four major themes of Dickinson's poetry: body, mediation, journey and gesture.

The first chapter situates Dickinson's preoccupation with the Word made flesh in the context of a New England literary and theological tradition which had long been preoccupied with the necessity of accommodating divine absolutes within the fallible relativity of human representation and perception. Drawing from contemporary liberal theology, American typological exegesis, Puritan incarnation theology and the extended symbolism of Dickinson's 'veil', I explain why Dickinson understood revelation and representation in similar terms and locate her sometimes playful and sometimes anguished poetic experiments in the theological terrain that she inherited.

The second chapter discusses the extent to which her fictions of naming are embedded in religious narratives ranging from Adam's absolute naming of the animals and Eve's fallen name to Babel and New Testament Baptism. It also explores the connection between sacramental mediation and Dickinson's poetic orientation towards the nameless, explaining the consequences of the mediatory and performative 'name' for the very texture and source of Dickinson's poetic language and personae.

Chapter 3 discusses the contemporary habit of comparative religion and explains that Dickinson would have understood the continuity between the sun-god, the transfigured Christ and sublime illumination. Light is both a commonplace Romantic symbol of the sublime and a biblical and mythological representation of divine presence, and this chapter suggests that Dickinson felt poetic inspiration to be equivalent to the spiritual effect wrought by transfiguration. This fed Dickinson's Romantic desire to see the poet as alternately possessed by divine light, writing in a kind of Dionysian ecstatic frenzy and as the origin of divine light, exerting Apollonian strength and power. This chapter sets poems in which Dickinson came closest to celebrating Emerson's idea of the poet's illuminated mind against those where she displays a more ambivalent feeling towards ideas of greatness and artistic longevity.

All too often Dickinson was left to fall back into the pain and struggle of a wandering existence. The fourth chapter revisits the questing journey as a fundamental part of Dickinson's aesthetic in the light of new work on her manuscripts and compositional practices. Rather than seeing Dickinson's poetic 'quest' as straining towards a rarefied poetic pearl, I look at the way Dickinson merged classical and religious quest narratives in order to depict the agony of the in-between as a place from which to write. These include the struggles of Jacob with the angel and Christ in Gethsemane and Christian narratives of conversion and crucifixion. Dickinson's questing motif also extends to Old Testament and classical notions of 'wilderness' and 'wandering' which, in the Romantic tradition, acquired a new artistic glamour. I suggest that Dickinson imagined journeying to the place of the dead as a way of comprehending a writer's life.

For Dickinson, Christ on the cross was the definitive image of the sacrifice needed to fulfil the poet's quest. Chapter 5 discusses the ways in which the narrative of sacrificial dying inspired Dickinson's sense of poetic performance, election and fulfilment. Dickinson's attitude towards sacrifice is ambivalent as she deals both ironically and sympathetically with the martyr's journey. However, sacrifice opens the paths between humanity and divinity and so brings into play a space of finite infinity that always allows for suggestion, incompleteness and future possibility. Calvary may be the fulfilment of Christ's redemptive function but it is not the end of the poet's quest narrative.

The narrative of finite infinity finds a more complete expression in the images surrounding resurrection. Chapter 6 explains the way in which

Christian and pagan notions of resurrection inspired Dickinson's poetic negotiations of loss, return and rebirth. For Dickinson, resurrection asks for a particular kind of faith, a faith in recognition to replace loss, to elide the difference between old and new. Her poetic explorations of the space opened by death focus the poet's attention on the epistemic absence at the heart of her own aesthetic, the experiences which her experiential verse can only imagine and which her characteristic verse forms can only begin to enact. Resurrection is the alpha and omega of religious narrative. It is fitting that it should have struck Dickinson as a symbol of both the limitations and expansive possibilities of her verse.

NOTES

1 '[My family] are religious – except me – and address an Eclipse, every morning – whom they call their "Father".' T. H. Johnson (ed.), *The Collected Letters of Emily Dickinson* (Cambridge, Mass.: Harvard University Press, 1986), p. 404. All further references are to this edition and are included in the text.
2 James McIntosh, *Nimble Believing: Dickinson and the Unknown* (Ann Arbor, Mich.: University of Michigan Press, 2000), p. 125.
3 See, for example, Jane Donahue Eberwein, *Dickinson: Strategies of Limitation* (Amherst, Mass.: University of Massachusetts Press, 1985); Roger Lundin, *Emily Dickinson and the Art of Belief* (Cambridge: Wm. B. Eerdmans Publishing Co., 1998); and Greg Johnson, *Emily Dickinson: Perception and the Poet's Quest* (Tuscaloosa, Ala.: The University of Alabama Press, 1985). The critical debate has generally been shaped by responses to Dickinson's personal ambivalence towards God. The following critics have emphasised the sympathetic tone of many poems in order to affirm their sense of Dickinson's own belief: Peggy Anderson, 'The Bride of the White Election: A New Look at Biblical Influence on Emily Dickinson', in *Nineteenth-Century Women Writers of the English-Speaking World*, ed. Rhoda B. Nathan (London: Greenwood Press, 1986), pp. 1–11; Elisabeth McGregor, '"Standing with the Prophets and Martyrs": Emily Dickinson's Scriptural Self-Defence', *Dickinson Studies, U.S. Poet*, 39 (1981), pp. 18–26, at p. 18. Others have seen poetry as a surrogate for religion: Vincent P. Anderson, 'Emily Dickinson and the Disappearance of God', *Christian Scholar's Review*, 11.1 (1981), pp. 3–17; Lundin, *Dickinson and the Art of Belief*. Dickinson has also been discussed as a mystic. Here, Wolosky's essay, 'The Metaphysics of Language in Emily Dickinson (as Translated by Paul Celan)', in *Trajectories of Mysticism in Theory and Literature*, ed. Philip Leonard (London: Macmillan, 2000), pp. 25–46, is excellent. Also useful are Michael R. Dressman, 'Empress of Calvary: Mystical Marriage in the Poems of Emily Dickinson', *South Atlantic Bulletin*, 42.1 (1977), pp. 39–43, and Hastings Moore, 'Emily Dickinson and the Apophatic Tradition', *Dickinson Studies, U.S. Poet*, 39 (1981), pp. 3–17. Dickinson's connections with oriental culture and religion have been explored by Christopher Benfey, 'A Route of

Evanescence: Emily Dickinson and Japan', *The Emily Dickinson Journal*, 16.2 (2007), pp. 81–93, and Hiroko Uno, 'Emily Dickinson's Encounter with the East: Chinese Museum in Boston', *The Emily Dickinson Journal*, 17.1 (2008), pp. 43–67.

4 See, for example, Shira Wolosky, *Emily Dickinson: A Voice of War* (New Haven and London: Yale University Press, 1984). Characterising Dickinson's response as hostile and embattled, Wolosky claims that her central poetic mode is blasphemy as humanity takes on Divinity in a violent reflection of the civil war. See also Rowena Revis Jones, '"A Royal Seal": Emily Dickinson's Rite of Baptism', *Religion and Literature*, 18.3 (1986), pp. 29–51. Jones concludes that Dickinson was doubtful of God and critical of the traditional doctrines of Congregationalist orthodoxy. She reads the Baptismal poems as a reorientation towards the goal of human happiness.

5 'The man enamoured of this excellency, becomes its priest or poet.' Ralph Waldo Emerson, 'Divinity School Address', in *The Collected Works of Ralph Waldo Emerson*, ed. Joseph Slater, Robert Spiller, Alfred R. Ferguson *et al.*, 6 vols. (Cambridge, Mass.: Harvard University Press, 1971–2003), vol. I, pp. 76–93, at p. 84.

6 Elisa New, *The Regenerate Lyric: Theology and Innovation in American Poetry* (Cambridge: Cambridge University Press, 1993).

7 Earlier studies of Dickinson's poetic identity have often emphasised the constructive role of gender. See, for example, Cristanne Miller, *Emily Dickinson: A Poet's Grammar* (Cambridge, Mass.: Harvard University Press, 1987); Sandra M. Gilbert and Susan Gubar, *The Madwoman in the Attic: The Woman Writer and the Nineteenth-Century Literary Imagination* (New Haven and London: Yale University Press, 1979), pp. 581–651; Margaret Homans, *Women Writers and Poetic Identity* (Princeton, NJ: Princeton University Press, 1980), pp. 162–214; Joanne Feit Diehl, *Dickinson and the Romantic Imagination* (Princeton, NJ: Princeton University Press, 1981); and Joanne Dobson, *Dickinson and the Strategies of Reticence: The Woman Writer in Nineteenth-Century America* (Bloomington and Indianapolis, Ind.: Indiana University Press, 1989).

One important work which invites consideration of religious influences is Sharon Cameron's *Lyric Time: Dickinson and the Limits of Genre* (Baltimore and London: The Johns Hopkins University Press, 1979). For Cameron, Dickinson's poetic identity is forged through an imaginative construction of unknown and impossible-to-know places, through a partial wresting of the unknown from the inner recesses of the human mind and from a tension between synchronic and diachronic meaning.

8 Plato, *The Republic*, trans. Desmond Lee (London: Penguin, 1987), pp. 256–64.

9 See Carolyn Lindley Cooley, *The Music of Emily Dickinson's Poems and Letters: A Study of Imagery and Form* (London: McFarland and Co., 2003).

10 These include Beth Maclay Doriani, *Emily Dickinson: Daughter of Prophecy* (Amherst, Mass.: University of Massachusetts Press, 1996), p. 34; Connie

Ann Kirk, 'Climates of the Creative Process: Dickinson's Epistolary Journal', in *A Companion to Emily Dickinson*, ed. Martha Nell Smith and Mary Loeffelholz (Oxford: Blackwell, 2008), pp. 334–48, at p. 335; Domhnall Mitchell, 'Emily Dickinson and Class', in *The Cambridge Companion to Emily Dickinson*, ed. Wendy Martin (Cambridge: Cambridge University Press, 2002), pp. 191–215, at pp. 206–9; Ruth Miller, 'Poetry as a Transitional Object', in *Between Reality and Fantasy: Transitional Objects and Phenomena*, ed. Simon A. Grolnik and Leonard Barkin (New York: Aronson, 1978), pp. 449–50; Elisa New, 'Difficult Writing, Difficult God: Emily Dickinson's Poems beyond Circumference', *Religion and Literature*, 18.3 (1986), pp. 1–27, at pp. 6–7, 10, 21–2; William H. Shurr, *The Marriage of Emily Dickinson: A Study of the Fascicles* (Lexington, Ky.: The University Press of Kentucky, 1983), p. 100; Judith Farr, *The Passion of Emily Dickinson* (Cambridge, Mass.: Harvard University Press, 1994), p. 50.

11 Eleanor Elson Heginbotham, *Reading the Fascicles of Emily Dickinson: Dwelling in Possibilities* (Columbus, OH: Ohio State University, 2003), p. 5.

12 Jean McClure Mudge has argued that, for Dickinson, the body was the most private house or chamber. Jean McClure Mudge, *Emily Dickinson and the Image of Home* (Amherst, Mass.: University of Massachusetts Press, 1975), p. 22.

13 New, *The Regenerate Lyric*, pp. 180–2.

14 Elizabeth Gaskell alludes to this common crisis in *Mary Barton* (New York: Penguin, 1977), pp. 85–6.

15 Sharon Cameron, *Choosing not Choosing: Dickinson's Fascicles* (Chicago: University of Chicago Press, 1992); Heginbotham, *Reading the Fascicles*. Papers from a 1997 round-table discussion of Dickinson's fascicles are available for view in the online archive (www.emilydickinson.org/fascicle_index. html) and scholarship in this area continues to grow.

16 Aliki Barnstone, *Changing Rapture: Emily Dickinson's Poetic Development* (Lebanon, NH, and London: University Press of New England, 2006).

17 For biographical material, any argument about Dickinson's religious imagination is indebted to Richard Sewall's comprehensive *The Life of Emily Dickinson* (Cambridge, Mass.: Harvard University Press, 1974); Cynthia Griffin Wolff's, *Emily Dickinson* (Cambridge, Mass.: Perseus, 1988) which pays close attention to Dickinson's religious education and Lundin's *Dickinson and the Art of Belief*, which is the lengthiest biographical approach to Dickinson's religious stance and argues that poetry was Dickinson's surrogate for religion.

18 For a discussion of the way in which Dickinson's cultural engagement enabled her adaptation of inherited religious beliefs, see Barton Levi St Armand, *Emily Dickinson and Her Culture: The Soul's Society* (Cambridge: Cambridge University Press, 1984).

CHAPTER I

A Word made flesh

The Word made flesh is the basis of the Gospel story. The incarnation implies the narrative of Christ's life, making it both a story for all time, the capitalised and absolute Word carrying the meaning of revelation in the body of Christ, and a tale that draws attention to the human and transitory conditions of existence. In Dickinson's poetry, the paradox of the Word made flesh underpins a tension between religious revelation and aesthetic representation. This chapter probes that tension and argues that this is the context from which Dickinson's poetic concern with embodiment derives its distinctive qualities. Dickinson was not only heir to a literary and theological tradition that merged the discourses of representation and revelation, she was also writing in a culture which had a particular interest in the body as a signifier of incorporeal meaning and in the duality of poetic consciousness. In Dickinson's poetry these problems are referred back to their theological origins in incarnation doctrine.

FROM REVELATION TO REPRESENTATION

In Puritan New England, the Word made flesh was the prime example of divine–human communication. In 1633 the English Puritan William Guild wrote: 'the Messiah ... was the resemblance, painting and pointing out that cleere Lampe and Lambe of God, the express Image and ingraven Character of the Father'.[1] Guild expresses a Calvinist preoccupation with the revelation of God in Christ. He makes no reference to Jesus's humanity so as to close the gap between Father and Son, the thing-in-itself and the image of the thing. However, he cannot avoid the language of imperfection: 'resemblance, painting ... Image and ingraven Character'. Despite Guild's implicit desire for it to be otherwise, God remains partly hidden, not fully revealed even in his own revelation. Calvinist orthodoxy required such a space between spirit and natural man. Divine revelation, even in the body of Christ, was of necessity imperfect. The gap between the thing-in-itself and the image of the thing, or the divine referent and its representational sign, could not be closed.

In Dickinson's century, revelation continued as a matter of theological and poetic concern, muddying the waters of the new liberal Christianity. Boston liberal dissatisfaction with Calvinist doctrine erupted in 1805 when the liberal Henry Ware was elected in a narrow vote as the Hollis Professor of Divinity at Harvard. In 1819, William Ellery Channing set out the liberal creed in a sermon entitled 'Unitarian Christianity' and the American Unitarian Association was formed in 1825. Unitarians professed to reason from the Bible alone. They still based their authority upon the revelation of God through Christ. But they maintained that this revelation was carried solely through human means. Christ was pure man and the Word transmitted through the words of human language. The Bible, though invested with divine authority, was in many ways a book like any other and needed to be read as such. Channing preached:

Our leading principle in interpreting Scripture is this, that the Bible is a book written for men, in the language of men, and that its meaning is to be sought in the same manner as that of other books. We believe that God, when he speaks to the human race, conforms, if we may say, to the established rules of speaking and writing. How else would the Scriptures avail us more than if communicated in an unknown tongue.[2]

Religion was that which appealed to the natural principles of common-sense and reason.

But, as Conrad Wright has argued, the choice was not simply between Natural Religion and Orthodox Calvinism.[3] If Unitarianism had obvious roots in the Enlightenment rationalism of the eighteenth century, it was also indebted to eighteenth-century sentiment. While eighteenth-century Deistic Rationalists maintained that the unassisted intellectual powers of man could discover the essential doctrines of religion (God's existence, ethical responsibility and Heaven and Hell) Supernatural Rationalists argued that Natural Religion existed but was insufficient without additional doctrines which came to man by a special divine revelation of God's will. In 1759, Ebenezer Gay wrote:

We should not depreciate and cry down Natural Religion, on Pretence of advancing the Honour of the Revealed, as if they were two opposite Religions, and could no more stand together in the same Temple that Dagon and the Ark of God ... They subsist harmoniously together, and mutually strengthen and confirm each other. Revealed religion is an *Additional* to the Natural; built, not on the Ruins, but on the strong and everlasting Foundations of it.[4]

This kind of eighteenth-century Supernatural Rationalism was not a sect in its own right, but invariably appeared in association with other doctrines. Like the Deists, Supernatural Rationalists emphasised historical evidence. The key difference was that they were persuaded by what seemed to be historical evidence for revelation, especially the miracles, which bore the burden of revealed religion.

So, despite the Unitarian emphasis on reasoned interpretation of the scriptures, revelation continued to have a place in liberal thought. Supernatural Rationalism framed Christian apologetics in the language of Enlightenment commonsense, drawing on post-revolutionary republican sympathies to maximise their potential menace to Orthodox Calvinism. But a new European vocabulary emerged in the 1830s and as German Idealism, Swedenborgianism and Coleridgean Romanticism began to usurp Scotch Realism, allowing intuition rather than empiricism to justify revelation, Unitarianism came under threat. Emerson's description of Jesus in 'History', which was in Dickinson's family library, exemplifies the split:

Jesus astonishes and overpowers sensual people. They cannot unite him to history or reconcile him with themselves. As they come to revere their intuitions and aspire to live holily, their own piety explains every fact, every word.[5]

Emerson is largely responsible for the view of Unitarianism as a cold and sober religion. He championed the sacred as a realm where imagination had power to change reality, giving unprecedented power to subjective perception. His objection to revelation was that it had become driven by doctrine rather than feeling and experience, proclaiming: 'the word Miracle, as pronounced by Christian churches, gives a false impression; it is Monster. It is not one with the blowing clover and the falling rain.'[6] This is not an objection to revelation so much as an objection to what he perceives as the corruption and stultification of revelation through dogma or reason. 'The blowing clover and the falling rain' has associations of freshness, newness and process. The present participles are important here. For Emerson, revelation needed to be a continuous, living experience. He protests: 'Men have come to speak of the revelation as somewhat long ago given and done, as if God were dead. The injury to faith throttles the preacher; and the goodliest of institutions becomes an uncertain and inarticulate voice.'[7] The corruption of the Word through doctrine becomes a corruption of the preached word and human language. Revelation needs therefore to be redeemed through poetic utterance not maintained through doctrinal stammering. For Emerson, the real duty of the minister or poet lay in prophetic utterance not parish calling or versification.

Emerson's purpose is moral; his only absolute is goodness. Emerson claims: 'The true Christianity, – a faith like Christ's in the infinitude of man, – is lost'.[8] He transfers faith in God to faith in man as a being in which 'infinitude' (the secularisation of Divinity) can be experienced. By this stage in Emerson's 'Address', 'man' has become an enlarged term and an idealised concept, a figure capable of 'illimitable' extension. Christ as prophet speaks of faith in *this* being as opposed to faith in the Father-God.

DICKINSON'S PLAY

Although there is no evidence to suggest that Dickinson heard Emerson lecture in Amherst or that she ventured next door when he was entertained in 1857 by her brother Austin and his wife Sue, she certainly read his work. She had a copy of Emerson's 1847 collection of poems and read a number of his works including *Representative Men, Essays* (first and second series) and *Nature, Addresses and Lectures* (containing the 'Divinity School Address') which was inscribed by Sue in 1869 and found in the Dickinson family library with corners turned in, possibly by Emily.[9]

The more liberal trends of contemporary culture certainly had their effect on her, allowing her to delight in the 'poison' of unorthodox opinion,[10] destabilising the authority of the Puritan Bible and transforming it into the 'Antique Volume' (Fr1577) of liberal exegetical practice while legitimising an emphasis on experiential process over doctrinal fixity. Yet she was far more sceptical about the blurring between revelation and representation. 'You constituted Time', written about late 1862 and included in fascicle 23, explores the problems of the revelation of God in man from the point of view of a disappointed lover. Dickinson is irreverent, playful and perhaps a little slight in this poem, but in many respects her practical blurring of the absolute and the relative and her emphasis on subjective attitudes as opposed to objective truths establishes her within a long-standing New England tradition.

In his seminal work on the New England mind in the seventeenth century, Perry Miller argued that 'the space between revelation and the inconceivable absolute ... was the portal though which ran the highway of [American Puritan] intellectual development'.[11] It was a space of possibility which had an enormous impact on theories of representation in the arts. According to the Puritan doctrine of technologia, the rules of art were supposed to be the rules of God, but in trying to understand the nature of human representation, Puritan theologians from Samuel Mather through to Jonathan Edwards struggled with the same problem reflected in the language of Guild's incarnation theology – the difficulty of holding humanity and divinity together in a single relationship. In their writing as well as their theology, the Puritans made repeated attempts to close the gap. Yet despite, or perhaps because of, their best efforts, the gap continued to widen and it both allowed for, and came to define, the shared theological and aesthetic vocabulary of the Word made flesh. A stereoscopic vision, born from a paradoxical desire to limit and indulge the imagination, shaped the development of New England thought.

With nothing of the earnestness of her Puritan forebears but much of the same intellectual interest in revelation, Dickinson wrote:

> You constituted Time –
> I deemed Eternity
> A Revelation of Yourself –
> 'Twas therefore Deity
>
> The Absolute – removed
> The Relative away –
> That I unto Himself adjust
> My slow idolatry –
>   (Fr488; J795)

On the one hand, the poem bears witness to the dangerous character of revelation, which makes you believe (perhaps falsely) that you are in the presence of divinity. There is also a parody of the Unitarian and Emersonian reconfiguration of divinity as humanity. The terms here are serious: absolute and relative, true God and false idols. But the speaker's manoeuvring of them is playful. Dickinson reveals a preoccupation with attitudes over objects. The force of the poem turns on the 'slow idolatry' of the last line. As the absolute has done away with the relative, the speaker must 'adjust', not end, her idolatrous attitude. Her compulsion to worship remains the same even as her understanding of the object of it changes. The temporal sense of the word 'slow' returns us to the first line – 'You constituted Time' – and also implies stupidity and unwillingness to learn (or really change). Arguably, nothing has actually changed with the removal of the relative by the absolute. Through playing with the two terms, Dickinson blurs the practical distinction between them. She was fascinated by the way we might comprehend the notion of an absolute, what we need to make it seem real to us and the mistakes that might arise from this need. 'You constituted time' is as much about exegetical practice as human disappointment. The first stanza makes the appearance of an absolute as good as an absolute to the speaker. The second stanza exposes the problem of such theology; the speaker's attitude remains the same even as the object of her devotions appears to change.

EXEGESIS AND PERCEPTION: FROM INCARNATE TRUTHS TO EMBODIED WORDS

Dickinson's embodied typology is one of the ways in which she responds poetically to the theological problems suggested by revelation as she gestures towards the unknown *beyond* experience. Behind her she had the weight of New England's exegetical tradition. The image of Christ's body and the problems of revelation implicit in the Word made flesh had come to inform the aesthetic values and structure of American writing long before her birth. The early Puritans, who relied on historical verifiability, used incarnate truths to guard against the dangers of the imagination. The writings of Cotton Mather and the sermons of Jonathan Edwards were still part of a church founded on exemplarism and therefore part of a religious community that, as Charles Cohen has explained, 'kindled together the affections which bound together a society that conceived itself as the embodiment of God's love'.[12] With Edwards's emphasis on the affections, embodied experience replaced incarnate truths, forming and interpreting God's Word. In 'Poetry and Imagination', Emerson later claimed embodied experience as a metaphor for spiritual and poetic liberation: 'the poet gives us the eminent experiences only, – a god stepping from peak to peak, not planting his foot but on a mountain'.[13]

Dickinson's main precursor in ideas was the eighteenth-century theologian Jonathan Edwards, but in order to understand the change he brought about we need to go back to early Puritan New England. Seventeenth-century Puritan writing almost invariably tried to understand the world in terms of the Bible, and of the fourfold system of medieval exegesis (literal, typological, moral and anagogical) the Puritans favoured typology. Typological exegesis interpreted the New Testament as the fulfilment or antitype of Old Testament types or events. From these historical connections, exegetes often drew parallels with their own lives. The Puritans liked it because typology seemed to enforce the strictest possible connection between the Bible and their everyday lives – meaning was defined by what could be *known* instead of imagined. Puritan typology thus began as an exegesis which relied on incarnate truths and a literary strategy which purported to cleanse fallible human perceptions. A type had to be a real figure of biblical history who had his fulfilment in the antitype, Christ. Types were distinguished from spiritualised or allegorised forms by their historical verifiability. They were safer because they were less likely to encourage an irrational imagination and they seemed to be closer to the absolute truth of God. Early Puritan typology was a theory of incarnation rather than representation – an exegetical and literary method which struggled to close the gap between absolute and relative, the thing-in-itself and the image of the thing, the Word and the flesh.

In 1681 the English Puritan Benjamin Keach published the *Tropologia: a Key to Open Scripture Metaphors ... Together with Types of the Old Testament*, which directly influenced the American Samuel Mather's *Figures or Types* (1683). Yet while Mather's typology strove to keep religious narrative within the safe confines of historical verifiability, it could not disguise the Puritan urge to see more – to interpret and suggest rather than dictate and restrict. Dickinson's poetry is a nineteenth-century manifestation of at least a 200-year-old dissatisfaction with the imaginative limits of iconoclastic doctrines. One of the most interesting early examples of this dissatisfaction is found among the gravestones of New England churchyards. On seventeenth-century headstones, it is usual to see an image of a skull with wings – symbolising the transition from mortality to eternal life. It was from this crude image that the cherub seen on eighteenth- and nineteenth-century gravestones evolved. The skull was fleshed out and the symbolic juxtaposition of death with eternal life became muted. Perhaps, as Melissa Mannon has implied, this softening should also be seen as part of a shift away from mystical iconography to classical symbols which gained new meaning in revolutionary and post-revolutionary America.[14]

Seventeenth-century carvers often employed symbols older than Christianity – Christ as the sun-god for example – in order to try to understand the mysteries of the afterlife. One suspects that gravestone engravings had to rely on the representative qualities of the symbol, rather than the incarnate truths of typology, because of the uncertainty and fear in what they were depicting. During the eighteenth century, New England produced a unique group of stones called symbols of transformation. They show the voyage of the soul through death in terms of becoming rather than a juxtaposition of states of being. Beginning with the winged skull and ending with a symbolic representation of the glorified soul in Heaven, these stone images depict numerous and strange in-between states. It seems that these carvers attempted to represent, in a series of frozen symbols, the fascinating *process* and not just the doctrinal definition of glorification.

The persistence of symbolism among gravestone engravings despite doctrines of iconoclasm in the Church suggests why the purity of Samuel Mather's *Figures and Types* did not last. A typology which relied exclusively on historical verifiability – an exact and singular connection between two known people or events – just did not satisfy the Puritan need for meaningful and relevant exegesis. It could not address that inconceivable absolute which occupied the space between the image and the thing-in-itself – that absolute which could not be fully revealed even in the incarnation narrative and which the symbol could at least begin to imagine. In the eighteenth century, American typological exegesis became detached from its historical moorings and representation began to be understood in terms that had once been confined to incarnation. Samuel's nephew, Cotton Mather, extended the meaning of figural types towards spiritual rather than literal fulfilment. The *Magnalia Christi Americana* (1702) used the Old Testament in two distinct senses: to emphasise the abrogation of types in Christ, and to make continuous associations between the Old Testament, the Ancients, and contemporary events. His typology was analogous and the freedom of analogy opened exegesis to more personal and suggestive readings.

The change that Cotton Mather had begun to make in the application of typology took a new direction in the writings of Jonathan Edwards (1703–58). As Shira Wolosky has noted, the enduring supposition among Dickinson scholars that she would not have known very much about Edwards is almost certainly false. Not only was Edwards's presence strongly felt within popular culture, affecting common thought and experience through sermons and discussion, his works were also frequently republished, circulated and discussed up to the last quarter of the nineteenth century. The publishing effort was driven by Edwards Amasa Park of Andover, a preacher in the Edwardsian style whom Dickinson particularly admired. On 21 November 1853, the 22-year-old Dickinson wrote to Austin:

We had such a splendid sermon from that Prof Park – I never heard anything like it and don't expect to again, til we stand at the great white throne, and 'he reads from the book, the Lamb's book.' The students and chapel people all came to our church, and it was very full, and still – so still, the buzzing of a fly would have boomed like a canon. And when it was over and that wonderful man sat down, people stared at each other and looked wan and wild, as if they had seen a spirit, and wondered they had not died. (*L*, p. 272)

In 1829, a ten-volume edition of Edwards's *Works* appeared, featuring many previously unpublished manuscripts as well as a long biographical memoir. It was acquired by Amherst College Library in that same year and was on the curriculum when Emily's brother was a student there in the 1840s. Moreover, Mary Lyon, the headmistress of Mount Holyoake Female Seminary, where she attended for two terms in 1847–8, was a committed Edwardsian and frequently preached and taught his texts.[15]

It was Lyon who expressed concern at Dickinson's religious apathy, and her Revivalist enthusiasm and hellfire preaching were probably responsible for the poet's undercutting of Edwards in a letter to her nephew Gilbert around 1881: '"All liars shall have their part" – / Jonathan Edwards – / "And let him that is athirst come" – / Jesus' (*L*, p. 701).[16] The apparent attribution of the first quotation, from Revelation 21.8, to Edwards associates him with the more violent side of her Puritan heritage and she is clearly encouraging the little boy towards the more welcoming humanity of Jesus. In the same letter, she encloses a poem 'for Gilbert to carry to his Teacher', claiming to prefer 'the divine Perdition / Of Idleness and Spring' to the Puritan's 'Industry and Morals / And every righteous thing'. The sin that Edwards and Lyon warned against appealed to her sense of humour as a 'distinguished Precipice' from which to fall and she made sure to send that wisdom to her other nephew Ned around 1882 (Fr1577). These late letters and poems, which were sent in an affectionate spirit to the nephews she was so fond of, exhibit the elderly Dickinson's desire to assure them a less frightening view of religion than she herself had been privy to as a child. Their tone echoes her ironic reconfiguration of Edwards's famous sermon, 'Sinners in the Hands of an Angry God', as 'A Pit – but Heaven over it –', written nearly twenty years earlier in 1863 (Fr508).

But although Dickinson repeatedly cast her ironic eye on the Puritan preoccupation with sin, she was fascinated from an extremely early age by the role of language in affective religion and this was probably why she was so appreciative of Park's sermon. Richard Sewall counts eight Edwardsian revivals in Amherst between 1840 and 1862.[17] The most powerful was in 1851 when ninety-five people joined the church, including Edward Dickinson. Emily, however, wrote to Austin: 'I have just come in from church very hot and faded! Our church grows interesting. Zion lifts her head. I overhear remarks signifying Jerusalem' (*L*, p. 120). The vividness of Dickinson's expression points towards an experience of Edwardsian intensity. However, the girl writes to her brother with a degree of amused detachment. 'Interesting' is suggestive of observation rather than participation and salvation is only rendered second-hand.

So, at the same time as she was sceptical about Revivalism, Dickinson could not help but admire the Edwardsian preaching style that inspired the Revivalist spirit. Edwardsian Revivalism remained particularly strong in outposts such as Amherst which were at one remove from the liberal theology growing up in Boston. At least three of the Edwardsian revivals in Amherst occurred when Dickinson was still attending church regularly, during the ministry of Aaron Colton. Colton took up his post when Emily was ten years old and soon became a favourite in the Dickinson family. A few years after his arrival in the parish, the child wrote to Abiah Root: 'we went to church in the morning and listened to an excellent sermon from our own minister' (*L*, p. 58). Colton was a preacher in the Edwards mould. His sermons employed Edwardsian style to make their content seem *real* to the congregation. In 'A Sermon on the Power of Habit', Colton brought the immediate danger of vice to life with skilfully imaginative use of metaphor and present-tense verbs:

[Our habits] steal upon us like a thief in the night. They creep with soft, velvety step. They take us unawares. That unguarded youth is all unconscious of the malign work going on in him: not a suspicion that he is forging chains and fetters with which the Philistines shall some day make him grind in their prison-house, and use him for their sport. It is a sapping and mining in the dark, at the seat and citadel of life – of all that makes life worth living. Putting that poison-cup to his lips – not a thought that he could ever be a slave to the drink-fiend. Not he; no, never, nor possibility of it. 'Why, man alive, do you think I am not my own master?' But you see him afterward – and how changed! How the demon has him, and mocks his groans and tears. Is this fiction? I wish it were. But no; it is just what you and I have seen and sorrowed over – the young, and beautiful, and strong, broken wrecked, stain upon their high places – sunk to depths from which we never see him rise.[18]

In true Edwardsian fashion he stresses the need for action in *this* life:

My dear young friends, will you not, like Moses, and like Mary, choose the good part? Will you not choose it now today, and so receive at last, and how soon, the welcome, Well done!'[19]

These kinds of sermons were able to create a different order of truth within consciousness, to enable people to experience ideas rather than simply hear about them. They implicitly emphasised subjective attitudes over objective truths.

Edwards's own turn towards experiential religion was intrinsically connected to his idea of typology as a tautology of representations that could conjure the *image* of absolute truth in the mind of the perceiver, rather than function as a historical incarnation of an abiding and absolute truth.

In 'Some Thoughts Concerning the Present Revival of Religion' (1742), Edwards argues that the expectation of a wholly good or wholly false representation of a mark of God on the soul is disingenuous because we live in an 'imperfect state and dark world, where so much blindness and corruption remains in the best'.[20] According to Edwards every human being is inwardly divided. Thus all human representations partake of doubleness and cannot be said to represent the integrity of good or evil. Edwards abandoned the notion of a site of representational purity along with an absolute outside of human experience. He regularly employed comparatives rather than superlatives. The 'truest representation' was that which could conjure an *image* of absolute truth in the mind of the recipient:

If the subject be in its own nature worthy of very great affection, then a speaking of it with very great affection is most agreeable to the nature of that subject, or is the truest representation of it, and therefore has most of a tendency to beget true ideas of it in the minds of those to whom the representation is made.[21]

Edwards claimed that, through an act of benign ventriloquism, the sensitive minister was able to translate the inarticulate language of being into the normative language of the regenerate and so raise language from its fallen state by closing the gap between being and representation, experience and expression. This is one of the reasons why Edwards is often seen as a forerunner of Emerson.[22] The Puritan Edwards, however, was even more careful than Emerson to hedge his claims. The minister's feeling had to be founded in true conviction lest Edwards warned,

through persons not distinguishing the wheat from the chaff … and laying great weight on the natural and imaginary part, and yielding to it and indulging of it, that part grows and increases and the spiritual part decreases; the Devil sets in and works the corrupt part, and cherishes it to his utmost.[23]

But the crucial point was not to make theological dogmas seem *true* but to make them seem *real*, and therefore relevant and affecting.

In this respect, Edwards set an important precedent for Dickinson, whose typology, as in 'The Province of the Saved' (1863), began in her own consciousness. The difference between this poem and 'You constituted Time' arises out of the distinction between attitudes derived from true conviction and attitudes born of foolish indulgence. Like Edwards, Dickinson was aware of the problems of false conversion and insincere emotion. Her strong scepticism may well have been why she was able to remain an enthusiastic observer (rather than an enthusiastic participant) of the Visible Church in the years when she still attended. Like Edwards she turned to the authenticity of embodied experience in order to negotiate the problem of falsity. Through 'endur[ance]' and 'acclimat[ion]' defeat is understood as a fleshy reality as opposed to an abstract concept. By contrast, the 'slow idolatry' of 'You constituted Time' leaves the speaker detached and uncomprehending:

> The Province of the Saved
> Should be the Art – to Save –
> Through Skill obtained in Themselves –
> The Science of the Grave
>
> No Man can understand
> But He that hath endured
> The Dissolution – in Himself –
> That Man – be qualified
>
> To qualify Despair
> To those who failing new –
> Mistake Defeat for Death – Each time –
> Till acclimated – to –
>
> (Fr659; J539)

As Robert Weisbuch has argued, what makes a type real in this poem is not that someone has existed, but that the subject has experienced. Only the man who has suffered despair can differentiate between the type and the antitype because he has some experience of the many endings which are types of death.[24] The repeated 'd's' poetically enact the typological relationship between 'dissolution', 'despair', 'defeat' and 'death'. Moreover, the poem withholds typological fulfilment. The final preposition is missing its object and this is one of the instances where Dickinson's characteristic dashes gesture towards the unknown and, it seems, the unknowable. Death is the relinquishing of the body and so beyond the scope of the poem where conscious experience is undeniably corporeal – 'dissolution' implies a physical as well as mental undoing at the centre of the self and 'acclimated' a physical adjustment. Dickinson's typology turns on the language of the body precisely because it is founded in subjective experience; in the diction that she inherited from Edwards and saw reflected in Emerson, that experience was undeniably corporeal.

EMBODIMENT, DUALITY AND DICKINSON'S DEBT TO CHRISTOLOGY

Embodiment reconfigured the problems of incarnation in a multitude of new ways. The distinction between incarnation and embodiment is partly temporal: incarnation is an older Christological notion and embodiment a modern and often secular concern, relating among other things to race, gender, violence and sex.[25] The distinction is also conceptual and experiential. Incarnation, the incorrupt Godhead made flesh, belongs to theology; embodiment, the implicitly corruptible or already corrupt soul-in-a-body, belongs to poetry and politics.

Many important critical considerations of corporeality in the nineteenth century return to the idea of the body as a signifier of incorporeal meaning – the problem articulated in Guild's description of Christ as 'the express Image and ingraven Character of the Father' and reconfigured in Edwards's emphasis on affective experience. For example, Sharon Cameron, whose work on this subject I discuss in more detail in Chapter 6, argues that relations between body and spirit give rise to literary questions about the definition of the literal and allegorical.[26] Marianne Noble's work on sentimental masochism discusses the body as the lexicon for earthly human understanding[27] and Karen Sanchez-Eppler points out that Dickinson's desire for embodiment constantly flounders on the unrecognisable and unspeakable nature of disembodied being.[28] So, moments of rhetorical embodiment endow emotional and conceptual abstractions with all the immediacy of bodily presence.[29]

In Dickinson's poetry the idea of the body as a signifier of incorporeal meaning is indebted to the conceptual vocabulary of Christology. When Dickinson invoked Christ's body, she did so in full awareness of its importance to the theological claim that Christ was not *only* human.[30] There is a long history of theological rationalisation for this contradiction and Dickinson would have been well schooled in its tenets. Midway through the first century the idea of two distinct natures held in hypostatic union within the single physical person of Christ became a crucial aspect of the incarnation.[31] Medieval theology then found the hypostatic union of utmost importance to understanding the incarnation. Aquinas's description of the hypostatic union emphasises the importance of Christ's physical person:

If the Word of God's human nature were not united to him in person it would not be united to him at all, and that would destroy all belief in the incarnation and undermine the whole Christian faith.[32]

In medieval terms, the incarnation was a theory of embodiment or personage.

Luther owed much to Aquinas's notion of Christ's person and believed that the union of the two natures in Christ was inseparable. In him, both

God and man suffered and died. So, the God-man became an essential part of Reformation theology and the Calvinist tradition to which Dickinson was heir. For Calvin, the context of the hypostatic union was Christ's salvific office – his role as mediator. Calvin emphasises that Christ was God in bodily form – a form we can comprehend:

For although all power is committed even unto his [Christ's] human nature by the Father, he still would not truly sustain our faith, unless he were God manifested in the flesh.[33]

The doctrine of the hypostatic union therefore conceives of two natures, one divine and one human, held together in a single physical body. Each nature has its own subjectivity. Inherent in the doctrine is the problem of how two subjectivities can be held in one relationship, and especially how this affects the agency of the physical body. The hypostatic union was one of the tenets which fundamentally divided Calvinist Trinitarians from Unitarians in the early nineteenth century. Channing, setting forth Unitarian beliefs in 1819, said:

we maintain that this [hypostatic union] is to make Christ two beings. To denominate him one person, one being, and yet to suppose him made up of two minds, infinitely different from each other, is to abuse and confound language, and to throw darkness over all our conceptions of intelligent natures. According to the common doctrine, each of these two minds in Christ has its own consciousness, its own will, its own perceptions. They have in fact no common properties. The divine mind feels none of the wants and sorrows of the human, and the human is infinitely removed from the perfection and happiness of the divine. Can you conceive of two beings in the universe more distinct? We have always thought that one person was constituted and distinguished by one consciousness. The doctrine, that one and the same person should have two consciousnesses, two wills, two souls, infinitely different from each other, – this we think an enormous tax on human credulity.[34]

For Channing, as for Emerson, who disparaged the way in which Christianity 'dwells, with noxious exaggeration about the *person* of Jesus',[35] Christ was pure man, entirely distinct from the Father-God, to whom he returned the benevolence that Calvinism had stolen for Christ alone.

Emerson's rejection of the hypostatic union was fundamental to his sense of the ideal poet as a man-god, comparable to his Jesus in 'History'. He writes:

when we describe man as poet, and credit him with the triumphs of the art, we speak of the potential or ideal man ... yet all men know the portrait when it is drawn, and it is part of religion to believe its possible incarnation.[36]

Calvinist incarnation theology is inverted; this is not God's condescension to be man but man's ability to be god. The same reasoning lies
behind Emerson's identification of a 'poet or priest'. Emerson may well
have opened Dickinson's mind to parallels between Christ and the poet.
But where Emerson imagines 'illimitable' man, usurping the minister's
role with poetic vocation, Dickinson reveals a very painful consciousness
of the difficulties of holding two subjectivities together.[37] For Emerson,
the poet ascends, melting boundaries and finding a home in the higher
regions of consciousness. For Dickinson, though she experimented with
this Emersonian power of rapt transfiguration, the poetic movement was
more frequently associated with struggle.[38]

   In Dickinson's creative experience of life as the point of *tension* rather
than *merger* between the immediacy of human experience and the distance of the divine beyond, she makes the Puritan God-man rather than
the Emersonian man-god a stronger basis for her poetic imitatio. In
'Life – is what we make it –' (1863) she makes Christ's body central to his
typological significance. The incarnation therefore becomes a way of rendering 'Distance' – a version of the beyond – accessible:

>Life – is what we make it –
>Death – We do not know –
>Christ's acquaintance with Him
>Justify Him – though –
>
>He – would trust no stranger –
>Other – could betray –
>Just his own endorsement –
>That – sufficeth Me –
>
>All the other Distance
>He hath traversed first –
>No New Mile remaineth –
>Far as Paradise –
>
>His sure foot preceding –
>Tender Pioneer –
>Base must be the Coward
>Dare not venture – now –
>   (Fr727; J698)

The speaker's trust is founded in her understanding of Christ's own bodily undertaking. In the first stanza death is personified so that Christ's
personhood is emphasised. The Christ of this poem is human and vulnerable, knowing to 'trust no stranger'. Christ's body is therefore conceived as a body among other bodies. He exists in a reciprocal relation

with the other bodies around him and with the speaker's own body. In the second half of the poem the speaker emphasises the actual corporeality of this body. 'He hath traversed', she says, pointing to the real and physical process of journeying. In that and 'His sure foot preceding' she implies that future bodily experiences were experienced by Christ because he was God made flesh. Dickinson makes Christ, not God, an exemplar for the speaker in this poem because he has a body, and it is only through that body that the speaker and, by implication, all of humanity, are able to understand the nature of eternity or death. The final stanza suggests that to 'venture' towards that meaning requires a kind of *imitatio Christi* that recognises the enabling condition of the body.

The empathic quality of this poem shows that Dickinson's point of contact was the human and it comes as no surprise that she was sympathetic to the Unitarian and Emersonian desire to humanise Christ completely. But her sense of poetic reach was expressed in a more traditional and distinct vocabulary of divine otherness, often made an uncomfortable and unknowable part of the self. So, the paradox of the God-man that the Unitarian minister William Ellery Channing dismissed as a ludicrous assault on human reason, retained, for her, its poetic appeal. Dickinson, truer in this respect to her Calvinist heritage, understood the struggle implied by such a paradox, writing repeatedly from about 1861 of the dangerous and painful condition of the split self: 'We don't cry – Tim and I' (Fr231), 'I felt a funeral in my brain' (Fr340) and 'Ourself behind ourself, concealed / Should startle most' (Fr407). For her, the fundamental problem of incarnation – the way in which two subjectivities can be held within one body – becomes a grounding principle of poetic duality.

Dickinson would also have been familiar with the figurative doubling of the self through the contemporary literary trope of 'double consciousness'. The term is Emerson's, first used in a sermon in 1833 to denote the outer and inner selves of man – one mortal, the other immortal.[39] Emerson's use of the term changes characteristically throughout his career. But he maintains that the fundamental divide is between solitude and society, or the spirit and the flesh. In 'Experience' he writes: 'consciousness in each man is a sliding scale, which identifies him now with the First Cause, and now with the flesh of the body'.[40] Henry David Thoreau's *Walden* uses 'double consciousness' in a typically Emersonian way:

[I] am sensible of a certain doubleness by which I can stand as remote from myself as from another. However intense my experience, I am conscious of the presence and criticism of a part of me, which, as it were, is not a part of me, but spectator, sharing no experience, but taking note of it; and that is no more I than it is you. When the play, it may be the tragedy, of life is over, the spectator goes his way. It was a kind of fiction, a work of the imagination only, so far as he was concerned.[41]

For Emerson and Thoreau, the rhetoric of 'double consciousness' was a way of gaining objectivity on the self, an ecstatic and fundamentally liberating experience. American 'double consciousness' was quite possibly a modern and secular manifestation of the rhetoric surrounding the hypostatic union – though Emerson was disparaging of the theological doctrine of two natures, he was eager to present Jesus as an example of humanity in which divinity was experienced and this is integral to the connection he forges between religious and poetic office. In Dickinson's poetry, however, I think the problem is most clearly referred back to its theological origins. Dickinson's idea of two subjectivities emerges through disjunction and limitation. As with Calvinist incarnation theology, the body is the necessary and often unhappy bind for doubleness. Thoreau explicitly makes imagination the faculty that enables double consciousness: 'it was a kind of fiction, a work of the imagination'. For Dickinson, too, the rhetoric was most likely a way of engaging with creative process. But Dickinson is no transcendentalist. Two poems, 'Me from Myself – to banish' (1863) and 'Like Eyes that looked on Wastes' (1863) show her wrestling with the difficulties of duality without transcendence. In 'Me from Myself – to banish' (1863) the body becomes an inescapable 'fortress':

> Me from Myself – to banish
> Had I Art –
> Invincible my Fortress
> Unto all Heart –
>
> But since Myself – assault Me –
> How have I peace
> Except by subjugating
> Consciousness?
>
> And since We're mutual Monarch
> How this be
> Except by Abdication –
> Me – of Me?
>
> (Fr709; J642)

If we read the fortress as part of a rhetorical figure for internal space, there is good reason to suppose that Dickinson imagined this space in bodily terms. Franklin notes the variant 'Impregnable' for 'Invincible' and this was the choice Johnson made in his 1955 edition of the *Poems*. The military and physical meanings of the word 'impregnable' evoke the metaphor of the body politic more clearly than 'Invincible' although the implication is there in both the variants. The word 'assault' in the second stanza reiterates the idea that the figure of the fortress can be understood in terms of the human body. 'Assault' implies physical as well as political, mental or emotional attack. The fortress's vulnerabilities are also the vulnerabilities of the flesh. The relationship between 'Me' and 'Myself', which takes place within internal space, relies on the speaker's depiction of that space as a physical constraint. Double consciousness, for Dickinson, is not a way of freeing the self from the constraints of the body; thus the poem ends with the image of two subjectivities trapped within a single fortress and a single person – a point emphasised beautifully by the way she retains the noun in the singular.

This poem may well have been influenced by Dickinson's reading of Shakespeare.[42] Its speaker has a parallel in Richard II who, in the final abdication of his throne, attempts to banish self from self. *Richard II* is concerned with exile from the start; Bolingbroke and Mowbray are condemned to tread 'the stranger paths of banishment'.[43] It is also concerned with the problems of the divine right of kings – Richard is 'God's substitute. His deputy anointed in his sight.[44] The rhetoric surrounding the divine right of kings centred on the king's two bodies – the personal body and the body politic. In Act 2 Scene 1, Richard of Gaunt refers to the body politic of Richard's Kingdom as 'this other Eden, demi-Paradise / this fortress built by Nature for herself'.[45] Linguistically as well as conceptually, Dickinson may have found her 'fortress' in Shakespeare.

The king's 'two bodies' recalls the 'two natures' of Christ far more immediately than the language of 'double consciousness'. Whereas 'double consciousness' is cerebral and transcendent, the 'two bodies' is incarnational. Ernst Kantorowicz explains that the medieval world raised the body politic to angelic heights because it represented the immutable incarnated within time.[46] The defence of the king's two bodies bears striking comparison with the hypostatic union: 'notwithstanding that these two Bodies are at one Time conjoined together, yet the Capacity of the one does not confound that of the other, but remain as distinct Capacities'.[47] Indeed, as Kantorowicz points out, 'we need only replace the strange image of the Two Bodies by the more customary theological term of the Two Natures in order to make it poignantly felt that the speech of Elizabethan lawyers derived its tenor in the last analysis from theological diction'.[48]

The fictions produced by the king's two bodies came, therefore, to enable interpretations of its problems that were similar to those produced by the doctrine of the hypostatic union. In Kantorowicz's opinion, *The Tragedy of Richard II* is the tragedy of the king's two bodies, the gradual breaking apart of the duality of natures. As Kantorowicz rightly points out, the tragedy reaches its climax in Act 4 Scene 1, when Richard's abdication enacts the banishment of his divinely appointed body from his human one. In the scene where he is asked for his crown, Richard's mortal body undoes its kingly counterpart: 'With mine own tears I wash away my balm, / With mine own hands I give away my crown, / With mine own tongue deny my sacred state, / With mine own breath release all duteous oaths'.[49] His banishment of self from self attempts what Dickinson's speaker so desires in the opening stanza.

Dickinson's speaker realises that she is a traitor to her own immortal body politic – her fortress: 'But since Myself – assault Me – / How have I peace / Except by subjugating / Consciousness?' Richard, in a similar move, claims: 'I find myself a traitor with the rest; / For I have given my soul's consent / To undeck the pompous body of a king'.[50] Shakespeare's portrayal of Richard as both victim and traitor was original and this particularity of the tragedy of Richard's dual personality is one that Dickinson's speaker echoes in 'Me from Myself – to banish'. Requesting a mirror in which he might see his face 'bankrupt of his majesty', Richard visually and symbolically externalises his double and the splintering of the mirror visually and symbolically shatters any possible duality. Bolingbroke's retort, 'the shadow of your sorrow hath destroy'd / The shadow of your face', emphasises how weak Richard's duality has become.[51] Dickinson, by contrast, retains the sense of two subjectivities trapped in one person; as 'mutual Monarch' her two subjectivities have equal power. Richard, in anticipation of his fate, turns to 'tell sad stories of the deaths of kings',[52] and Dickinson's self-abdication hints at Shakespeare's tragic resolution. For, death is the undoing of the king's two bodies as it is the undoing of the two natures of Christ on the cross at Calvary.

Dickinson's two selves are locked despairingly together. In 'Like Eyes that looked on Wastes', which again merges the discourses of two bodies, two natures and two consciousnesses, the sense of entrapment is even more apparent. The poem was also written in late 1863, although included in a different fascicle:

> Like Eyes that looked on Wastes –
> Incredulous of Ought
> But Blank – and steady Wilderness –

Diversified by Night –
Just Infinites of Nought –
As far as it could see –
So looked the face I looked upon –
So looked itself – on Me –

I offered it no Help –
Because the Cause was Mine –
The Misery a Compact
As hopeless – as divine –

Neither – would be absolved –
Neither would be a Queen
Without the Other – Therefore –
We perish – tho' We reign –

(Fr693; J458)

While the mirror scene enacts Richard's undoing of self, reflection, in this poem, is static. As if holding a mirror that *cannot* be broken, Dickinson's speaker is forced into a 'compact', a bond whose verbal character is underscored by the reflective structure of the poem – the rhyme of 'ought' and 'nought', the repetition of 'neither' and the pivotal act of looking in the second stanza. As Heinz Ickstadt has written, this is a self 'split into mirror halves'.[53] Ickstadt comments on the interesting relevance of the incarnation to Dickinson's strategies of verbal condensation – the poem's 'compact'. For Ickstadt, the poem is a locus for both revelation and incarnation. But faced with a duality that is both divinity and despair, Dickinson's poem is not a yearning towards wholeness in the midst of absolute rupture.[54] It is not simply a frustrated expression of desire for the Word made flesh in and through words, but a poem of self-exploration that is also an exploration of the painful condition of the incarnation. As with incarnation theology, the language of division is part of the vocabulary of unity. The speaker of this poem, like that of 'Me from Myself – to banish', remains 'mutual monarch': 'Neither – would be absolved –/ Neither would be a Queen / Without the Other – Therefore / We perish – tho' we reign'. The speaker's suffering is as much the result of the mirroring bond as the mirroring split. The mirroring is not exact; and just as identity is verbally condensed, so is difference. 'Ought' and 'nought' differ only by a letter, but it is a fundamental change. 'Ought' is anything; 'nought' is nothing. The poem's mirroring structure reflects imbalance as well as impasse. Nothingness quickly dominates.

The hypostatic union may have been a way for early Christian writers to clarify and simplify incarnation theology but, for Dickinson, it was a painful predicament. In 'I am afraid to own a Body –' (composed slightly later in 1865) she again uses the language of inheritance to depict duality as an unexpected and questionable gift:

> I am afraid to own a Body –
> I am afraid to own a Soul –
> Profound – precarious Property –
> Possession, not optional –
>
> Double Estate – entailed at pleasure
> Upon an unsuspecting Heir –
> Duke in a moment of Deathlessness
> And God, for a Frontier.
>   (Fr1050; J1090)

As a monarch inherits his throne, and a duke inherits his duchy, the speaker inherits the 'double estate' of body and soul. The law of entail restricts property to a linear descendant and, like the 'monarch' of 'Me from Myself – to banish' and the 'queen' of 'Like Eyes that looked on Wastes', the 'unsuspecting heir' of this poem has a parallel in Jesus Christ, who inherits his Father's incorrupt Godhead and his human form as 'precarious property'. Like Christ's humanity and divinity, body and soul remain equal and distinct. But the heir – subject to laws beyond his control – does not choose to inherit. In the archaic sense of the word, 'precarious' means dependency on another's will.[35] The word is derived from the Latin 'precarius', which means 'obtained by begging'. Given undeservedly, the property may be taken away. So, in the last line of the first stanza, Dickinson not only implies unwilling possession of body and soul but also unwilling dispossession. The 'moment of deathlessness' suggests both a time which is not death (life) and a time when death is no longer possible (a moment of immortality). The force of these equivocations has a similar effect to the poem's play on the dual sense of 'frontier' as expansive possibility and limiting enclosure. Christ must return to God in death. The Gospels tell the story of this return, but while Christ strives to rejoin God, God keeps him embodied and therefore exiled from heaven. Dickinson's twist is that enclosure, or embodiment, may itself be the expansive possibility – as in 'Like Eyes that looked on Wastes', 'a Compact / As hopeless – as divine –'.

POETICS: THE VEIL OF FLESH

At the centre of the Puritan church was the pulpit (not the altar) and the verbal character of Dickinson's 'Compact' owes much to her New

England heritage. For the Mathers and for Jonathan Edwards, Christ's redemptive mission was verbally, not visually, expressed. Christ was the Word made flesh and preaching embodied and consolidated that Word in and through the language of words. Ironically, Emerson's reaction against Calvinism was fuelled by a desire to release the Word from what he perceived to be stultifying incarnation theology through the literary power of words. He appreciatively called an essay on Coleridge, published in the *Christian Examiner*, a 'living leaping logos'.[56] In his 'Divinity School Address', Jesus appears as a 'holy bard' and the poet or priest ascends to free him from doctrines by which the church has forced him into slavery for their own ends. Emerson had no doubt as to how true revelation came about: 'If utterance is denied, the thought lies like a burden on the man. Always the seer is a sayer.'[57]

Living in a culture that maintained in various ways the connection between the revelation and human language, it is not surprising that the poet's love of language and her imagination of Christ endlessly fed off each other. In a play on the opening to John's Gospel, Dickinson explores the incarnation from the loving, consensual relationship she has with language.[58] The Word becomes mortal as soon as it becomes incarnate. By implication, when God assumes the person of Christ, the Word is made flesh, or language becomes part of poetic communication, the distinction between humanity and divinity becomes blurred. Dickinson recalls that God now has 'the power to die'. We are reminded, perhaps, of the striking end to 'My Life had stood – a Loaded Gun': 'For I have but the power to kill, / Without – the power to die –' (Fr764). In both poems, mortality is strength rather than weakness. Mortality is human and so brings with it the power of feeling and emotion. The consent of a word to become part of human language makes it mortal; weaker in its divine purity and stronger in its human feeling than when it 'breathes distinctly' or exists apart. As language consents to become part of human communication, words, like the condescension of God in Christ, become humanly rather than divinely empowered – and they are stronger for it.

> A Word made Flesh is seldom
> And tremblingly partook
> Nor then perhaps reported
> But have I not mistook
> Each one of us has tasted
> With ecstasies of stealth
> The very food debated
> To our specific strength –

A word that breathes distinctly
Has not the power to die
Cohesive as the Spirit
It may expire if He –

'Made Flesh and dwelt among us'
Could condescension be
Like this consent of Language
This loved Philology.

                                        (Fr1715; J1651)

The last two lines point suggestively to 'This' poem. Language has consented to be part of human communication and it is both the condition and object of the poet's love. 'Philology' is a considered choice. It has its etymological roots in *philos* (love) and *logos* (the creative principle associated with speech or action). So, Dickinson's love of language reflects an affinity with the verbal character of Christ and an awareness of the continuity between pagan and early Christian symbolism. In the first centuries CE, Jesus was commonly perceived and represented as the logos because as a secondary principle the logos, like Christ, was a way of understanding an absolute.

Dickinson's 'loved philology' acknowledges writing to be a similar compromise and it is through her own poetic relation to a notional absolute that she tries to understand the incarnation. But if philology is loved in this poem, then it is also loving. This is a poem about relationship as opposed to doctrine. 'Partook' and 'tasted' imply physical consumption and exploration of the body of Christ in the sacrament of the Eucharist and they emphasise participation and singularity. The power of the Eucharist, here, lies in Christ's ability to remain distinct in the flesh of each individual – the food is consumed 'to our specific strength'. Partaking in the sacrament is characterised by human experiences of nervousness and awe. Trembling is theologically resonant; there are thirty-three references to 'trembling' in the King James Bible. The theological context is probably best known to a modern audience through Kierkegaard's appropriation of the phrase 'Fear and Trembling' for his meditation on the story of Abraham's test of faith. There are, indeed, many occasions in the Bible when 'trembling' is coupled with 'fear', but the pairing is not without distinction. Psalm 2, for example, commands: 'serve the Lord with fear; rejoice with trembling'. Fear and trembling are companionable states and both reflect a nearness to God, but trembling is the appropriate expression of *happiness*, not terror, in the presence of the absolute. 'Tremblingly partook' implies an ecstatic state of being.

But why, one feels compelled to ask, the emphasis on secrecy and rarity? Puritanism did not outlaw the Eucharist as they did many of the Catholic sacraments and the Eucharist would have been performed in Dickinson's own church. In part, perhaps, Dickinson's emphasis on secrecy is to express something sacred, something beyond normal human reach. But it goes beyond that. Calvin had emphasised that the body and blood of Christ were received in a spiritual, not physical, manner. The speaker's sacrament is characterised by 'ecstasies of stealth' – a physical pleasure in the tantalising possibility that she may be caught at the forbidden shrine. The 'Word made Flesh' is the only way the divine can enter the human, just as words must consent to be part of language and language must consent to be part of human communication. Flesh refers both to the flesh of Christ and to our human flesh. The connection between writing and divine revelation is forged in the transgressive physical pleasure of the Eucharist. For Dickinson, both are acts of erotic participation in divine power.

Consumed 'to our specific strength', Dickinson suggests the Word becomes incarnate in each individual poetic body. This sense of poetry as an embodied medium is carried elsewhere in her work through the image of the veil, which appears variously as 'vail', 'cocoon' and half-open 'door', and is a midway image between Puritan understandings of the incarnation and Romantic aesthetics of representation. Barton Levi St Armand explains:

the veil in all of its manifestations, whether it be the cloak of nature, the robe of deity, or the garb of the spiritualist medium, was a basic metaphor for dealing with the problem of the sublime – what Kant had defined in eighteenth-century terms as 'an outrage of the imagination'.[59]

Dickinson's friend, the minister Charles Wadsworth, uses the image in this sense in his sermon 'The Treasures of Wisdom'. Wadsworth writes: 'look up from the grave's black shadow, to the radiant shapes that go by, behind the half-parted veil. You can almost see the beloved forms – almost hear the clear voices. And when that veil parts, and those clouds dissolve, ye shall walk with them in white robes, and be satisfied.'[60] The image of the veil as the last barrier between humanity and God is derived from Exodus 26, which dictates the way in which the curtains of the tabernacle should be made. A veil separated the tabernacle into two parts, outer and inner, Holy and Most Holy.[61] To walk beyond the veil was symbolically to enter a perfected state of grace. In the Christian tradition, the doctrine of resurrection replaces the Hebraic custom of passing through the veil. Hebrews 10.20 identifies Christ's body with the veil of the tabernacle, allowing humanity to 'enter into the holiest by the blood of Jesus, by a new and living way, which he hath consecrated for us through the veil, that is to say, his flesh'. The Gospel of Matthew describes the tearing of the veil after Christ's death: 'And behold the veil of the temple was rent in twain from the top to the bottom'.[62] Thus, through the blood of Jesus, instead of through the veil, man can enter safely and boldly into the region of God's manifold presence.

Here again, Dickinson's religious imagination is of a distinctly older cast than that of Emerson, who urges his followers in the 'Divinity School Address' to 'love God without mediator or veil'.[63] The veil, or its antitype, the body of Christ, is necessary because, in Hebraic tradition, direct contact with God requires some destruction of ordinary human nature. Dickinson refers to this tradition in 'No man saw awe' (two manuscripts, one lost, the other dated *c*.1874). Dickinson used both Old and New Testament vocabularies of divinity to explore the intensity of poetic experience. 'No man saw awe', 'To pile like Thunder' (two manuscripts, one lost, the other dated *c*.1875) and 'I cannot live with you' (1863) show the skill with which she brought the language of the Old and New Testament into play in order to imagine poetry as a veil of flesh. Dickinson's Old Testament vocabulary in 'No Man saw awe' and 'To pile like Thunder to its close' suggests that the unmediated experience of love, poetry or God will not allow anyone to emerge unscathed. The paradoxically revealing and concealing door she evokes in 'I cannot live with You' allows an encounter precisely because, like the veil or the incarnation, it also allows a separation:

> No man saw awe, nor to his house
> Admitted he a man
> Though by his awful residence
> Has human nature been.
>
> Not deeming of his dread abode
> Till laboring to flee
> A grasp on comprehension laid
> Detained vitality.
>
> Returning is a different route
> The Spirit could not show
> For breathing is the only work
> To be enacted now.
>
> 'Am not consumed,' old Moses wrote,
> "Yet saw him face to face" –
> That very physiognomy
> I am convinced was this
>
> (Fr1342; J1733)

The poem recalls Moses's encounter with the burning bush in Exodus 3.2–6:

And the angel of the Lord appeared unto him in a flame of fire out of the midst of a bush: and he looked, and, behold, the bush burned with fire, and the bush was not consumed. And Moses said, I will now turn aside, and see this great sight, why the bush is not burnt. And when the Lord saw that he turned aside to see, God called unto him out of the midst of the bush, and said, Moses, Moses. And he said, Here am I. And he said, Draw not nigh hither: put off thy shoes from off thy feet, for the place whereon thou standest is holy ground. Moreover he said, I am the God of thy father, the God of Abraham, the God of Isaac, and the God of Jacob. And Moses hid his face; for he was afraid to look upon God.

Moses has good reason to be frightened. In the entire Old Testament, he is the only man to encounter God directly and live to tell the tale. Dickinson's speaker imagines the event as an experience of death in life – a temporary suspension of breath and time. In the Bible story, as in Dickinson's poem, God surprises Moses when he is unprepared and unsuspectingly tending his flock in the desert. The arbitrary and terrifying will of the Old Testament God, whose only predicate, in this poem, is the 'awe' he inspires in mortal man, both appals and entices her. There is no sense of the friendly and companionable Christ – the accessible revelation of the incarnate God. This is the Old Testament God, distinctly void of human nature and corporeal life.

Miraculously, Moses's human nature remains; although after journeying to a place of death he does not remain unhurt. The speaker's strangely stilted depiction of Moses's subsequent breathing as 'work enacted' implies that his return to life is laboured and unnatural. Moses is forced to pretend the life he once lived so easily. Returning again to 'this' poem in the final stanza, Dickinson forges a clear connection between Moses and the poet, which leads St Armand rather optimistically to suggest that 'a romantic poet touched by the sublime must become, like Moses himself, a burning bush, glowing with the light of supernatural vision, yet with his human nature miraculously unconsumed'.[64] However attractive this reading is, I think that in claiming this for Dickinson (and perhaps for Romanticism) St Armand claims too much and so misses the real tension of Moses's miraculous survival. Dickinson's vision is far more uncomfortable than he makes out as Moses painfully clings to his humanity after being touched by divinity.

In 'To pile like Thunder to its close' which can be read (thematically) as a companion poem to 'No man saw awe', the consuming power of divine fire is reimagined as the experience of both poetry and love.[65]

To pile like Thunder to its close
Then crumble grand away
While everything created hid
This – would be Poetry –

Or love – the two coeval come –
We both and neither prove –
Experience either and consume –
For None see God and live –
                              (Fr1353; J1247)

There is something of the eclipse about the darkness in which creation
hides its common face. The intensity involved in reading (or perhaps writing) poetry is both religious and erotic. As Cristanne Miller points out in
her reading of this poem, 'consume' is an uninflected verb. In the context
of this poem, it could mean either 'to be consumed' (i.e. destroyed) or
'to consume' (i.e. take in divine power). Miller therefore emphasises the
tentativeness with which Dickinson approaches the 'coeval' experiences
of poetry, love and the divine.[66] Acknowledging this excellent reading,
McIntosh argues that this ambiguity represents the difference between
the abstract world of Dickinsonian absolutes and the human world of
Dickinsonian feeling. He writes:

Awe and love and poetry are too much for us. Yet in the actual world of human
feeling we regulate our responses; we die and become again; we survive spiritu-
ally by consuming. In 'No man saw awe' Moses both sees awe and doesn't. In
'To pile like Thunder' 'we' experience poetry and love and yet fail to experience
them. 'We both and neither prove –'.[67]

McIntosh also sees a connection between this paradox and the tasting of
the Eucharist in 'A Word made Flesh'. For him, these are all expressions
of a story Dickinson told over and over again – the story of encounter
between human nature and the unfathomable, beautiful darkness of the
'awesome unknown'.[68]

   McIntosh's generalisation is pertinent and his analysis of abstract absolutes and human relativisms lends clarity to the difficult paradox of this
poem. There is every reason to believe that Dickinson repeatedly told this
story because it symbolised poetic encounter with 'a divine physiognomy'
and that she associated the poetic experience born of this encounter with
the extreme metamorphosis and boundary crossing of death and ecstasy.
In 'Nature – sometimes sears a Sapling – ' she writes: 'We – who have the
Souls – / Die oftener' (Fr457). She begins another poem: 'My Life closed
twice before its close' (Fr1773) and of course, in 1870, Higginson reported
her as saying: 'If I read a book [and] it makes my whole body so cold no

fire can ever warm me I know *that* is poetry. If I feel physically as if the top of my head were taken off, I know that is poetry'.[69]

The paradox of this experience which is both abstract and absolute and human and relative is born out of the tension between Old and New Testament theology. The consuming fire of the Old Testament lay ready-to-hand for Dickinson as the expression of a power that overwhelms humanity. In 'To pile like Thunder' that power is 'poetry'. From the perspective of 'poetry', even the cumulative and heavy thundering which often accompanies divine revelation in the Bible is reduced to a bathetic 'crumble' – the aural failure emphasised by the physical dissolution. Creation hides its common face just as Moses rushed to hide his face from the burning bush. Poetry and love come 'coeval' because they are equally dangerous. Direct contact with either, as with the God of Hebraic tradition, requires some kind of destruction of ordinary human nature. But in the Christian tradition, which links religious ecstasy and the experience of death, Christ, as a mediatory veil of flesh, allows for repeated death and resurrection, 'to die and become again' as McIntosh says. In the Pauline writings, this accommodation of human feeling to an understanding of the absolute is a direct result of the incarnation. Paul says: 'I protest by your rejoicing which I have in Christ Jesus our Lord, I die daily'.[70] McIntosh's analysis of 'To pile like Thunder' convinces precisely because Dickinson's poetry is coming out of this very Christian tradition which accommodates the absolute to the relative in the Word made flesh. Bringing the Word to life in the fleshy form of poetry, Dickinson knows that 'We both and neither Prove'.

The equation between poetry and love becomes clearer if we look at the way Dickinson depicts erotic desire in the final stanza of 'I cannot live with You':

> So We must meet apart –
> You there – I – here –
> With just the Door ajar
> That Oceans are – and Prayer –
> And that White Sustenance –
> Despair –
>
> (Fr706; J640)

The lovers in this poem are separated by the same barrier which exists to protect man from God. 'The Door ajar' – another manifestation of the veil – emphasises that this barrier is also an invitation to enter. However, the full rhyme with 'are' is arresting. The 'door ajar' may almost be no invitation at all, so vast and insuperable seems the gulf of distance across the 'Oceans'. This moment of arrest is both aided and broken by Dickinson's dash which, after holding the reader back, then pushes him/ her on to the half-rhyme of 'prayer'. Prayer is a way of orienting oneself towards the absolute, an attitude which aims to transcend an unbridge- able distance between subject and object. There is some hope here, and the subsequent dash encourages us to linger in that hope. Our desire for hope is temporarily rewarded by the 'white sustenance' of the penulti- mate line. A small sense of spiritual elevation, the buoying hope reserved for the faithful, teases its way in here. But the unexpected 'despair', a full rhyme with 'prayer' which stands in subtle but meaningful contrast to the half-rhyme with 'ajar', quickly and cruelly returns us to a sense of the speaker's overwhelming remoteness.

Are we to feel caught out by Dickinson's undercutting of hopeful prayer with despair? There is certainly a sense that despair may be a more hon- est orientation towards the absolute, a more honest condition of prayer. Dickinson's complicated rhyming, broken rhythms and fragmented lines poetically enact a separation forced upon, and paradoxically willed by, the speaker. The paradox is echoed in her desire to 'meet apart' – separation is all that will allow the revelation of one to the other. The final 'des- pair' could so easily be substituted with the word 'desire' that Dickinson implies they are parallel states. Were Jacques Lacan suddenly parachuted into the world of Dickinson's poem, he would find, in the speaker's separ- ation from her lover, the very lack he argues is the premise of desire.

In his theological rationalisation of despair, Dickinson's contemporary Søren Kierkegaard also forged a connection between despair and desire. He wrote: '[the] torment of despair is precisely the inability to die'.[71] Kierkegaard develops his thesis from a theory of relational being, which he describes as a 'synthesis of the infinite and the finite, the temporal and the eternal, of freedom and necessity'.[72] For Kierkegaard, despair is born out of the condition of relational being, which is impossible as a condi- tion of being because it is always a process of becoming. For Kierkegaard, as for Dickinson, despair is both merit and defect, a condition of want which bears an important structural similarity to desire. In Dickinson's love poem, despair and desire mean the inability to die, to live, to be saved, damned, united or even properly sundered. Any concrete state, any point of arrival that would breach the condition of paradox, is impossible. The paradox is fundamental because, in its true form, love (like Poetry or God) will not allow for the compromising conditions of the mortal world. In the line, 'You there – I – here –', Dickinson visually positions her speaker as close to her lover's location 'there' as to her own 'here'.

The 'I' is separated in both cases only by a single dash. However, 'You there – I – here –', also maintains a sense of inescapable distance, a distance which is as much a product of desire as it is of despair.

In this chapter I have argued that Dickinson's confrontation with embodiment is part of an imaginative tradition in American writing in which the incarnation has archetypal significance. Dickinson opens up the relationship between religious and artistic interpretations of the Word made flesh, probing the tensions between revelation and representation, referring poetic duality back to the language of incarnation and developing notions of poetic encounter through the typology of the 'veil' or 'door ajar'. The following chapter takes Baptism, the second communication event of the Gospel story, as a basis for discussing the way Dickinson's fictions of naming are embedded in religious narratives. It explores the connection between sacramental mediation and Dickinson's poetic orientation towards the nameless, explaining the consequences of the mediatory 'name' for the very texture and source of her poetic language.

NOTES

1 William Guild, 'Epistle Dedicatorie' to *Moses Unvailed, or those Figures which Served Unto the Patterne and shadow of Heavenly Things, pointing out the Messiah Christ Jesus, Briefly Explained*, quoted in Mason I. Lowance, *The Language of Canaan: Metaphor and Symbol in New England from the Puritans to the Transcendentalists* (Cambridge, Mass.: Harvard University Press, 1980), p. 33.

2 William Ellery Channing, 'Unitarian Christianity' (1819), in *The Unitarian Controversy 1819–1823*, 2 vols., ed. Bruce Kuklick (London: Garland Publishing, 1987), vol. I, pp. 3–47, at p. 5.

3 Conrad Wright, *The Liberal Christians: Essays on American Unitarian History* (Boston, Mass.: Beacon Press, 1970), p. 5.

4 Ebenezer Gay, *Natural Religion, as Distinguished from Revealed* (Boston, 1759), quoted in Wright, *Liberal Christians*, p. 11.

5 Ralph Waldo Emerson, 'History' (1841), in *The Collected Works of Ralph Waldo Emerson*, ed. Joseph Slater, Robert Spiller, Alfred R. Ferguson *et al.*, 6 vols. (Cambridge, Mass.: Harvard University Press, 1971–2003), vol. 2, pp. 1–25, at p. 16.

6 Ralph Waldo Emerson, 'Divinity School Address', p. 81.

7 *Ibid.*, p. 84.

8 *Ibid.*, p. 89.

9 Harvard University, Houghton Library, MSS *AC85.Aℓ191.Zz847e2; EDR 132; EDR 152; EDR 153; and EDR 255.

10 In response to reading Theodore Parker's *Two Christmas Celebrations*, a fable about the redemptive capacity of human kindness that sought to return

Jesus to history and messianic activity to the human sphere, she wrote: 'I heard that he was "poison." Then I like poison very well' (*L*, p. 358).

11 Perry Miller, *The New England Mind: The Seventeenth Century* (Cambridge, Mass., and London: Harvard University Press, 1939), p. 21.

12 Charles Lloyd Cohen, *God's Caress: The Psychology of Puritan Religious Experience* (Oxford: Oxford University Press, 1986), p. 161.

13 Ralph Waldo Emerson, 'Poetry and Imagination', in *Letters and Social Aims* (Boston, Mass.: Houghton Mifflin Co., 1903), pp. 3–75, at p. 10.

14 Melissa Mannon, *Gravestones: A Reflection on American Lifestyles* (1991–2001): www.mannon.org/gravestones.

15 Wolosky, 'The Metaphysics of Language in Emily Dickinson', p. 28.

16 Dickinson was never persuaded to join the church and she notoriously remained seated at school when all girls who yearned to be Christians were asked to stand. Sewall, *Life*, p. 360n.

17 Sewall, *Life*, p. 24.

18 Rev. A. M. Colton, 'A Sermon on the Power of Habit', in *The Old Meeting House and Vacation Papers Humorous and Other, collected for publication by his brother G. Q. Colton* (New York: Worthington Co., 1890), pp. 270–98, at pp. 278–9. This sermon was included in the publication at the request of friends and is undated.

19 *Ibid.*

20 Jonathan Edwards, 'Some Thoughts Concerning the Present Revival of Religion in New England', in *The Great Awakening*, ed. C. C. Goen (New Haven and London: Yale University Press, 1972), pp. 289–530, at p. 314.

21 *Ibid.*, p. 387.

22 Perry Miller was the first to argue that the gap between Edwards and Emerson was not as great as the latter might have imagined, *Errand Into the Wilderness* (Cambridge, Mass.: Harvard University Press, 1956).

23 *Ibid.*, pp. 289–530, at p. 467.

24 Robert Weisbuch, *Emily Dickinson's Poetry* (Chicago and London: University of Chicago Press, 1972), p. 87.

25 See, for example, Sharon Cameron, *The Corporeal Self: Allegories of the Body in Melville and Hawthorne* (Baltimore and London: The Johns Hopkins University Press, 1981); Marianne Noble, *The Masochistic Pleasures of Sentimental Literature* (Princeton, NJ: Princeton University Press, 2000); Karen Sanchez-Eppler, *Touching Liberty: Abolition, Feminism, and the Politics of the Body* (Berkeley, Los Angeles and London: University of California Press, 1993); and Homans, *Women Writers*.

26 Cameron, *Corporeal Self*, p. 2.

27 Noble, *The Masochistic Pleasures*, has a chapter on Dickinson, pp. 147–90.

28 Sanchez-Eppler, *Touching Liberty*, p. 117.

29 In support of her point, Sanchez-Eppler quotes Dickinson's famous letter to Joseph Lyman: 'Space and Time are things of the body and have little or nothing to do with our selves. My Country is Truth.' Sanchez-Eppler, *Touching Liberty*, p. 105.

30 In September 1877, Dickinson sent a letter of consolation to Higginson on the death of his wife. Comforting him in his grief, she wrote: 'To be human is more than to be divine, for when Christ was divine he was uncontented till he had been human' (*L*, p. 592).

31 In October 451 the Council of Chalcedon agreed the following definition: '[Christ] is one and the same, the same in perfect divinity, the same in perfect humanity, true God and true man, consisting of a rational soul and a body, consubstantial with the Father in divinity and consubstantial with us in humanity'. F. Ocáriz, L. F. Mateo Seco and J. A. Riestra, *The Mystery of Jesus Christ: A Christology and Soteriology Textbook* (Dublin: Four Courts Press, 1991), p. 97.

32 Thomas Aquinas, *Summa Theologiae: A Concise Translation*, ed. Timothy McDermott (London: Eyre and Spottiswoode, 1989), p. 479.

33 John Calvin, *Genesis*, ed. Alister McGrath and J. I. Packer (Nottingham: Crossway Books, 2001), p. 249.

34 Channing, 'Unitarian Christianity', pp. 19–20.

35 Emerson, 'Divinity School Address', p. 82.

36 Emerson, 'Poetry and Imagination', p. 26.

37 Emerson, 'Divinity School Address', p. 79.

38 Further discussion of Dickinson's debt to Emerson can be found in Chapter 3, below.

39 A. C. McGiffert, *Young Emerson Speaks* (Boston, Mass.: Houghton Mifflin Co., 1938), p. 200.

40 Ralph Waldo Emerson, 'Experience' (1844), in *The Collected Works of Ralph Waldo Emerson*, ed. Joseph Slater, Robert Spiller, Alfred R. Ferguson *et al.*, 6 vols. (Cambridge, Mass.: Harvard University Press, 1971–2003), vol. 3, pp. 25–49, at p. 42.

41 Henry David Thoreau, *Walden* (1854; Oxford: Oxford University Press, 1997), p. 123.

42 For a detailed discussion of Dickinson's Shakespeare, see Páraic Finnerty, *Emily Dickinson's Shakespeare* (Amherst, Mass.: University of Massachusetts Press, 2006).

43 1.3.415.

44 1.2.37–8.

45 2.1.43–4.

46 Ernst H. Kantorowicz, *The King's Two Bodies: A Study in Mediaeval Political Theology* (1957; Princeton, NJ: Princeton University Press, 1997), pp. 8–9.

47 Edmund Plowden, *Commentaries or Reports* (London, 1816), 233a. Kantorowicz, *The King's Two Bodies*, p. 12.

48 Kantorowicz, *The King's Two Bodies*, p. 16.

49 4.1.196–200.

50 4.1.238–40.

51 4.1.282–3.

52 3.2.152.

53 Heinz Ickstadt, 'Emily Dickinson's Place in Literary History; Or, the Public Function of a Private Poet', *The Emily Dickinson Journal*, 10.1 (2001), pp. 55–69, at p. 63.

54 Ickstadt argues that it is, in support of Shira Wolosky, 'A Syntax of Contention', in *Emily Dickinson*, ed. Harold Bloom (New York: Chelsea House Publishers, 1985), p. 172. Ickstadt, 'Emily Dickinson's Place', pp. 55–69, at p. 64.

55 Dickinson used *Webster's American Dictionary*. In the 1841 edition, the full entry for 'precarious' reads: 'a. [L. *precarius* from *precor*, to pray or entreat; primarily, depending on request, or on the will of another.] 1. Depending on the will or pleasure of another; held by courtesy; liable to be changed or lost at the pleasure of another. A privilege depending on another's will is *precarious*, or held by a *precarious* tenure. 2. Uncertain; held by a doubtful tenure; depending on unknown or unforseen causes or events. Temporal prosperity is *precarious*; personal advantages, health, strength and beauty, are all *precarious*, depending on a thousand accidents. We say also, the weather is *precarious*; a phrase in which we depart not more from the primary sense of the word, than we do in a large part of all the words in the language.' Noah Webster, *An American Dictionary of the English Language; First Edition in Octavo, containing the whole vocabulary of the Quarto, with corrections, improvements and several thousand additional words to which is prefaced an introductory dissertation on the Origin, History and Connection of the languages of Western Asia and Europe, with an explanation of the principles on which languages are formed*, 2 vols. (New Haven: Published by the Author, 1841), vol. 2, p. 339.

56 Robert D. Richardson Jr., *Emerson: The Mind on Fire* (Berkeley, Los Angeles and London: University of California Press, 1995), p. 166.

57 Emerson, 'Divinity School Address', p. 84.

58 The manuscript was lost so dating is impossible.

59 Barton Levi St Armand, 'Veiled Ladies: Dickinson, Bettine, and Transcendental Mediumship', in *Studies in the American Renaissance*, ed. Joel Myerson (Charlottesville, Va.: University Press of Virginia, 1987), pp. 1–53, at p. 21.

60 Quoted in St Armand, 'Veiled Ladies', p. 22.

61 Patrick Fairbairn, *The Typology of Scripture*, 2 vols. (Grand Rapids, Mich.: Zondervan Publishing House, 1967), vol. 1, p. 342.

62 Matt. 27.51.

63 Emerson, 'Divinity School Address', p. 90.

64 St Armand, 'Veiled Ladies', p. 25.

65 James McIntosh, *Nimble Believing: Dickinson and the Unknown* (Ann Arbor, Mich.: University of Michigan Press, 2000), p. 109. The poems are thought to have been written about a year apart, in 1874 and 1875 respectively.

66 Cristanne Miller, *Emily Dickinson: A Poet's Grammar* (Cambridge, Mass.: Harvard University Press, 1987), pp. 127–30.

67 McIntosh, *Nimble Believing*, p. 109.

68 *Ibid.*

69 Thomas Wentworth Higginson, in a letter to his wife dated Amherst / Tuesday 10 p.m. (*L*, pp. 473–4).

70 1 Cor. 15.31.
71 Søren Kierkegaard, *The Sickness Unto Death*, trans. Alastair Hannay (London: Penguin, 2004), p. 48.
72 *Ibid.*, p. 43.

CHAPTER 2

Beginning from the name

Following the story of the Gospel, this chapter takes inspiration from Christ's Baptism. This is the first time the Word made flesh allows for verbal communication between God and man as God names Christ his 'son'.[1] As a naming event that looks forwards to the 'son['s]' return to Heaven, it also opens up the same tension between the absolute Word and the mortal flesh that was the focus of the previous chapter. Dickinson drew from the way in which the incarnation informed the Puritan ritual of Baptism to explore her sense that the poetic possibilities of sacramental mediation lie in the compromised vision suggested by the given 'name'. Her sense of this compromised vision was rooted in a fundamental post-lapsarian opening between essence and representation. While Dickinson played with the idea of essential nameless truths, she could never reconcile her handling of them. So she found inspiration for the shifting texture of her poetic voice in the mediatory Baptismal 'name'. The poems discussed here simultaneously enact the difficulty of voicing namelessness and invite reflection on the theological meaning of sacramental mediation.

FICTIONS OF NAMING

The poet who wrote to Thomas Wentworth Higginson, 'I enclose my name – asking you, if you please – Sir – to tell me what is true?' clearly understood the sense of identity that a name implied. On the one hand, names signify fixity. They tie you to your family and your family's expectations. They are the means by which you are known and by which you know others. They stand as your representative but they can also be changed, adopted, discarded and manipulated to seal others into a relationship with you. Philosophers from Plato onwards have considered the name to be a shifting signifier of meaning. Dickinson, too, knew the power a name could hold.

This was the first letter she sent him. It was written in response to Higginson's 'Letter to a Young Contributor', which was the lead article in the April edition of *The Atlantic Monthly* and offered practical advice to novice authors. It was not out of place, therefore, for Dickinson to ask for assistance. But the tone of the letter is extraordinarily intimate:

15 April 1862
Mr Higginson
Are you too deeply occupied to say if my Verse is alive?
The Mind is so near itself – it cannot see, distinctly – and I have none to ask –
Should you think it breathed – and had you the leisure to tell me, I should feel quick gratitude –
If I make the mistake – that you dared to tell me – would give me sincerer honor – toward you –
I enclose my name – asking you, if you please – Sir – to tell me what is true?
That you will not betray me – it is needless to ask – since Honor is its own pawn –

(*L*, p. 403)

This is more than a request; it is an act of self-surrender. Her first line dares Higginson to look away from her, to find her insignificant and irritating. It dares him to feel embarrassed by her and her pleading confession, 'I have none to ask'. Dickinson is breathy and flirtatious, exchanging 'honor' for 'truth', an exchange which is so sexually suggestive one imagines that Higginson, on receiving this, might feel as if he had been enticed into a clandestine affair of love not tutelage – a feeling which could only have been heightened by the poet's assurance that he would not 'betray' her. Leaving the letter unsigned and enclosing her 'name' along with four of her poems, Dickinson enacts a poetic giving of self, pretending to surrender to his greater authority while actually establishing control. In this first letter, Dickinson laid the foundations for a relationship which was to exist entirely on her terms and yet would continue to maintain the pretence of Higginson's superior authority.

In the nineteenth century, an author's name was often a conscious literary device. Many of Dickinson's female contemporaries used pseudonyms. Those 'yorkshire girls' (the Brontës; *L*, p. 437) Dickinson so admired were renowned for it. Marian Evans and Helen Fiske Hunt were among other prominent women on both sides of the Atlantic who adopted male pennames. These women used pseudonyms so that they could enter the male-dominated world of publication more easily. But others used pseudonyms as part of a philosophical play on the meaning of the name. Kierkegaard, for example, took on the name of Johannes de Silentio as the author of

Fear and Trembling. Kierkegaard's mask is aesthetic rather than practical. Johannes de Silentio is simultaneously a comment on the book and an interrogation of authorship: 'the present author is no philosopher, he is *poetice et eleganter* (to put it in poetic and well-chosen terms), an occasional copyist who neither writes the System nor makes any *promises* about it, who pledges neither anything about the System nor himself *to* it'.[2] As Jacques Derrida claims in his analysis of this passage, Kierkegaard's disclaimer, absolving the man of silence from responsibility, emphasises the relevance of Kierkegaard's pseudonym to a book where both God and Abraham keep silent about their reasons.[3]

For Dickinson, like Kierkegaard, a pseudonym was anything but a practical resource. She assumed fictional names as easily as she assumed poetic personae and her letters, like her poems, often have a distinctly theatrical quality.[4] Her correspondence with Higginson provides some of the best, although not the only, examples of this. In February 1863, she finished a letter to Higginson, 'Your Gnome' (*L*, p. 424). Johnson notes that Higginson could never explain the reason for the signature. He writes: 'one conjectures that perhaps he [Higginson] had earlier commented on the gnomic quality of the verse' (*L*, p. 424). Dickinson's pseudonym seems to have been deliberately designed to mystify Higginson, subverting the act of submission implicit in the possessive pronoun and lending her correspondence its characteristic air of ironic humility.

In another letter to Higginson, written about 1863, she says:

Dear friend –
  You were so generous to me, that if possible I offended you, I could not too
    deeply apologise.
  To doubt my High Behaviour, is a new pain – I could be honourable no
    more – till I asked you about it. I know not what to deem myself – Yesterday
    'Your Scholar' – but might I be the one you tonight, forgave, 'tis a Better
    Honour – Mine is just the Thief's Request –
  Please, Sir, Hear

                                                                    'Barabbas'
                                                                   (*L*, p. 425)

Again, Dickinson's pseudonym not only allows her to inhabit a persona but creates a role for the recipient. She plays Barabbas to Higginson's Christ. 'Scholar' is also the metonymic extension of 'disciple'. As Marietta Messmer points out in her reading of this letter, Higginson is not only Christ, he is also Pilate, who will release Barabbas in spite of his guilt.[5] While Dickinson claims (unconvincingly) that she 'knows not what to deem [herself]', she seems to know very well what to deem Higginson.

As Pilate or Christ, he is her forgiver. As with the 'gnome' signature, Dickinson's power lies in her ability to use the pseudonym of 'Barabbas' to create a dynamic of her choosing. The quotation marks emphasise that Barabbas is just a role she is assuming; Dickinson implies that it is therefore one role she can just as easily discard.

Higginson clearly felt uncomfortable occupying the subject position that Dickinson outlined for him. Reflecting on his correspondence with the poet in 1890, he observed that she was 'always persistently keeping up this attitude of "scholar" and assuming on my part a preceptorship which it is almost needless to say did not exist'.[6] In 1869 Higginson wrote to Dickinson as his superior, expressing his desire to meet her: 'you ... enshroud yourself in this fiery mist and I cannot reach you, but only rejoice in the rare sparkles of light' (*L*, p. 461). In her response, Dickinson refuses to let him dismantle her carefully constructed power imbalance and elevates him even further:

You were not aware that you saved my Life. To thank you in person has since been one of my few requests. The child that asks my flower 'Will you' – he says – 'Will you' – and so to ask for what I want I know no other way. You will excuse what I say, because no other taught me? (*L*, p. 460)

Again, casting herself as his untutored disciple, Dickinson also makes Higginson her saviour, her Christ. Rather than inviting him on his terms and allowing him to feel as if he is privileged to uncover her mystery, she humbles herself and issues the invitation as if it would put her in his debt. There is, of course, a characteristic irony to this humility. She makes Higginson her saviour to outwit him and retain control of their relationship, something which she knew Christ's disciples would never presume to do.

Most critics agree that Dickinson's pseudonyms were a way of sealing her recipient into a relationship. Messmer notes that Dickinson's choice of alias is frequently based on the recipient's (often literary) background and interests.[7] Jane Eberwein sees her pseudonyms as 'a device for establishing a privileged relationship with the particular reader', and Judith Farr, picking one example, writes: 'if she could identify Sue with Cleopatra, Dickinson was willing to see herself in Anthony'.[8]

PRE- AND POST-LAPSARIAN LANGUAGE

Dickinson's fictions of naming, which became essential to her performative poetics, developed from a childhood interest in pre- and post-lapsarian language. Adam first speaks in Genesis when naming the animals:

And out of the ground the Lord God formed every beast of the field and every fowl of the air; and brought them unto Adam to see what he would call them; and whatsoever Adam called every living creature, that was the name thereof. And Adam gave names to all cattle, and to the fowl of the air, and to every beast of the field; but for Adam there was not found an help meet for him.[9]

Most biblical commentators assume that this is the first time Adam has ever spoken and so human language comes into being as an act of naming that imitates God's creation of the world. One does not have to take the interpretation of this passage very far to arrive at the idea that naming (or language) creates Adam's world. In the Adamic tradition, naming can be a world-making tool.

The reality which follows language is one where the relationship between essence and representation is paramount. If Adam learns language directly from God then the names he grants are inherently appropriate and, in the pre-lapsarian Garden of Eden, there is perhaps no difference between word and thing. Any pre-lapsarian theory of language would therefore be a theory of being. If Adam gives names at random and the parallel with God is one of contrast, then perhaps this gives credence to humanity's right to impose arbitrary signs and signifiers. For Dickinson, Adam's naming of the animals would almost certainly have been associated with true speech and she was familiar with many of the writers who grappled with the implications of Adam's language for the post-lapsarian world. She loved Shakespeare, whose Caliban rails against Prospero with the words: 'You taught me language; and my profit on't / Is, I know how to curse. The red plague rid you / For learning me your language'.[10] Prospero, in a clear echo of Adamic tradition, teaches Caliban 'how to name the bigger light, and how the less'.[11] Dickinson also read Emerson, who invokes Adam's 'true language' in his essay on 'The Poet', describing the poet as 'the Namer or Language-Maker' who gives to everything 'its own name and not another's'[12] and Milton who, as John Leonard has pertinently argued, dramatised the distinction between pre- and post-lapsarian naming in *Paradise Lost*.[13]

Milton's Adam begins to name his world as soon as he recognises the life in his own body:

> My self I then perus'd, and Limb by Limb
> Survey'd, and sometimes went, and sometimes ran
> With supple joints, and lively vigour led:

> But who I was, or where, or from what cause,
> Knew not; to speak I tri'd, and forthwith spake,
> My Tongue obey'd and readily could name
> What e'er I saw.[14]

Milton's Adam finds his power of naming at the very moment at which he tries to understand his own origins. When God presents the animals 'two and two' (350), Adam names them and then immediately asks after the name of God:

> O by what Name, for thou above all these,
> Above mankinde, or aught then mankinde higher,
> Surpassest farr my naming, how may I
> Adore thee, Author of this Universe,
> And all this good to man, for whose well being
> So amply, and with hands so liberal
> Thou hast provided all things: but with mee
> I see not who partakes.[15]

As Leonard explains, Adam's asking after God's name and his asking for a companion with whom to share the bounty of creation both result from his naming of the animals.[16] Adam's act of naming forces him to confront both the unnameable and incomprehensible nature of God and his own human nature and needs – a reference to Genesis 2.20: 'but for Adam there was not found an help meet for him'. In Milton's portrayal of the Adamic tradition, pre-lapsarian language signifies human ability to recognise things as they truly are – not only the things of the natural world but also humanity's own peculiar condition, exalted above the rest of creation and yet far from understanding the glory of the Creator-God. Milton's theory of pre-lapsarian language is indeed a theory of pre-lapsarian being. Adam understands his unique position in the world shortly after he finds the power of speech 'readily' in his mouth.

Reading Genesis and Milton, Dickinson would have understood pre-lapsarian language to be synonymous with truth and post-lapsarian language to be synonymous with equivocation and deception. If Adam initiates a language where things are what they are called, Eve is the first to question the relationship between sign and signified when she establishes the sin of disobedience, trusting the serpent's words over God's: 'But of the fruit of the tree which was in the midst of the garden, God hath said, Ye shall not eat of it, neither shall ye touch it, lest ye die. And the serpent said unto the woman, ye shall surely not die.'[17] Satan is not only 'guileful' with words but misleading in his movements: 'He leading swiftly rolled / In tangles, and made intricate seem straight, / To mischief swift.'[18] His movements parallel the linguistic deception with which he tempts Eve to disobedience with 'persuasive words, impregned / With reason, to her seeming, and with truth.'[19] And disobedience to God's dictum opens up new possibilities for human authorship – distanced for the first time from the Creator-God who, in Milton's terms, is 'Author of this Universe'. For Milton, Eve's sin releases a diabolic gift of fluency and performance. She launches immediately into an interior monologue, praising the Tree of Knowledge and making an idol of it:

> Thus to herself, she pleasingly began.
> O sov'reign, virtuous, precious of all trees
> In Paradise, of operation blest
> To sapience, hitherto obscured, infamed,
> And thy fair fruit let hang, as to no end
> Created; but henceforth my early care,
> Not without song, each morning and due praise
> Shall tend thee, and the fertile burden ease
> Of thy full branches offered free to all.[20]

Milton's Eve delights in her fiction and her eloquent speech recalls the serpent's words. And after Adam falls, the entire human language becomes associated with stances, disconnections and distance: 'Adam, estranged in look, and altered style, / Speech intermitted thus to Eve renewed'.[21]

Arguably, we could locate any theatrical or meta-theatrical writer in this Old Testament tradition of naming and language. It would not seem so pertinent to Dickinson if she had not shown, from childhood, a desire to place herself within it. In a letter to Abiah Root, written on 12 January 1846, Dickinson claimed that she was 'Eve, alias Mrs Adam' (*L*, p. 24). Dickinson would have known that Eve only comes by her name after she and Adam are cursed by God:

Unto the woman [God] said, I will greatly multiply thy sorrow and thy conception; in sorrow shalt thou bring forth children; and thy desire shall be to thy husband and he shall rule over thee. And unto Adam he said, Because thou hast hearkened unto the voice of thy wife, and hast eaten of the tree of which I commanded thee, saying, Thou shalt not eat of it: cursed is the ground of thy sake; in sorrow shalt thou eat of it all the days of thy life; Thorns also and thistles shall it bring forth to thee; and thou shalt eat the herb of the field; In the sweat of thy face shalt thou eat bread, till thou return unto the ground; for out of it wast thou taken: for dust thou art, and unto dust thou shalt return. And Adam called his wife's name 'Eve'; because she was the mother of all living.[22]

Not only is the name 'Eve' associated with a post-lapsarian distance from God in the inception of mortality, it is also coincidental with the fallen state of marriage, so Dickinson's joke creates another alias in 'Mrs Adam'. Immediately after Adam names his wife, he and Eve are given skins to clothe their nakedness and hide their newfound shame. The humorous duplicity of the alias 'Mrs Adam' is another indication that Dickinson is playing on the equivocal nature of language after the Fall. As 'Eve – alias Mrs Adam', she is party to a marriage founded in sin and concealment rather than innocence and transparency.

As Dickinson was well aware, in the fallen world names can be dangerous because they can lead us to false meanings. Her statement that she is 'Eve, alias Mrs Adam' is part of a letter in which she makes a joke of the metonymic capacity of the imagination: 'I have just seen a funeral procession go by of a negro baby, so if my ideas are rather dark you need not marvel' (*L*, p. 24). Margaret Homans charts Dickinson's literary process of becoming through her identification with Eve in these early letters, observing that the transition from religious metaphor to questions of fiction making is not fortuitous; they converge in ideas of truth. On 28 March 1846, Dickinson responded to the news of Abiah's conversion, presenting her friend's orthodoxy and her own fall from it as fictive:

I think of the perfect happiness I experienced when I felt I was an heir of heaven, as of a delightful dream, out of which the Evil one bid me wake and return again to the world and its pleasures. Would I not had listened to his winning words! … I determined to devote my whole life to [God's] service and desired that all might taste of the stream of living water from which I cooled my thirst. But the world allured me and in an unguarded moment I listened to her siren voice … I felt my danger and was alarmed in view of it, but I had rambled too far to return and ever since my heart has been growing harder and more distant from the truth and now I have bitterly to lament my folly. (*L*, pp. 30–1)

Quite possibly, as Homans suggests, Dickinson's insistence in these religious passages that there is such a thing as the truth may be a defence against the growing knowledge that there is no absolute truth or literal meaning.[23] The passage echoes the style of an Edwardsian sermon and the girl who resisted Revivalism is aware of the ease with which figurative language can deceive and she is also aware that the Bible is itself figurative. Perhaps, at fourteen, it still disturbed her that the fictions she delighted in were indistinguishable from the words of the 'Evil one', although the relish with which she elaborates upon her temptation suggests she rather liked to fall. By April 1850, however, her ambivalence had dissipated: 'I have heeded beautiful tempters, yet do not think I am wrong' she wrote to Jane Humphreys (*L*, p. 95). Before Dickinson was out of her teens, she had shed the moralism of Puritan piety and embraced the possibilities of post-lapsarian language.

Like her contemporary Walt Whitman, who wrote 'If I worship one thing more than any other it shall be the spread of my own body, or any part of it',[24] Dickinson found her poetic voice in the self's ability to permeate other selves, take possession of them and inhabit their name. In 'I'm Nobody! Who are you?', which Franklin dates to late 1861, she dramatised the absurd juxtaposition of silliness and seriousness in the poet who has no one name. To be 'Nobody' could enable one to be many bodies – to live the experience of the little girl, the amorous lover, the new bride, the martyr, the King, the human Jesus or any other of the myriad personae Dickinson inhabited. It recalls Emerson's transparent eyeball – 'I am nothing. I see all' – of which 'I'm Nobody' could be a reformulation.[25] But Dickinson's comic stance is central. The silliness of the poem, a refusal to be taken seriously, is a way of distancing herself from the earnestness of Transcendentalism. The tone suggests a parody of Emerson, yet in the parodic appropriation of his words, she demonstrates the ability of a 'nobody' to inhabit the bodies and voices of others.

> I'm Nobody! Who are you?
> Are you – Nobody – too?
> Then there's a pair of us!
> Don't tell! They'd banish us – you know!
>
> How dreary – to be – Somebody!
> How public – like a Frog –
> To tell your name – the livelong June –
> To an admiring Bog!
>
> (Fr260; J288)

Naming herself 'Nobody', Dickinson also makes a joke of the biblical connection between 'name' and 'reputation', writing 'How dreary – to be – Somebody!' In the Christian tradition, the connection is found in Philippians 2.5–9:

Let this mind be in you, which was also in Christ Jesus. Who being in the form of God, thought it not robbery to be equal with God. But made himself of no reputation, and took upon himself the form of a servant, and was made in the likeness of men: And being found in fashion as a man, he humbled himself, and became obedient unto death, even the death of the cross. Wherefore, God also hath highly exalted him, and given him a name which is above every name.[26]

Making himself 'of no reputation', Christ is rewarded with 'a name which is above every name'. Christ's humility stands in direct contrast to the Old Testament sin of overreaching, the offence committed by the Israelites in building the tower of Babel: 'And they said, Go to, let us build us a city and a tower, whose top *may reach* unto heaven; and let us make a name, lest we be scattered abroad upon the face of the whole earth'.[27] The story of Babel contrasts with other examples of human–divine communication in Genesis and Exodus which take place upon a mountain – a natural (and in the biblical worldview God-given) halfway house between heaven and earth. The man-made 'tower', however, is a symbol of humanity's arrogance (as opposed to God's condescension) as is the 'name' that they want to build with it. Moreover, 'scattering', in the Old Testament, is always a divine punishment and, in their vain hope that a 'name' (or reputation) may preserve their unity, the Israelites set themselves in defiance against God.

Christ is rewarded through language with a name of God's choosing – 'a name which is above every name' – and trying to build a 'name' for themselves, the Israelites are punished with confounded language and scattering:

And the Lord said, Behold the people is one, and they have all one language; and this they begin to do: and now nothing will be restrained from them which they imagine to do. Go to, let us go down, and confound their language, so they may not understand one another's speech. So the Lord scattered them abroad from thence upon all the face of the earth.[28]

In the post-lapsarian Bible, the power to create and destroy names, to give and confound language, is divine. God tells Moses: 'Whosoever hath sinned against me, him I will blot out of my book'.[29] He threatens to 'blot out the remembrance of Amalek from under Heaven' but not to 'blot out the name of Israel'.[30]

Dickinson's speaker openly ridicules the humble way in which Christ makes 'himself of no reputation'. The speaker takes on Christ's role in the spirit of disobedience rather than obedience. The silly tone, in its refusal of conformity, adds to the sense of the speaker's delight in this disobedience. Dickinson's fictions of naming and her desire to be 'nobody' are disobedient acts which subvert the idea that, as a process of naming and bonding into Christ's obedient sacrifice, Baptism undoes original sin. 'Don't Tell!' has the feel of a bond among thieves. The two voices could be those of Adam and Eve after they ate the apple. 'Banish' suggests the exile from Eden and Franklin notes 'advertise' as a variant for 'banish us' (and this is the variant that Johnson chooses). To 'Advertise' Adam's and Eve's sin would, after all, be to effect their banishment. In both Genesis and Milton, Adam and Eve try to hide their crime from God. Dickinson's colloquial 'Don't Tell!' and her silly 'frog' and 'bog' parody the Edenic

landscape. The story of the sin of disobedience becomes a tale of child-
ish naughtiness as Dickinson's 'Nobody' manifests the little girl persona
again, delightedly preserving her difference from the adult world.

Unlike the rebels of Genesis and *Paradise Lost* and the humble self-
emptying of Christ, Dickinson's two outsiders celebrate their exclusion.
Within this space of exclusion, the poet's jovial speaker names herself
'nobody', subverting the fixity implicit in a socially conferred 'name' or the
equative naming of pre-lapsarian Eden. She begs her double not to 'tell'
because this would surrender control of her name – 'they'd advertise' – and
destroy the inwardness symbolised by the bond to secrecy. Having read
Genesis and Milton, Dickinson would have been familiar with the idea
that the original sin of disobedience opened the space between essence and
representation, allowing a realm of inwardness to emerge. Asserting her
naughtiness, here, she protects that realm from intruders.

PERFORMING THE SELF: THE BAPTISMAL TRANSLATION

Dickinson's well-known poems on Baptism are rooted in this post-
lapsarian opening between essence and representation. In the Puritan
ritual of Baptism, children are given their own names at the same time
as they are baptised into the name of Christ. The *Westminster Shorter
Catechism* (1647), from which Dickinson would have been instructed,
gives the following description:

Baptism is a sacrament wherein the washing with water in the name of the
Father, and of the Son, and of the Holy Ghost, doth signify and seal our ingrafting into Christ, and partaking of the benefits of the covenant of grace, and our
engagement to be the Lord's.[31]

In Puritan doctrine, therefore, the sacrament of Baptism was the sign of
a bond marked by humanity's passivity and reception into the name of
God. As an experience in the Christian child's life, Baptism was also a
rebirth into promise. Baptised 'in the name of the Father, of the Son and
of the Holy Ghost' and 'ingraft[ed] into Christ', the child could hope
for, although not be sure of, salvation. The process of naming into God
allowed for a physical and interpretative translation – a cleansing of body
and a cleansing of mind and perception. This translation, which has its
roots in Gospel narrative and Calvinist theology, became the hallmark
of Dickinson's Baptism trope as she found, in the theology of Baptism,
a metaphor for her own poetic identity, repeatedly translating itself and
inhabiting new names.[32]

Translation can refer to a bearing of body and a bearing of meaning and usually involves some form of mediation to enable communication between two parties or movement between two places. In the Calvinist tradition sacraments are just such acts of mediation. Calvin wrote: 'The sacraments may be called the gate of Heaven, because they admit us into the presence of God'.[33] As a sacrament, Baptism opens the channels of communication and allows for a translation of human and divine speech. There is a scriptural basis for this: Christ's Baptism is the first time the incarnation clearly allows for communication between humanity and God; it is the first time that God speaks in the Gospels. As an 'ingrafting into Christ', Baptism enables the child to participate in the sacrament of the Word made flesh and, as we saw in the previous chapter, Dickinson's imagination of the Word made flesh and her understanding of poetic encounter endlessly fed off each other. The naming event of Baptism also appealed to her understanding of poetic election because of its mediatory possibilities.

Her most famous Baptism poem, 'I'm ceded – I've stopped being Their's –' (1862) explores a process of initiation that relies on an essential namelessness and a vital ability to choose and inhabit new names. If this poem is about Dickinson's conscious choosing of her own adult identity, quite possibly the identity of the poet her family did not expect her to be, then it is also about the poetic possibilities of sacramental mediation. In choosing her life as a poet – her adult Baptism and her new name – Dickinson's speaker does not let go of the sense that she is being born again in the 'supremest name' of God and into Christ's body, which must be crucified as well as resurrected. She also does not relinquish the idea that she is entering a covenant comparable to her childhood Baptism. The change is in her new-found consciousness of what she is doing. Poetic power resides in the ability to choose each name she inhabits.

> I'm ceded – I've stopped being Their's –
> The name They dropped upon my face
> With water, in the country church
> Is finished using now,
> And They can put it with my Dolls,
> My childhood, and the string of spools,
> I've finished threading – too –
>
> Baptized, before, without the choice,
> But this time, consciously, Of Grace –
> Unto supremest name –
> Called to my Full – The Crescent dropped –
> Existence's whole Arc, filled up,
> With one – small Diadem –

My second Rank – too small the first –
Crowned – Crowing – on my Father's breast –
A half unconscious Queen –
But this time – Adequate – Erect,
With will to choose
Or to reject,
And I choose, just a Crown –

(Fr353; J508)

In her essay on Dickinson's Baptismal imagery, Jones argues that the poet finds the experience 'overwhelmingly passive'.[34] Beginning with the 'name They dropped upon [her] face / With water', Dickinson draws from the orthodox position of passivity but she cannot help subverting it. The conscious formation of a new identity relies on the dynamic between passivity and activity, although asserting her authority does not necessarily bring her closer to an authentic sense of self. Celebrating her freedom from her given 'name' and therefore from her expected identity, Dickinson's speaker reaches for more symbols.[35] The language of majesty, here a 'Crown' and 'Diadem', reflects a barrier as well as a nearness to God. The diadem (a crown) only represents election. It is, like the sacrament of Baptism, an outward sign of inward spiritual grace. The speaker wears the mark of divinity, but the qualifying 'just' opens up a space between the crown and what it represents. The 'Will to choose, / Or to reject' is the freedom to inhabit the 'supremest name –,' a name that is not essentially hers. Dickinson is profoundly aware that, as a sacrament, Baptism is a sign and symbol of a grace that cannot be fully realised in this world.

The speaker's conclusion that she chooses 'just a Crown –' implies, in part, the compromise inherent in the sign of divinity, a compromise that Calvin acknowledged in his understanding of the sacraments as signs by which God manifests himself imperfectly in the world. Therefore, part of Dickinson's election is the awareness of an overwhelming absolute that cannot be properly grasped. The symbol is the only tangible means by which Dickinson may begin to comprehend the intangible, or incomprehensible, absolute – the nameless name. And the diadem also illustrates the poverty of symbolism; it can only represent and reflect divinity rather than be it.

Dickinson's attraction to the symbol of the diadem may have been influenced by Charles Wadsworth's sermons. According to Wadsworth:

The value of a gem is not in its composition, but in its crystallization. Even the diamond is composed mainly of carbon, and differs from the black coal of our furnaces only in this mysterious transfiguration ... But the spiritual man has through gracious crystallization, become a gem, *reflecting Divine light, and thus fitted for a diadem.*[36] (emphasis added)

So the diadem also illustrates the compromising necessity of symbolism. The sign of divinity, which makes us so aware of its essential absence, is all there can be of its presence.

As we saw in the previous chapter, Dickinson inferred a vital similarity between religious narratives and poetics in the use of compromised vision (such as the Word made flesh) to give the absolute a space within the relative. So, she employed various manifestations of the veil as a midway image between Puritan understandings of the incarnation and Romantic understandings of the imagination. Like a veil, poetics mediate between experience and an exalted or absolute notion of 'Poetry', which, through her own artifice, she thought 'We both and neither Prove'. In this instance the poetic paradox is expressed through a space that is both concrete, like a crown or diadem, and beyond the reach of the speaker who wears the crown. Thus, at the moment Dickinson's speaker asserts her agency she renders the effort of assertion empty with a passive construction by saying 'The name They dropped ... Is finished using' rather than choosing a more active construction such as 'I have finished using'.

The spatial narrative of the poem helps to explain this compromise. One of the implications of the circular 'spools' is that the destiny conferred on the baby was to inhabit a circle, and go round and round without breaking free of her given identity. Yet, the speaker says that her name was 'dropped' upon her face. The vertical movement implies that the speaker's infant Baptism was already part of a linear narrative. The circle appears to have been broken from the start, something the speaker emphasises with the image of the incomplete 'Crescent', which she also describes as 'dropped'. The imperfect circle that represents the infant Baptism contrasts with the diadem that she consciously chooses as an adult. The speaker's mature decision allows her to enter the circle, represented by the round diadem, far more successfully than her infant Baptism and the perfect circle suggests a further analogy with the poetic vocation that Dickinson described to Higginson as 'circumference' (*L*, p. 410). However, accepting her own existence as a series of compromised positions appears to be part of this new election. The diadem that fills existence is 'small'. As a child she was 'half-unconscious' and as an adult she stands 'erect' and in 'second rank', acknowledging through the vertical movement that she is climbing back up the line along which her childhood name and arc had 'dropped'.

The speaker perceives the compromise of election as a sacrifice and describes her second Baptism as a death. 'I'm ceded –' immediately suggests that she is dead, given up, finished. 'They' lay aside her name, dolls, and spools as a person's belongings are collected and packed away after her death. The image of 'the string of spools, / [She's] finished threading –' compounds the sense that this is a death-scene. Like the third of the Moraie, the Greek goddesses of fate and destiny, she has cut the thread of life.[37] Dickinson's speaker controls her own fate; she finishes threading her own spool; she chooses her own death. The crown for which she reaches at the end can be seen not only as the crown of election, but also as the crown of thorns. The compromise, which is part of her election, is equated with dying. Dickinson frequently used dying to express the intensity of reading poetry, and here it seems that she conceived of her poetic election in the same terms. As a death she chooses and controls, it is a sacrifice of self. So, the narrative of sacrificial dying expresses the compromise that allows her to harness her poetic power. This acknowledgment of compromise does not detract from the boldness of her art. The last line is also strikingly and knowingly audacious. She'll choose 'just a Crown –' as if it's a modest start! One should never underestimate Dickinson's ability to merge serious purpose with comic ambition, and she partly anticipates a hubristic end here.

Dickinson's aesthetic of Baptism can be seen to rely on the kind of enabling constraint (or veil) that the persona or fictional 'name' provides. The poet herself highlighted this theatricality with a natty disclaimer to Higginson in July 1862: 'When I state myself, as the Representative of the Verse – it does not mean – me – but a supposed person' (*L*, p. 412). Partly, of course, this is a way of protecting herself from biographical intrusion. But it also suggests that Dickinson valued the performative quality of her verse because the mask or veil that it provided liberated her from the limitations of her personal experience and so allowed her a fuller manifestation in art.

In other words, the supposing, staging and naming of the self were the result of both a conscious awareness of the compromise that the artifice or artistry of poetics entails, and a sense that such acts of compromised naming might begin an orientation (however hubristic) towards a 'supremest name'. In the Baptismal narrative which moves from the slavery of sin to the freedom of salvation, the name is an orientation towards, not a state identical with, true being. Puritan Baptism acknowledges a post-lapsarian opening between essence and representation and Dickinson exploited that opening repeatedly in her performative poetic stance.

In 'I am ashamed – I hide –' (1863) Dickinson consciously reworks the conversion narrative – a movement from helpless contrition and humility to powerful joy and love – to express the formation of a new performative self, baptised, in this poem, 'a Bride':

> I am ashamed – I hide –
> What right have I – to be a Bride –
> So late a Dowerless Girl –
> Nowhere to hide my dazzled Face –
> No one to teach me that new Grace –
> Nor introduce – My soul –
>
> Me to adorn – How – tell –
> Trinket – to make Me beautiful –
> Fabrics of Cashmere –
> Never a Gown of Dun – more –
> Raiment instead – of Pompadour –
> For Me – My soul – to wear –
>
> Fingers – to frame my Round Hair
> Oval – as Feudal Ladies wore –
> Far Fashions – Fair –
> Skill – to hold my Brow like an Earl –
> Plead – like a Whippowill –
> Prove – like a Pearl –
> Then, for a Character –
>
> Fashion My Spirit quaint – white –
> Quick – like a Liquor –
> Gay – like Light –
> Bring Me my best Pride –
> No more ashamed –
> No more to hide –
> Meek – let it be – too proud – for Pride –
> Baptized – this Day – A Bride –
>
> (Fr705; J472)

William Shurr has argued that the marriage day comes to symbolise a day exalted above any other for Dickinson, and that this poem begins with a humble celebration of the event.[38] Yet, as is so often the case with Dickinson, humility seems to be something in which the speaker luxuriates. She is, in the spirit of the Puritan conversion experience, ashamed before us, and she delights in the publicity of the display. The provocative irony of 'I hide –', as she places herself centre-stage, suggests the dynamic of humiliation and exaltation is enacted rather than felt, and it signals forward to the poem's concern with the performance of the self.

Dickinson's Baptismal imagery again acknowledges that a renaming of self calls authenticity into question. Here, Dickinson adds nuance to this concern with the desire for authenticity expressed in the second line and the speaker's recognition that the claim to authenticity rests on social signifiers like dowries. The focus on adornment and clothing is part of Dickinson's engagement with staged authenticity. The speaker's regret that there is no one to 'introduce – [her] Soul –' and her longing for someone to advise her on the right wardrobe 'For me – My soul – to wear' suggests a self that cannot be directly rendered, but must be staged and mediated by another.

The poem becomes clearer if we compare it with a letter Dickinson wrote to Sue on 12 March 1853. Lamenting Sue's absence from Amherst, she writes:

All life looks differently and the faces of my fellows are not the same they wear when you are with me. I think it is this, dear Susie; you sketch my pictures for me, and 'tis their sweet colourings, rather than this dim real that I am used, so you see when you go away, this world looks staringly at me, and I find I need more vail – Frank Pierce thinks I mean berage vail,[39] and makes a sprightly plan to import the 'article' but dear Susie knows what I mean. (*L*, p. 229)

Dickinson's game of dress-up in 'I am ashamed' casts the self into imaginative figures which bear comparison with the 'sweet colourings' of Sue's 'sketch[ed] … pictures'. As the 'vail' of artistic imagination lends the 'dim real' of everyday existence a greater clarity and protects her from the face-to-face confrontation of 'staring' banality, the self that is fashioned comes closer to its essence than that which is innocently unformed. So, the speaker's new name, 'Bride', also relies on performance for its authenticity. Her entry into 'that new Grace –', which has been granted as a gift, must also be learnt and performed in order to be realised. Thus, in the first two stanzas, the speaker appears sceptical that she can *be* rather than *borrow* her new self. The similes in the third stanza compound this. Yet the pun that haunts 'Far fashions – Fair –' and is repeated in 'Fashion My Spirit' hints that this borrowing may be all there is of creative action. 'Fashion', meaning both 'mode' and 'shape', implies that the speaker's guise is her shaping force.

If, in the first three stanzas, the idea of an authentic conversion to 'Grace' is consistently parodied by the language of theatricality, the final stanza acts as a pivot between a failed conversion or Baptism and a successful one. Desiring her spirit to be 'Quick – like a Liquor –', the speaker of 'I am ashamed' elides the difference between the sensation of burning and the sensation of life. It is, paradoxically, the recognition that she cannot *have* grace, but must surrender herself to the borrowing of it that allows for the change in tone. In the final stanza, she does not reach for the language of apparel. She seems, instead, to adopt an essence. The penultimate line suggests she is beyond the dynamic of the Puritan conversion experience: 'Meek – let it be – too proud – for Pride –'. The speaker's successful Baptism hints at the borrowing of Christ's own power, which she describes as a kind of ecstasy.[40] The Baptism of fire figuratively kills and divinely empowers (or enlivens) her. In this sense, the poem repeats the paradigm we saw in 'I'm ceded' of passivity and activity. The speaker, who is initially 'dazzled', finally chooses 'light'. Interestingly, her active choice then subsides into passive surrender, suggesting a similar compromise to the election of 'I'm ceded'. In the final stanza, she actively calls for her own Baptism and is passively 'Baptized' just as the active choosing of a 'Crown' is undercut by the passive construction 'Is finished using'. Yet, there can be no doubt that she is surrendering to something greater: a trial by suffering, a Baptism of fire.

'[W]hite' not only suggests purity and death, it recalls the 'Soul' of 'Dare you see a Soul at the *White Heat?*' which is 'Forge[d]' as the speaker's spirit is here 'Fashion[ed]'. 'Fashion'd' and 'Forg'd' both suggest that the deliberate activity of poetic craft (which Dickinson likens elsewhere to the pang which is 'wrought') is integral to the self's process of becoming.[41] In 'Dare you see a Soul at the *White Heat?*' (*c.*1862) Dickinson's speaker explores a short-lived triumph of essence over performance.

> Dare you see a Soul at the *White Heat?*
> Then crouch within the door –
> Red – is the Fire's common tint –
> But when the vivid Ore
> Has vanquished Flame's conditions,
> It quivers from the Forge
> Without a colour, but the light
> Of unannointed Blaze.
> Least village has its Blacksmith
> Whose Anvil's even ring
> Stands symbol for the finer Forge
> That soundless tugs – within –
> Refining these impatient Ores
> With Hammer, and with Blaze
> Until the Designated Light
> Repudiate the Forge –
>
> (Fr401; J365)

'Tint' and 'conditions' are the way in which fire makes itself visible to the eye and known in the world. This poem depicts heat as the essential being of flame. Marked by the absence of its signifiers, it is 'without a colour'. It also 'quivers', recalling, in its movement, Philippians 2.12, where the disciples are asked to work towards their salvation in 'fear and trembling'. Dickinson's naked, unannointed, unconditioned and colourless fire is extremely vulnerable. The quivering white heat articulates an essence which has vanquished its way of being known. The reader's invitation into a circumscribed and dangerous space ('crouch' also implies that the space may be small) allows for the idea that, in the position of a witness, we are in the place of the sacred. The Prometheus myth, which Dickinson knew well, may also be an influence on this poem. Prometheus stole fire from Hephaestos's forge in order to benefit mankind (by making the power of fire known in the world). In doing so, he violated the sanctity of the gods.[42]

The second half of the poem emphasises the difficulty of ushering into language the nothingness (in the sense of no-one-thing) of infinite being. The more reflective generalisation, 'Least village has its Blacksmith', is another way of knowing the absolute that is this poem's subject in experiential terms. Dickinson's speaker attempts to force the white heat back into the 'symbol', the very means of being known that it has vanquished, even before she acknowledges the way it is ironically undercut by the named or 'Designated' light. Like the 'crown' or 'diadem', the 'symbol for the finer forge' depicts the limited capability of the overreacher and the poet, who both desire to name or know that which they know naming destroys. There is a close connection, therefore, between the artistry and compromise of the symbol and the artistry and compromise of the name.

TOWARDS THE NAMELESS

Dickinson admits something of the overreacher in the poet who deals in essences, but as with the girl who chooses 'just a Crown –' she implies that the compromises she makes and the repeated translations of self that she performs are, like the 'Vail', a way of orienting herself beyond the name towards the nameless. Her poetic capability begins from the name as both this point of orientation and a shifting signifier of meaning which playfully and poetically enacts the difficulty of voicing namelessness. In 'The Sun went down – no Man looked on –' (1865) she depicted a 'nameless bird' which partly belies the ironic wit of 'I'm Nobody!' and the ironic disclosures of 'Dare you see a Soul at the *White Heat?*'

The Sun went down – no Man looked on –
The Earth and I, alone,
Were present at the Majesty –
He triumphed, and went on –

The Sun went up – no Man looked on –
The Earth and I and One
A nameless Bird – a Stranger
Were Witness for the Crown –

(Fr1109; J1079)

Again, this poem uses secrecy to give a sense of the sacred. 'No Man looked on' echoes the experiences of Abraham, Moses and Christ's disciples, who all shielded their faces from the blinding light of divinity. The sun, here, participates in the symbolism of divine presence, and the speaker stands privileged above humanity insofar as she is able to witness it. Dickinson identified her vocation as that of a 'warbling teller' or 'songbird'. This bird, which appears at the rising of the sun, may also represent Dickinson's poetic self, embodied apart as a kind of Holy Ghost. As it shares in her privilege, it at least implies that namelessness and the strange, the guises of the unknown, are the conditions of sacred witness. Like the Old Testament God, the speaker of this poem has no predicates. She refers to herself only as 'I'.

The 'nameless Bird – a Stranger', is also reminiscent of the dove in which the Holy Spirit descends during Christ's Baptism (prefigured in the dove which symbolises God's covenant with Noah after the flood).[43] The inverted movement of the setting and rising sun seems to mirror the movement of his Baptism; he lowers himself to be baptised by John and afterwards rises immediately out of the water, accompanied by the opening of the heavens, and the descent of the Holy Spirit in the form of the dove. The final 'Witness for the Crown' uses the divine symbolism of the sun to conflate the image of Christ's Baptism with the coronation imagery resonant of the Puritan election to grace. But 'witness' implies the speaker stands at one remove from the sacred which is also revealed symbolically (and therefore at a second remove) as a 'Crown'.

Namelessness metaphorically hovers in this poem, embodied apart from Dickinson's speaker and yet seeming to pertain directly to her unnamed identity. Dickinson displays a desire to be close to it, a sense perhaps that it manifests the very source and texture of her poetic language but she cannot, in the end, remove herself from the vocabulary of revealed religion (which must be witnessed in order to be true) and the Baptismal translation.

In 'The last of Summer is Delight –' (*c*.1875–6) she beautifully expressed her poetic dilemma:

> The last of Summer is Delight –
> Deterred by Retrospect.
> 'Tis Ecstasy's revealed Review –
> Enchantment's Syndicate.
>
> To meet it – nameless as it is –
> Without celestial Mail –
> Audacious as without a Knock
> To walk within the Vail.
>
> (Fr1380; J1353)

Dickinson played about with this poem but this was the version finally transcribed into set 14 and enclosed in a letter to Higginson in 1876. In all its variant forms this poem presents two different scenarios. It begins as a poem of definition, a naming of event and experience – variants of that naming include 'The last of Summer is a Time / For chastened Retrospect' and 'The last of Summer is Result / Subdued to Retrospect'. In all these variant forms, the speaker's act of naming brings the sense of removal inherent in a 'name' into focus. 'Delight – / Deterred by Retrospect' frames the experience in compromising memories of the height of summer. 'Ecstasy's revealed Review – / Enchantment's Syndicate' confirms the compromised vision implicit in the naming of experience. It also links this compromise to that of revealed religion. Sarcastic as ever about doctrinal surety, Dickinson suggests that naming this experience bankrupts it of meaning.

The alternative with which the second stanza opens, 'To meet it – nameless as it is –', uses the present tense of the verb 'to be' to emphasise the unmediated nature of the encounter. Unlike the 'Delight – / Deterred by Retrospect', this experience is not put off to the future or framed in the lens of memory. The impenetrability of 'Mail' also serves to emphasise the inadequacy of revealed religion and the naming of experience. As the 'Vail' is a type of Christ's body and a symbol of the mediate quality of the imagination, armour is the symbol by which God makes himself known in the world – a point clarified by the rhyme of 'Mail' and 'Vail'. 'To walk within the Vail' without acknowledging the necessity of separation is dangerous. The 'knock' allows the 'Vail' to be seen as a door, emphasising that the boundary is simultaneously a barrier and an invitation to enter (as in the 'door ajar'). But to enter this space requires a kind of dying – a sacrifice of self – because 'To walk within the Vail' is the privilege of the dead. 'Audacious' also suggests the danger of passing beyond the 'Vail' without the conventional politeness of the 'knock', an acknowledgment of a displaced position, which the first stanza describes and which Dickinson's fictions of naming explore, is part of its attraction.

The namelessness to which Dickinson aspired animated the poses she adopted and the personae she inhabited. It is the same namelessness that she owns in her description of the 'eclipse' her family 'call their "Father"'. Dickinson's credulous family need a name for God, a name by which they can understand their relationship to him. Their attitude is hardly unique. In religious discourse, God frequently becomes father to the child, master to the servant and shepherd to the lost sheep. Dickinson often satirised this need to name 'Papa above' (Fr151) and in her sense of her own vocation, the namelessness or epistemic absence of God is a poetic force without equal. It is a force which manifested itself most frequently in images of light (such as the rising, setting or eclipsed sun). The following chapter explores how, through imagining encounters with light, Dickinson brought poetry and divinity to a reckoning.

NOTES

1 'The heavens were opened unto him, and he saw the Spirit of God descending like a dove, and lighting upon him: And lo a voice from heaven, saying, "This is my beloved Son, in whom I am well pleased".' Matt. 3.16–17. The wording in Mark and Luke is almost identical. John writes: 'Upon whom thou shalt see the Spirit descending, and remaining on him, the same is he which baptizeth with the Holy Ghost' (1.33).
2 Søren Kierkegaard, *Fear and Trembling*, trans. Alastair Hannay (1843; London: Penguin, 2005), p. 6.
3 Jacques Derrida, *The Gift of Death*, trans. David Wills (Chicago and London: University of Chicago Press, 1992), p. 58.
4 For further discussion of Dickinson's personae, see John Emerson Todd, *Emily Dickinson's Use of the Persona* (The Hague: Mouton, 1973). For further discussion of Dickinson's letters, see Marietta Messmer, *A Vice for Voices: Reading Emily Dickinson's Correspondence* (Amherst, Mass.: University of Massachusetts Press, 2001).
5 Messmer, *A Vice for Voices*, p. 137.
6 *Ibid.*, p. 128.
7 *Ibid.*, p. 138.
8 Jane Donahue Eberwein, *Dickinson: Strategies of Limitation* (Amherst, Mass.: University of Massachusetts Press, 1985), p. 49, Farr, *Passion*, p. 175.
9 Gen. 2.19–20.
10 1.2.365–7.
11 1.2.337.

12 Emerson, 'The Poet' (1844), in *The Collected Works of Ralph Waldo Emerson*, ed. Joseph Slater, Robert Spiller, Alfred R. Ferguson *et al.*, 6 vols. (Cambridge, Mass.: Harvard University Press, 1971–2003), vol. 3, pp. 1–25, at p. 13.

13 John Leonard, *Naming in Paradise: Milton and the Language of Adam and Eve* (Oxford: Clarendon Press, 1990). For Dickinson's knowledge of Milton and Emerson, see Jack Capps, *Emily Dickinson's Reading: 1836–1886* (Cambridge, Mass.: Harvard University Press, 1966), pp. 12, 34, 71–2, 180 (Milton) and pp. 92, 101, 111–18, 121, 127, 145, 173–4 (Emerson).

14 8.267–270.

15 8.357–364.

16 Leonard, *Naming in Paradise*, p. 25.

17 Gen. 3.3–4.

18 9.655 and 631–3.

19 9.737–8.

20 9.794–802.

21 9.1132–3. The sense of disconnection is heightened in the Old Testament story of Babel where, as we will see later in this chapter, God's punishment for humanity's foolish attempt to build themselves up a name equal to his own, is an even greater confounding of (a once pure) language.

22 Gen. 3.16–20. In Gen 2.23, Adam says, 'she shall be called Woman, because she was taken out of Man'.

23 Homans, *Women Writers*, p. 168.

24 Walt Whitman, 'Song of Myself' (1855), in *Complete Poems and Prose of Walt Whitman* (Philadelphia: Ferguson Bros & Co., 1881), pp. 29–79, at p. 49.

25 Emerson, 'Nature', in *The Collected Works of Ralph Waldo Emerson*, ed. Joseph Slater, Robert Spiller, Alfred R. Ferguson *et al.*, 6 vols. (Cambridge, Mass.: Harvard University Press, 1971–2003), vol. 1, pp. 7–45, at p. 10.

26 In nineteenth-century Germany, this passage inspired a group of theologians to consider the idea that, in becoming human, God the son in some way limited himself or temporarily emptied himself of some of the properties thought to be divine prerogatives. This became known as kenotic theology, from the Greek verb κενό ('keno' meaning 'to empty') and emphasised Christ's humility. See Stephen C. Evans (ed.), *Exploring Kenotic Christology: The Self-Emptying of God* (Oxford: Oxford University Press, 2006).

27 Gen. 11.4.

28 Gen. 11.6–8.

29 Exod. 32.33.

30 Deut. 25.19, 2 Kings 14.27.

31 Jones, '"A Royal Seal"', p. 31.

32 Linda Freedman, '"Meadows of Majesty": Baptism as Translation in Emily Dickinson's Poetry', *The Emily Dickinson Journal*, 17.1 (2008), pp. 25–43.

33 Jean Calvin, Commentary on Gen. 28.17, cited in Ronald S. Wallace, *Calvin's Doctrine of the Word and Sacrament* (Edinburgh: Scottish Academic Press, 1995), p. 23.

34 Jones, '"A Royal Seal"', p. 33.

35 Her expected identity is reflected in the 'dolls' and 'spools'. As Jane Eberwein points out, dolls prepare a little girl for motherhood and threading spools train small hands for manual labour or fancy needlework. Eberwein, *Strategies of Limitation*, p. 189.

36 Charles Wadsworth, *Sermons* (Philadelphia, 1882), p. 77, cited in Mary Elizabeth Barbot, 'Emily Dickinson's Parallels', *The New England Quarterly*, 14.4 (1941), pp. 689–96, at p. 690.

37 One spun the thread of life, one determined the length of the thread of life and one cut the thread of life. The weird sisters in *Macbeth*, which Dickinson read and loved, were based on this myth.

38 Shurr, *Marriage of Emily Dickinson*, p. 109.

39 A fashionable covering for the face.

40 John the Baptist says: 'I indeed baptise you with water unto repentance: but he that cometh after me is mightier than I, whose shoes I am not worthy to bear: he shall baptise you with the Holy Ghost, and with fire'. Matt. 3.11.

41 Fr665.

42 Dickinson's familiarity with the Prometheus myth is discussed in greater detail in Chapter 4, below.

43 Gen. 8.8–11. The flood is an Old Testament type for New Testament Baptism.

CHAPTER 3

Encounters with light

In the synoptic Gospels, the transfiguration connects Baptism with crucifixion because all are events of extreme metamorphosis and boundary crossing.[1] The transfiguration is a moment when the disciples witness Jesus shining with divine light. The synoptic accounts of Jesus's transfiguration all focus on his sudden and apparent brightness. Matthew writes: 'His face shone like the sun and his raiment was white as light'.[2] Mark says: 'And his raiment became shining, exceeding white as snow; so as no fuller on earth can whiten them'.[3] Luke tells how: 'his raiment was white and glistering'.[4] The light of transfiguration has no limits. It is uncreated divine light.[5] In the transfiguration story Jesus is beheld as the centre of this light. He makes the eternal manifest to the disciples. The transfiguration resonates thematically with other examples of divine appearance. There have been several studies which suggest the transfiguration story is a misplaced resurrection story.[6] Other studies have proposed the transfiguration prefigures the resurrection or cite it as a post-resurrection story of ascension.[7]

The transfiguration has been seen as a foreshadowing of Christ's glorification. Both Mark and Matthew stress the unnatural brightness of Jesus's clothing during his transfiguration.[8] The apocalyptic transformation of the cosmos is associated with magical garments throughout the Bible. Matthew and Mark specifically echo Enoch 14.20, where the 'gown' of the 'Great Glory' is said to be 'shining more brightly than the sun, and ... whiter than any snow'. Enoch 71.1 also talks of the 'sons of the holy angels' whose 'garments were white ... and the light of their faces was like snow'. Christ's clothing at the moment of his transfiguration parallels the transformative garments of the heavenly seers. At the moment of Christ's transfiguration the heavenly fabric which tears at the Baptism and crucifixion manifests itself as his garment, whole and intact. The part of death prefigured in the transfiguration is, therefore, the process of dying – the means by which a redeemed man is able to enter heaven.

Dickinson's encounters with light describe inspiration as a mental change that is similar to the spiritual change wrought by transfiguration. Although the Gospel story provides the imaginative impetus for many of these descriptions, her understanding of the trope extends beyond it, fuelled by an awareness of other religions. Mythological sun-gods and Old Testament fires fuse with New Testament transfiguration to dramatise inspiration as the intrusion of eternity into time. This chapter explores the way in which Dickinson derives her ideas about inspiration and poetic longevity from her understanding of encounters with light as experiences of eternity within time or death within life.

Although Dickinson's moments of inspiration are fleeting, they gesture towards the possibility of a more lasting realm of illumination. Briefly transfigured, her speakers are left to contemplate that realm in terms that call both Heaven and poetic posterity into question. In this respect, her encounters with light are starkly different to the kind of boundary crossing we find in poems where notions of quest and sacrifice, the central themes of Chapters 4 and 5, predominate. They deal with the moment as opposed to the journey; they imagine brief intrusions of eternity into time rather than the slow and frequently painful process of poetic wandering. Light therefore emerges as a desired but often untrustworthy source of the poet's creative power and a half-desired, half-despised symbol of poetic posterity.

COMPARATIVE RELIGION

Dickinson understood the continuity between the sun-god, the transfigured Christ and sublime illumination. The comparative religious study that uncovers such parallels was an essential part of the growing transatlantic liberalism in the nineteenth century. The writings of F. C. Baur, Ludwig Feuerbach and David Friedrich Strauss questioned the historicity of Christ and allowed for the idea that archetypes, based ultimately on psychology, were deducible from comparative religious study. Baur's first work, published in 1824, focused on the symbolism and mythology of the ancient world and its relation to Christianity. For Feuerbach, the study of God was to be found in the study of man. He wrote: 'I accept the Christ of religion, but I show that this supernatural being is nothing more than the product and reflex of a supernatural mind'.[9] Strauss's *Life of Christ*, which, like Feuerbach's *Essence of Christianity*, was brought into the English language by George Eliot, argues for a religious and theological truth in the Gospels which is mythical rather than historical. In translation through Eliot's works, the German contribution to comparative religious study found its way into American intellectual society.

In his ministerial role, Emerson articulated the liberal idea that religious sentiment was the same 'whether the individual honor Jove or Brahma or the Holy Virgin or Saint' but became 'disordered by the corruptions' of cult and culture.[10] His divergence from Unitarianism was due, in part, to a feeling that it was just another such cult but he continued to emphasise comparative religion as a legitimiser of essential human truths. In 1838, he accused 'historical Christianity' of converting Jesus into a 'demigod, as the Orientals or Greeks would describe Osiris and Apollo'.[11] His growing attraction to 'the devout and contemplative East', which intensified from the 1840s, also helped him validate his own sense of the material world as an image of the God within.[12]

In 1850, the English Charles Southwell (1812–60) translated *Origines de tous les cultes* by François Dupois (1742–1809) which explained that Christianity was still the worship of nature, especially of the sun, and Christ was the same hero as Osiris.[13] Southwell, who had spent time in prison for blasphemy, wrote a virulent attack on the Christian church in which he made it clear that the history of the Christian God and Christ is another 'solar fable' in which light vanquishes darkness and Christ appears as a sun-god. As the century progressed, the interest in the mythological origins of Christianity and in the parallels between liberal Christianity and Asiatic religions increased in Europe and America. In 1870 Channing gave an address on the religions of China in which he furthered Unitarian beliefs by emphasising both the individual and societal presence of reason and sensibility in oriental thought and practice.[14] In 1873, the Oxford Professor Friedrich Max Muller dedicated his *Introduction to the Science of Religion* to Emerson. Muller's book has been called 'the foundation document of comparative religion in the English speaking world'.[15] In 1918, Williston Walker, an American church historian who graduated from Amherst College in 1883 (a few years before Emily Dickinson's death in 1886) published *A History of the Christian Church*, in which he wrote:

December 25 ... celebrated the victory of light over darkness, and the lengthening of the sun's rays at the winter solstice. This assimilation of Christ to the sun god ... was widespread.[16]

In the Gospels, Christ's transfiguration is the clearest example of the prevalence of this sun-god myth among the early Christian writers. But all major religious traditions see light as emanating from divine beings which is why early religious myths and stories usually involve some kind of sun-god and the characteristics of later deities are often indebted to early sun-god myths. The Greek Helios (known to the Romans as Sol) and Apollo, the Egyptian Ra and the Persian Mithra were all gods of sun or light and so important to early mythology that, in the first centuries CE, Jesus was commonly perceived and represented as the Logos, a cosmic power of harmony underlying the order of the universe, whose central emblem was the sun, a source of reality, light and life.[17] The most commonly used type for Christ – the ram or the lamb – was also the celestial sign of Aries. The sun passed through Aries in March and began to lead the world back to the long days of summer. The yearly return of the sun to the celestial lamb occurred in spring and was therefore associated with the regeneration of nature. Ancient sun-worshippers celebrated the victory of the lamb over the Prince of Darkness. The priests wore white, the colour of Christ's clothes in the transfiguration story (and Emily Dickinson's uniform dress). The Persians chanted the renewal of all things, and the Trojans annually sacrificed a white lamb to the sun.

Dickinson, influenced by contemporary trends, often imagined transfigurative encounters with light in mythological or abstractly emotional terms. From her knowledge of typology, she would have also understood the way in which the transfiguration narratives are indebted to Old Testament stories of divine illumination. Matthew – Dickinson's favourite Gospel writer – amalgamates motifs from Moses and Daniel in his version of the story. One biblical commentator, A. D. A. Moses, suggests that Matthew portrays the transfiguration as a magnified version of the events on Sinai. After Moses's encounter on Sinai, his face shines with the reflected glory of God. Daniel, by contrast, has a vision of an angel whose face is 'like the appearance of lightning' – a manifestation, rather than reflection, of divine presence.[18] For A. D. A. Moses, it is precisely because Jesus is the Danielic Son of Man, shining with divine light and not simply reflecting it, that he is a new and greater Moses and the transfiguration is a new and greater Sinai event.

THE TRANSFIGURING EXPERIENCE

Dickinson was well aware that the sun could be a scorching and destructive power that withered life as well as a vital radiance that nourished the world. Her descriptions of transfiguration gain their force from this paradox. As a young woman, early in June 1852, she wrote to Susan Gilbert of the sun's terrible strength. Here, Dickinson's sun is a god, personified as the 'man of noon'. Dickinson herself, the innocent trusting flower, both desires and fears possession by sunlight – the transfiguring experience that will leave her irrevocably altered:

You have seen the flowers at morning, *satisfied* with the dew, and those same sweet flowers at noon with their heads bowed in anguish before the mighty sun; think you these thirsty blossoms will now need nought but – *dew*? No, they will cry for sunlight, and pine for the burning noon, tho' it scorches them, scathes them; they have got through with peace – they know that the man of noon, is mightier than the morning and their life is henceforth to him. Oh, Susie, it is dangerous, and it is all too dear, these simple trusting spirits, and the spirits mightier, which we cannot resist! It does so rend me, Susie … that I tremble lest at sometime I, too, am yielded up. (*L*, p. 210)

Dew – recalling the Christian's passive Baptism – is nothing compared to this extreme glorification. Dickinson dismisses '*satisf[action]*' as the humble position of those who know no better, of innocence and ignorance, the blind contentment of people whom Sylvia Plath would condemn in 1963 as 'The tame flower-nibblers, the ones / Whose hopes are so low they are comfortable'.[19] One could easily read Dickinson's 'thirsty blossoms' as part of a nineteenth-century preoccupation with death.[20] But, while death is certainly present in the image, what seems to set Dickinson apart, here, is the suggestion that she will be 'yielded up' to life. The flowers are scorched – scathed but not killed by their sun-worship. The intensity of the burning noon is the moment to which they will consecrate their lives. The real contradiction here is the suggestion that life is intensified at the moment eternity, or death, enters time, or mortality. What the flowers undergo, and what Dickinson fears and desires, is not death but transfiguration.

In the biblical tradition, the real paradox of sun symbolism lies in the fact that the sun's withering and destructive power is part of the symbolism of divine revelation. In Moses's encounter with the burning bush, God appears as a terrifying force of fire. When the Israelites are gathered at the foot of Mount Sinai, the mountain becomes wrapped in a dark smoke because God descends on it in fire. Only Moses is privileged enough to approach the darkness which shrouds God's fiery presence.[21] Similarly, in Ezekiel's vision of God's glory, divine beings appear in the middle of an oddly bright cloud: 'a great cloud, and a fire infolding itself, and a brightness was about it, and out of the midst thereof as the colour of amber, out of the midst of the fire'.[22] As Christ radiates divine light during his transfiguration, his brightness is again accompanied by an overshadowing paradoxical 'bright cloud'.[23]

Fire breeds smoke just as God breeds danger, and light may be a religious metaphor for divine truth, strength and goodness but stories of divine illumination often include suggestions of darkness because they focus on the actual and threatening experience of divine encounter rather than the abstraction of divine goodness. So, too, Dickinson's sun-worshipping flowers feel the presence of the sun as intense and visceral. They 'thirst' after his power, expressing spiritual longing as physical and erotic desire for the 'man of noon'; they bow their heads submissively and painfully in 'anguish'; they 'cry' and 'pine' as would abandoned children, lovers or widows. '[T]hey have got through with peace' writes Dickinson, acknowledging the permanent rupture brought about by the encounter with light. These flowers will never know peace again. The poet's passions are moved here by the same sense of excitement and horror that inspires her retelling of Moses's encounter with the burning bush in 'No Man saw Awe'. Moses, we might remember, survives but he does not remain unhurt.

> Not deeming of his dread abode
> Till labouring to flee
> A grasp on comprehension laid
> Detained vitality.
>
> Returning is a different route
> The Spirit could not show
> For breathing is the only work
> To be enacted now.

Like the flowers who are 'yielded up', Moses's life is momentarily suspended in the presence of the absolute and is never quite the same again. In both instances, Dickinson describes the quintessential religious narrative of an encounter with light. Like Moses, her flowers (avatars of herself) are glorified and that experience includes physical harm and emotional abasement.

In 'He touched me, so I live to know' (1862), Dickinson describes another transfiguring experience, fusing religious imagery with Romantic notions of the sublime in the story of a lover's embrace. Here, her speaker's transfiguration is carried by an erotic search for light in the midst of cloudy darkness. Light gives shape to experience but the darkness of sex and the sea, of dreams and imagination, of the womb and the depths of the mind, has its own creative power and, beginning with a lover's embrace and a sea-image of coital union, Dickinson establishes a fertile and inviting darkness:

> He touched me, so I live to know
> That such a day, permitted so,
> I groped opon [*sic*] his breast –

It was a boundless place to me
And silenced, as the awful Sea
Puts minor streams to rest.

And now, I'm different from before,
As if I breathed superior air –
Or brushed a Royal Gown –
My feet, too, that had wandered so –
My Gypsy face – transfigured now –
To tenderer Renown –

Into this Port, if I might come,
Rebecca to Jerusalem,
Would not so ravished turn –
Nor Persian, baffled at her shrine
Lift such a Crucifixal sign
To her imperial Sun.

                                    (Fr349; J506)

Like the 'thirsty blossoms', the speaker's experience of transfiguration is
strongly sensual. She knows through touch not sight, and can only grope
blindly. 'Grope' suggests both a search for something by feeling (especially, Webster notes, in the dark or like a blind person) and the search
for knowledge in mental darkness. Franklin and Johnson note that
Dickinson's suggested variations for lines 2–3 are 'persuaded so / I per-
ished' and 'accepted so – / I dwelt'. The suggested changes remained mar-
ginal so the emphasis is on darkness and uncertainty. But Dickinson was
considering death when she wrote these lines and she retained a death
image in the 'boundless place' which 'silenced as the awful sea / Put
minor streams to rest'. As an experience of death in life, this transfiguration is also an experience of sensual and sexual delight. The touch of the
unknown awakens body and mind, forging through sense-experience the
connection between bodily life and mental knowledge and so the speaker's life is overwhelmed by the memory of dark feelings: 'He touched me,
so I live to know / That such a day, permitted so, / I groped upon his
breast –'.

The poem hunts the darkness of the opening stanza to uncover the
light of transfiguration. A new gentleness, a metaphorically 'lighter'
look graces the speaker's visage: 'My Gypsy face – transfigured now – /
To tenderer Renown'. If darkness is erotic, uncertain, alien and fruit-
ful, light is associated with an exalted return home and so the speaker
talks of a roving 'Gypsy' existence in the past tense: 'My feet, too, that
had wandered so'. The poem ends with two equally strong images of

submission: Rebecca, foremother of Christ, elected by God, submitting to the divine,[24] and the Persian priestess worshipping the sun. The consecutive images link the divine touch to that of the archetypal sun-god given form in Christ. But Dickinson, a fan of the simile – 'as if I breathed superior air' – and the conditional 'if' – 'if I might come' – implies that the submissive return home is not assured. Dickinson's speaker, here, has little power to choose. Striking a more submissive tone than she uses in any of her Baptism poems, Dickinson asks for permission to return and her request recalls the permission she received to '[grope] upon his breast'. Like the flowers in Dickinson's letter to Sue, the speaker would surrender her life to the divine moment of touch – an encounter with light in the midst of erotic darkness.

In the terms of the Romantic sublime, she yearns to rekindle the numinous experience she had that day; she wants to be lost again inside a power infinitely greater than herself and yet she tries to control that power as the Persian priestess may appease the power of the sun through ritualistic worship. Sublime experience owed much to the duality of fear and relief – fear at the threat to one's life and relief at having been preserved from that threat – and the experience of the sublime was frequently associated with a particularly awesome type of physical environment like a storm or the sea. Dickinson's image of the stream meeting the sea (or man meeting his maker) evokes that sublime threat. But, as Gary Stonum has argued, enlisting Dickinson as a poet of the sublime says nothing new about her; the difference is in how she adapts it. For Stonum, the orthodox Romantic sublime necessitates a poetics of mastery in which the poet's authority resides in their sublime transfiguration at the end of the poem. Dickinson, by contrast, works to circumvent the complicity between sublimity and mastery, deliberately avoiding a sense of formal closure and thematic coherence. Stonum suggests that, in Dickinson, the encounter with alterity that forms a major part of sublime experience is a confrontation with an alien subjectivity not a neutral object. Two subjectivities, self and other, vie for power.[25]

In 'He touched me', the other takes on the alien subjectivity of a lover. The sea also had peculiarly animate resonances for Dickinson. Sewall notes how, in 1850, she ran straight towards the open sea crying loudly to a pious friend, 'I love the danger!'[26] The sea, evocative of dark and mysterious origins, primeval and surging depths, erotic and procreative power, holds the danger of life as well as death. Dickinson clearly enjoyed provoking her pious friend with unladylike and unorthodox behaviour but her outburst reveals a genuine excitement at the danger of death which could invigorate, and even enable, life. Noticeably, her transfiguration story in 'He touched me' displays no relief at having been preserved from danger and every desire to return to it, perhaps knowing that, like the 'thirsty blossoms', she has 'got through with peace'.

Stonum's emphasis on the 'alien subjectivity' of Dickinson's sublime encounters indicates one of the ways in which her religious imagination modifies her notion of the Romantic sublime. For Rebecca and the Persian priestess, submission and worship are empowering because they forge a relationship with divinity. For Christ, too, the transfiguration is a moment of submission, as he becomes possessed by his own alien subjectivity (or divine nature), and empowerment, as he shines with godly radiance. Christ's transfiguration is simultaneously the moment when his authority is confirmed as the disciples witness his divine nature and God claims him as his son, and the point at which his sacrificial and submissive role in the divine plan is foreshadowed in the idea of his future death and resurrection. The 'transfigured' return Dickinson imagines at the end of this poem implies an even greater empowerment than she has yet known, a creative fruitfulness born of dark eroticism.

CREATIVE TENSIONS: APOLLONIAN LIGHT AND DIONYSIAN DARKNESS

The tension between the poet as a source of divine light or power and the poet who surrenders to divine possession has a parallel in Nietzsche's concept of Apollonian and Dionysian principles, which he derived, in part, from Emerson.[27] Apollo – the God of Light – lends his name to all types of form or structure. Dionysus – the God of Wine – possesses the ecstatic subject in a frenzy of dark intoxication. Emerson claimed that: 'The poet knows that he speaks adequately then only when he speaks somewhat wildly ... not with the intellect alone but with the intellect inebriated by nature ...'.[28] Emerson's language on the subject of poetic utterance also turns repeatedly on images of light. In 'The Method of Nature' he claims that, 'the poet must be a rhapsodist: his inspiration a sort of bright casualty'.[29] In 'Self-Reliance' he urges that, 'a man should learn to detect and watch that gleam of light which flashes across his mind from within'.[30]

Arguably, the sun-god myth created an archetypal patterning structure for sublime encounter which informed the Romantic oracular tradition and in which Dickinson's poetry participates. Her poetry frequently situates itself at the point of tension between the powers of Dionysus and

Apollo. Her art, as Camille Paglia was one of the first to notice, some-times rises out of her control and, like the Pythia seated at the Temple of Delphi, she seems to become possessed by its prophetic tones.[31] The Apollonian manifests itself as order and control, forcing the unruly into patterns of poetic form and structure, harnessing the light that inspires in the midst of a sublime darkness. 'I would not paint – a picture –' (1862) bound together with 'He touched me' in fascicle 17 explores this ten-sion between light and dark, power and surrender in relation to artistic endeavour:

> I would not paint – a picture –
> I'd rather be the One
> It's bright impossibility
> To dwell – delicious – on –
> And wonder how the fingers feel
> Whose rare – celestial – stir –
> Evokes so sweet a Torment –
> Such sumptuous – Despair –
>
> I would not talk, like Cornets –
> I'd rather be the One
> Raised softly to the Ceilings –
> And out, and easy on –
> Through villages of Ether –
> Myself endued Balloon
> By but a lip of Metal –
> The pier to my Pontoon –
>
> Nor would I be a Poet –
> It's finer – own the Ear –
> Enamoured – impotent – content –
> The License to revere,
> A privilege so awful
> What would the Dower be,
> Had I the Art to stun myself
> With Bolts of Melody!
>
> (Fr348; J505)

After desiring the Dionysian role throughout the poem, Dickinson inverts the pattern in the last few lines. Shifting her focus from the superhuman force which will possess her to her power to possess nature and art, she moves from passivity to activity. She may well have been experimenting, here, with her reading of Emerson. Poetic inspiration is divine lightning but the attack is internal, recalling 'that gleam of light which flashes across [a man's] mind from within'.

For Dickinson, as for Emerson, light was associated with the prophetic power of divine fire, energy and wonder. But, light was also part of a quasi-mystical, quasi-scientific vocabulary. Dickinson's speaker wonders what it would be like to float 'Through villages of Ether'. For Dickinson and her contemporaries, ether was not quite matter (Newtonian science emphasised that matter had to be inert and could only be animated by ether) and not quite spirit (which was a divine substance). Ether was also thought to be the medium of light. So this is another one of Dickinson's illuminated encounters. But what kind of encounter is it? Ether was part of contemporary science but it caught the literary imagination of a number of writers. Emerson used ether to express the essential disembodied truth of history: 'Time dissipates to shining ether the solid angularity of facts'.[32] Dickinson twice imagined an 'ether sea' – a shining gulf or perhaps bridge between two worlds.[33] Floating 'Through villages of Ether', her speaker wonders what it would be like to inhabit passively the medium of light, not encounter it directly or assume any of its power. Returning to (lightning) 'Bolts of Melody' at the end, she harnesses the power of light for herself. Lightning bolts – the natural vocabulary of the Romantic sublime – win over a passive involvement in the medium of ether that, Dickinson implies, rather lacks the Promethean urge.

Dickinson's desire to float through the ether expresses the limits as well as the reach of the Dionysian experience. She reveals a kind of wonder at the mechanics of the balloon which can be held aloft in the ether by 'but a lip of metal'. But Dionysian possession is inferior to Apollonian control, which emphasises the poet's own ability to bring about an encounter with light through the creative act. Shifting her focus from the super-human force which will possess her to her power to possess nature and art, Dickinson's speaker moves from passivity to activity, imagining that she is the source and culmination of light.

THE READING EXPERIENCE: SOURCES OF INSPIRATION AND DARK TRANSFIGURATIONS

Wherever there are issues of possession and origin in Dickinson's encounters with light, there are questions about the divine or dark sanction of creative power. About 1863, while recalling the experience of reading Elizabeth Barrett Browning's poetry for the first time, she described a transfiguring encounter with light that hints at diabolic, as opposed to divine, influence.[34] The poem conceives of inspiration as a mental change that is equivalent to the spiritual effect wrought by transfiguration, but this transfiguration hinges on the closeness between creative and destructive power:

I think I was enchanted
When first a sombre Girl –
I read that Foreign Lady –
The Dark – felt beautiful –

And whether it was noon at night –
Or only Heaven – at noon –
For very Lunacy of Light
I had not power to tell –

The Bees – became as Butterflies –
The Butterflies – as Swans –
Approached – and spurned the narrow Grass –
And just the meanest Tunes

That nature murmured to herself
To keep herself in Cheer
I took for Giants – practising
Titantic Opera –

The Days to Mighty Metres stept –
The Homeliest – adorned
As if unto a Jubilee
'Twere suddenly confirmed –

I could not have defined the change –
Conversion of the Mind
Like Sanctifying in the Soul –
Is witnessed – not explained –

'Twas a Divine Insanity –
The Danger to be Sane
Should I again experience –
'Tis Antidote to turn –

To Tomes of solid Witchcraft –
Magicians be asleep –
But Magic – hath an Element
Like Deity – to keep –

(Fr627; J593)

This encounter with light begins with another and sensual experience of darkness, hunting it, as in 'He touched me', to recover a transfiguring illumination. But here the initial darkness bears the mark of sorcery. Reading 'that Foreign Lady' sounds like the activity of an enchanted fortune teller and becomes tantalisingly exotic. England, we know, was far from 'Foreign' to her. She felt sympathetic companionship with her 'yorkshire girls' (the Brontës) and she read Romantic and contemporary British writers as, if not more, avidly those of her native country.[35] Describing

Barrett Browning as a 'Foreign Lady', Dickinson emphasises the wandering nature of her reading experience. This encounter with light is not a homecoming but, like the 'Gypsy' rovings in 'He touched me', a lunatic (or lunar) divergence. This is the only time the word 'lunacy' appears in Dickinson's lexicon. Her depictions of blinding or disorientating light are usually associated with the sun and not the moon. If sunlight is indicative of divine presence, moonlight, and its association with madness, suggests a warped imitation of divine power. The pace over the following three stanzas increases to a diabolic frenzy and the metamorphoses the speaker describes are not natural.

The poem suggests that poetic inspiration distorts the mind and, as McIntosh rightly emphasises, this only makes claim for the experience more convincing.[36] But, it is a very particular distortion: a 'Lunacy of light' echoed later as a 'Divine Insanity'. The poem's 'Lunacy of light' carries the theme of a dark transfiguration, mirrored in the strange and wonderful metamorphoses of the bees and butterflies. This is a dark brightness, an indication that creative power can easily become destructive. As McIntosh has argued, the experience of reading Browning's poetry is presented as 'an outrageous but plausible alternative to the Calvinist conversion experience'.[37] Thus, like Christ's transfiguration and the Calvinist conversion experience, it is 'witnessed – not explained –'. The speaker's concession, 'The Danger to be Sane', is telling. To be conscious of poetic inspiration, as to come face to face with God without shielding one's eyes, is dangerous.

The difference is, of course, that this appears to be a conversion generated by witchcraft as opposed to God.[38] Religion leaves humanity passive in the face of supernatural powers but magic empowers human beings through their command of the supernatural, and Dickinson suggests Browning's poetry shares that power. Thus, reading is 'like Sanctifying in the Soul' as 'Magic' is 'like Deity'. But these are analogous, not identical, terms. In other words, there may well be a difference between the enchanting power of poetry and the divinely sanctioned conversion to grace but, in the thrall of reading, it is hard or even impossible to discern.

In early New England, this issue of the origin of power was one of the main concerns which underlay ministerial objections to magic. Magic was both a challenge to ministerial authority and God's control of occult realms. Clergymen argued that the knowledge and power magic offered was blasphemy against God's omnipotence and design, especially as magic was thought to be the direct result of diabolic intervention.[39] Fear of diabolic witchcraft intensified in New England in the mid-seventeenth century and peaked in the infamous Salem Witchcraft Trials of 1692–3.

However, by the eighteenth century the witch-hunts had diminished and, for the first time in New England's history, a magistrate considered submitting the accusers to a medical examination to determine whether or not they were sane.[40] By the nineteenth century, people had ceased to believe in witchcraft as something that was unquestionably real and had begun, like Dickinson, to associate magic with insanity.

Dickinson implies that poetic inspiration may insanely rather than divinely empower us. Or, perhaps, since the connection is not oppositional, divine empowerment must be madness and human creativity a dark transfiguration. She may have been influenced, in this respect, by her reading of Nathaniel Hawthorne, who plays on the idea of a 'dark transfiguration' in *The Scarlet Letter*.[41] Hawthorne's minister displays:

> all that violence of passion, which … was, in fact, the portion of him which the Devil claimed, and through which he sought to win the rest. Never was there a blacker or a fiercer frown that Hester now encountered. For the brief space that it lasted, it was a dark Transfiguration.[42]

Throughout the book a prophetic spiritual light of truth is associated with the sun. The image of burning sunlight occurs repeatedly and, significantly, it will not let go of Pearl (the illegitimate offspring of an ill-fated union and symbolically named to recall the 'pearl of great price' of redemption and eternal life). When Pearl and her mother, Hester, go into the forest the child says: 'Mother … the sunshine does not love you … let me run and catch it' (*SL*, p. 138). Pearl does catch it and stands 'in the midst of it, all brightened by its splendour' (*SL*, p. 138). The child is beheld as the centre of light, but as her mother approaches and tries to grasp the light: 'the sunshine vanished; or to judge from the bright expression that was dancing on Pearl's features, her mother could have fancied that the child absorbed it into herself, and would give it forth again' (*SL*, p. 138).

Pearl radiates light. Clothed in scarlet and gold, she is obviously the scarlet letter invested with life. But, she is not simply the concrete manifestation of the sin her mother wears emblazoned in a red 'A' on her chest. In her transfigured state, she gives face (somewhat ironically) to the state of redeemed man. However, around Pearl, the light of redemption is dangerously fugitive. Later in the forest scene, she is perceived in a 'streak of sunshine … [which] quivered to and fro, making her figure dim or distinct, – now like a real child, now like a child's spirit' (*SL*, p. 153). Pearl, like Christ, bridges two worlds and, in the world of spirit, her divine light is safe, but in the world of the flesh, it becomes darkened. The minister's

'dark Transfiguration' stands in direct contrast to Pearl's spiritual illumination. Encounters with light, Hawthorne suggests, have their dark
reflection in human corruption.

'I think I was enchanted' blurs the boundary between corruption and
creation. Dickinson reminds us that the power to create can become the
power to destroy and that the veil the poem provides can just as easily
enable an encounter with the devil as with the divine. Poets stand at one
remove from the force which animates their work and so their creation,
be it the poem or persona, is the only way in which that force can be
encountered. But, in the throes of the sublime experience that is poetic
inspiration, Dickinson does not care about origins. Moonlight is the
dark reflection of sunlight. 'Lunacy of Light' may be what comes off the
veil of art but Dickinson is not pious and her retrospective and slightly
self-deprecating awareness that she must have been 'enchanted' does not
lessen her desire to forget herself again. Artistic transport may be a crazy
enchantment but it is a magical and transfiguring one.

Bringing retrospection to the fore, this poem casts an ironic eye on the
enchantment of the reading experience. But the final stanza sets a limit
to the self-conscious irony of the aftermath. Dickinson's tone is a little
embarrassed, but there is still some 'Element' to magic that, 'like Deity',
refuses to be known. At the end of the poem, Dickinson's speaker has not
forgotten that poetic language brought about a transfiguring encounter
with light. It enacted marvellous changes in her mental state and could
make her believe it was 'noon at night –'.

THE TRANSITUS

Dickinson did not always render her sense of poetic power with ironic
or lunatic configurations of light. Many of Dickinson's literary contemporaries, as well as her Puritan ancestors, used the moment of death
to confirm the existence of an afterlife with an image of shining light.
Medieval theologians referred to the passage from life to death as the
'transitus'. In the nineteenth century the process was sometimes referred
to as the 'crossover'.[43] The transitus was a period of temporal compres-
sion, when all time, eternity, was experienced diachronically, as journey.
In 'The Sun kept setting – setting – still' (1863), the experience of light
in darkness, or 'noon at night', forges an analogy between poetic inspiration and the transitus:

> The Sun kept setting – setting – still
> No Hue of Afternoon –

Opon [*sic*] the Village I perceived –
From House to House 'twas Noon –

The Dusk kept dropping – dropping – still
No Dew upon the Grass –
But only on my Forehead stopped –
And wandered in my Face –

My Feet kept drowsing – drowsing – still
My fingers were awake –
Yet why so little sound – Myself
Unto my Seeming – make?

How well I knew the Light before –
I could not see it now –
'Tis Dying – I am doing – but
I'm not afraid to know –

(Fr715; J692)

The transitus was a popular subject for poets, and Tennyson expressed it in the death of a nun in 'St Agnes' Eve'. In the copy of Tennyson's *Poems* found in the Dickinson library, there are light markings by the side of 'St Agnes' Eve', exhibiting, as Judith Farr comments, an interest in the poem's sentiments.[44] The entire following passage is marked:

He lifts me to the golden doors;
The flashes come and go;
All heaven burst her starry floors,
And strews her lights below,
And deepens on and up! The gates
Roll back, and far within
For me the Heavenly Bridegroom waits,
To make me pure of sin.
The sabbaths of Eternity,
One sabbath deep and wide –
A light upon the shining sea
The Bridegroom with his bride!

Dickinson's moment of sublime transformation reads differently to Tennyson's, partly because of the way in which she keeps her speaker glued to the temporal world. Dickinson's slow rhythm and probing questions reflect a dawning awareness of this moment of greatness. By contrast, Tennyson's tone is celebratory and dramatic. Where he imagines the bursting of cosmic fabric and the happy union of the nun with God, Dickinson's narration is suspended uneasily on the brink of time and eternity. Tennyson's nun joyfully enters eternity; Dickinson's speaker waits curiously on the doorstep.

Tennyson's narrative progresses to the point of eternity, which resolutely holds all time within it: 'One sabbath deep and wide'. But Dickinson expresses the transitus in the repeated action at the end of each stanza's first line, followed by the word 'still'. We talk of life stilled by death, meaning stopped. However, 'still' also means 'ongoing'. The verbal repetition simultaneously paralyses the narrative and pushes it forward and Dickinson heightens the paradox by using the progressive past, disrupting the recounted narrative to suggest the prolonged significance of that moment in time, rather than the final arrival in Heaven.

In the midst of another 'Noon at night', the supernatural luminosity that characterises the final sunset of life or the death-in-life encounter of poetic inspiration, the second stanza exploits a religious tableau that we can easily recognise as one of Dickinson's favourites. The speaker is anointed with dew in the manner of Old Testament priests.[45] She is baptised into death and simultaneously reborn into a new life. The Baptismal imagery offers a way of reading the third stanza:

> My Feet kept drowsing – drowsing – still
> My fingers were awake –
> Yet why so little sound – Myself
> Unto my Seeming – make?

In the previous chapter we saw how Baptism helped Dickinson express her poetic vocation. She found in its theology a way of understanding the complex relationship between the self's essence and representation; she found a way of understanding the relationship of 'Myself / Unto my Seeming'. Dickinson wrote most of her poems at night in the privacy of her little bedroom and it is no coincidence that as her feet 'drows[e]', her fingers come alive. Writing in the quiet of the night, her poetry is deaf even to her own physical presence, and poetic inspiration becomes an encounter with light that is akin to 'Dying', the transitus from time to eternity and the beginning of knowledge that remains, at this point, beyond the scope of the poem. So, the final verb is missing its object. *What* she is 'not afraid to know' can only be represented by one of Dickinson's dashes, a concrete manifestation of epistemic absence, because, while poetic inspiration manifests itself as an experience of the transitus, arrival on the other side defies expression.

POETIC POSTERITY

Dickinson's sense of poetic power is sometimes tempered by her ironic reflections on its delusionary nature and sometimes curious as to its reach.

Her ambivalence is reflected in the tone of the spiritual experience she describes. So, in 'I felt I was enchanted' she is both eager and embarrassed about the raptures of reading as they remind her of the delusions of the converted and of magical enchantment. By contrast, the experience in 'The Sun kept Setting' claims far less, and darkness replaces the light she 'knew' so well before. This, together with a fearless acknowledgment that she does not yet 'know', gestures beyond through the space of possibility and blindness. And in acknowledging the epistemic limits of both spiritual and poetic experience, Dickinson's tone abandons irony in favour of a stoic anguish.

Franklin dates both poems to late 1863, so it is impossible to attribute the difference in tone to a change in feeling over time. There is a similar conflict in the way Dickinson used images of light to express poetic achievement and posterity. Between 1858 and 1864 she made neat copies of more than 800 of her poems, gathered them into forty groups and bound each of those gatherings together with strings to form booklets. After this point she continued to arrange poems into sets and she increasingly wanted to send poems out in or as letters to her friends and family. We can never know whether these activities were intended to secure her some measure of literary posterity. However, four poems written between 1862 and 1865 use images of light to question the way a poet's life might continue through her work.

When Dickinson considers poetic achievement and reputation, she does so in terms which deliberately juxtapose poetic longevity with eternal life. 'I reckon – when I count at all –' (1863) appears to glorify poets as the highest of all creators only to imply that their surety masks a desire for something more. But while this poem turns against fame, 'The Poets light but lamps' (1865) casts poetic posterity in a more appealing light as Dickinson suggests that poems have the power to inspire future generations after their creators have gone. Although she voiced a desire for such lasting light, Dickinson struggled to maintain her faith in either poetic or religious arrival. 'The Spider Holds a Silver Ball' (1863) is sarcastic about the poet enraptured by his own creative act while 'Me – come! My dazzled face' (1862) deals ironically with both poetic and religious arrival.

Dickinson was taught to see the world and everything natural or mortal (including poets) as illustrative of God's great design. But in 'I reckon – when I count at all –' she proudly reorganised the traditional hierarchy:

> I reckon – when I count at all –
> First – Poets – Then the Sun –
> Then Summer – Then the Heaven of God –
> And then – the List is done –

> But, looking back – the First so seems
> To Comprehend the Whole –
> The Others look a needless Show –
> So I write – Poets – All –
>
> Their Summer – lasts a Solid Year –
> They can afford a Sun
> The East – would deem extravagant –
> And if the Further Heaven –
>
> Be Beautiful as they prepare
> For Those who worship Them –
> It is too difficult a Grace –
> To justify the Dream –
>
> (Fr533; J569)

Evoking a schoolroom setting, Dickinson's speaker mimics the lesson learnt as a child. Dickinson's old teacher, Edward Hitchcock, would have been appalled. He regularly warned his charges at Amherst College about the dangerous allure of ungodly and arrogant intelligence, believing young and curious minds to be especially vulnerable to its charms. In the first half of this poem Dickinson exalts poetry in precisely the manner that Hitchcock deemed sinful, setting it first above the signs of God's greatness, then above Heaven itself and, finally, rendering all but poets a 'needless Show'. The human light of poetry rivals divine light. But the rivalry is just that and, still short of triumph, Dickinson's confidence falters slightly when she comes up against 'the Further Heaven'. Dismissing it, she only emphasises the hold it has on her imagination. 'If [it] … / Be Beautiful' she says, allowing the poetic stress to fall on the adjective while pretending, unconvincingly, that beauty means little. Dickinson's 'Poets' suffer a lapse in courage, absorbing themselves in their own greatness, the dazzling 'Grace' of inspiration, because the other is 'too difficult'. Dickinson can barely hide her anguish and self-reproach. 'Poets', here, are pampered, indulged creatures, choosing comfort over struggle, a failing made even more acute by their awareness of a 'Beautiful … Dream' that may haunt them as it haunts the speaker of this poem.

Unjustified, Dickinson's 'Dream' remains unsanctified and her regret seems to be that this is not enough, that she rejects the fragile beauty of hope in favour of the 'Solid' summer of poetic greatness.[46] The surety of her conviction, 'So I write – Poets – All –' does not last and the change in tone possibly reflects the personal conflict of the poet who almost never published and who seemed to give up her 'Solid' summer.

'The Poets light but Lamps' shows Dickinson exploring the notion of poetic posterity with greater sympathy:

> The Poets light but Lamps –
> Themselves – go out –
> The Wicks they stimulate –
> If vital Light
>
> Inhere as do the Suns –
> Each Age a Lens
> Disseminating their
> Circumference –
>
> (Fr930; J883)

This poem describes the nurturing warmth of poetry rather than the violent encounter of poetic inspiration. Poets may be mortal but the result of their inspiration – their divine spark – endures. Poets, like God or the gods, project themselves through the objects of their creation. They make themselves known through poetry, or 'circumference', just as divine beings make themselves known through the spherical sun.

Despite occasions like this where she exhibited a desire for lasting influence in terms of 'vital Light', she could not help being ironic about the sense of arrival and achievement implicit in both the earthly immortality of poetic production and the eternal life of heavenly salvation. 'The Spider Holds a Silver Ball' provides another example of the way in which the poet may suffer delusions of grandeur in the experience of poetic production:[47]

> The Spider holds a Silver Ball
> In unperceived Hands –
> And dancing softly to Himself
> His Yarn of Pearl – unwinds –
>
> He plies from nought to nought –
> In unsubstantial Trade –
> Supplants our Tapestries with His –
> In half the period –
>
> An Hour to rear supreme
> His Continents of Light –
> Then dangle from the Housewife's Broom –
> His Boundaries – forgot –
>
> (Fr513; J605)

The spider-poet, absorbed in his work, weaves his own paradise, forming 'Continents of Light' out of his pearly thread. Pearls are not just precious, they are symbols of eternal life, recalling the 'pearl of great price' in Matthew's Gospel: 'the kingdom of heaven is like unto a merchant man seeking goodly pearls: who when he had found one pearl of great price, went and sold all that he had and bought it'.[48] Unchecked, the spider-poet can forget the transience of his creation, delighting in it so much that he believes it to be divine. So, too, Dickinson suggests, can the enraptured observer or reader who is recalled quite suddenly to the mundane cobweb in the penultimate line. 'Dangle' emphasises a sudden loss of dignity and agency as the poet-spider is recalled to the real world. Unlike the poets who 'light but Lamps', the cobweb does not last. The artwork is not only destroyed but forgotten, a timely reminder, perhaps, of the limitations of earthly endeavour.

In 'Me – Come! My dazzled face' (1862) she also implies that fame may be a delusion of paradise or, perhaps, a delusion as great as paradise:

> Me – Come! My dazzled face
> In such a shining place!
> Me – hear! My foreign Ear
> The sounds of Welcome – there!
>
> The Saints forget
> Our bashful feet –
>
> My Holiday, shall be
> That They – remember me –
> My Paradise – the fame
> That They – pronounce my name –
> (Fr389; J431)

This is a dream, a delusion of joy and longing, beginning with an exaggerated celebration that parodies the Christian's arrival in Heaven and ending as a drift of unfulfilled desire. Sitting uncomfortably on the border of hope and despair, Dickinson cannot hide the feeling that paradise and poetic longevity might be twin illusions, simple tricks of light.

Dickinson's many encounters with light, glorifying, erotic, empowering, enchanting or beautiful, describe momentary experiences of poetic inspiration that reflect a mental change as terrifying and vitalising as the spiritual light, and accompanying darkness, of divine presence. However, encounters with light do not last. Poets may project their glory in the objects of their creation, the 'Suns' of their 'Solid' summer, but the inspirational encounter is fleeting, often embarrassing, and the immortality of fame a poor substitute. Encounters with light are, like the transitus, experiences of all eternity compressed into a single instant of time. Dickinson's speakers, like the 'thirsty blossoms' in her letter to Sue, bear testimony to the fact that, having been transfigured, they can never be quite the same again.

Encounters with light lead us to another kind of poetry. These momentary and often delusional experiences of eternity may have broken through the barriers of time but, as a mortal poet, Dickinson was left to collapse into the intense and human pain of a 'wander[ing]' existence. The poems in the following chapter express another kind of poetic engagement, one which was agonisingly aware of place and time, of journey, progress and failure, of human solace and lonely suffering. In these poems, she wrote about the troubling awareness of the liminal, of the constraints of the body and the reach into death. This was a dark journey far from the dazzling light of divine encounter but it, too, was a fundamental part of her poetic vocation and religious imagination.

NOTES

1 John omits the transfiguration.
2 Matt. 17.2.
3 Mark 9.3.
4 Luke 9.29.
5 The uncreated light is the pure light of divine presence as opposed to the created light: candles, lamps, the sun, etc.
6 See, for example, C. E. Carlston, 'Transfiguration and Resurrection', *Journal of Biblical Literature*, 80.3 (1961), pp. 223–40. There have been a number of studies opposing this theory, notably R. Stein, 'Is the Transfiguration (Mark 9:2–8) a Mis-placed Resurrection Account?' *Journal of Biblical Literature*, 95.1 (1976), pp. 76–96.
7 For a general discussion of this theory, see G. H. Boobyer, *St Mark and the Transfiguration Story* (Edinburgh: T & T Clark, 1942); M. E. Thrall, 'Elijah and Moses in Mark's Account of the Transfiguration', *New Testament Studies*, 16.4 (1969–70), pp. 305–17, and, more recently, G. J. Davies, 'The Prefigurement of the Ascension in the Third Gospel', *Journal of Theological Studies*, 6.2 (1955), pp. 299–333.
8 Matt. 17.2, 'and his raiment was white as the light'. Mark 9:3, 'And his raiment became shining, exceeding white as snow; so as no fuller on earth can white them'.
9 Ludwig Feuerbach, *The Essence of Christianity*, trans. George Eliot (1854; New York: Prometheus Books, 1989), p. xxi.
10 *Complete Sermons of Ralph Waldo Emerson*, 4 vols., ed. Ralph H. Orth, Susan Sutton Smith, Ronald A. Bosco and Glen M. Johnson (Columbia, Mo.: University of Missouri Press, 1989–92), vol. 2, p. 138.
11 Emerson, 'Divinity School Address', p. 82.
12 *Ibid.*, p. 80. For a discussion of Emerson's religious radicalism and interest in comparative study, see Lawrence Buell, *Emerson* (Cambridge, Mass.: Harvard University Press, 2003), pp. 158–99.

13 Charles Southwell, *The Origin, Object and Organization of the Christian Religion* (London: William Friend, [?1850s]), pp. 8–55.

14 William Henry Channing, *Religions of China: Address before the Free Religious Association*. Boston, 27 May 1870 (Boston, Mass.: Press of John Wilson and Son, 1870).

15 Eric J. Sharpe, *Comparative Religion: A History*, 2nd edn (London: Duckworth, 1986), p. xi, cited in Buell, *Emerson*, p. 173.

16 Williston Walker *et al.*, *A History of the Christian Church*, 3rd edn (Edinburgh: T & T Clark, 1976), p. 155. There is no evidence that Dickinson knew Walker, but his work is indicative of the degree to which liberal Christianity had filtered into Amherst College by the late century. Dickinson would have been most familiar with comparative religion from Emerson and the Unitarian Christianity represented here by Channing.

17 David Fideler, *Jesus Christ, Sun of God: Ancient Cosmology and Early Christian Symbolism* (Wheaton: Theosophical Publishing House, 1993), p. 2.

18 Dan. 10.6.

19 Sylvia Plath, 'Mystic', in *Collected Poems* (London: Faber, 1981), p. 269.

20 Albert Gelpi does this in his analysis of the letter in *Emily Dickinson: The Mind of the Poet* (Cambridge, Mass.: Harvard University Press, 1965), p. 42.

21 'And Mount Sinai was altogether on a smoke, because the Lord descended on it in fire', Exod. 19.18.

22 Ezek. 1.4.

23 Matt. 13.5.

24 See Rom. 9.4–13.

25 Gary Lee Stonum, *The Dickinson Sublime* (Madison, Wisc., and London: The University of Wisconsin Press, 1990), pp. 189–93.

26 Sewall, *Life*, p. 105.

27 Michael Lopez, *Emerson and Power: Creative Antagonism in the Nineteenth Century* (DeKalb, Ill.: Northern Illinois University Press, 1996), p. 139. For more on the connections between Emerson and Nietzsche, see George J. Stack, *Nietzsche and Emerson: An Elective Affinity* (Athens, OH: Ohio University Press, 1992); David Mikics, *The Romance of Individualism in Emerson and Nietzsche* (Athens, OH: Ohio University Press, 2003); and Irena S. M. Makarushka, *Religious Imagination and Language in Emerson and Nietzsche* (London: Macmillan, 1994).

28 Emerson, 'The Poet', p. 16.

29 Emerson, 'The Method of Nature' (1841), in *The Collected Works of Ralph Waldo Emerson*, ed. Joseph Slater, Robert Spiller, Alfred R. Ferguson *et al.*, 6 vols. (Cambridge, Mass.: Harvard University Press, 1971–2003), vol. 1, pp. 117–41, at p. 132.

30 Emerson, 'Self-Reliance' (1841), in *The Collected Works of Ralph Waldo Emerson*, ed. Joseph Slater, Robert Spiller, Alfred R. Ferguson *et al.*, 6 vols. (Cambridge, Mass.: Harvard University Press, 1971–2003), vol. 2, pp. 25–53, at p. 27.

31 Camille Paglia, *Sexual Personae: Art and Decadence from Nefertiti to Emily Dickinson* (New Haven and London: Yale University Press, 1990), p. 646. See

also Beth Maclay Doriani, *Emily Dickinson: Daughter of Prophecy* (Amherst, Mass.: University of Massachusetts Press, 1996).

32 Emerson, 'History' (1841), in *The Collected Works of Ralph Waldo Emerson*, ed. Joseph Slater, Robert Spiller, Alfred R. Ferguson *et al.*, 6 vols. (Cambridge, Mass.: Harvard University Press, 1971–2003), vol. 2, pp. 1–25, at p. 6.

33 Fr571 and Fr1599.

34 Both Franklin and Johnson note that this poem was a tribute to Elizabeth Barrett Browning whose death on 30 June 1861, Johnson writes, 'had moved ED deeply'. She wrote two other commemorative poems for Elizabeth Barrett Browning: 'Her "last Poems"' (J312) and 'I went to thank her' (J363); Thomas Herbert Johnson (ed.), *The Poems of Emily Dickinson: Including Variant Readings Critically Compared with all Known Manuscripts*, 3 vols. (Cambridge, Mass.: Belknap Press, 1955), vol. 2, p. 455; Ralph William Franklin (ed.), *The Poems of Emily Dickinson: Variorum Edition*, 3 vols. (Cambridge, Mass.: Belknap Press, 1998), vol. 1, p. 618.

35 Jack Capps, *Emily Dickinson's Reading: 1836–1886* (Cambridge, Mass.: Harvard University Press, 1966), pp. 60–100.

36 McIntosh, *Nimble Believing*, p. 134.

37 *Ibid.*, p. 133.

38 *Ibid.*, pp. 132–4.

39 Richard Godbeer *The Devil's Dominion: Magic and Religion in Early New England* (Cambridge: Cambridge University Press, 1994), pp. 59–60.

40 Carol F. Karlsen, *The Devil in the Shape of a Woman: Witchcraft in Colonial New England* (London: W. W. Norton and Co., 1998), p. 45.

41 Capps, *Dickinson's Reading*, pp. 19, 25, 123.

42 Nathaniel Hawthorne, *The Scarlet Letter* (1850; Ware, Herts: Wordsworth, 1992), p. 145. All further references are to this edition and are included in the text.

43 Farr, *Passion*, p. 6.

44 Farr notes the markings, *ibid.*, p. 39.

45 'It is like the precious ointment upon the head, that ran down upon the beard, even Aaron's beard: that went down to the skirts of his garments; As the dew of Her-mon, and as the dew that descended upon the mountains of Zion: for there the Lord commanded the blessing, even life for evermore.' Psalm 133. 2–3.

46 In the Calvinist conversion experience, justification precedes sanctification.

47 Dickinson's affection towards the spider as a fellow artist surfaces in a number of poems, the most well known of which begins:

> The Spider as an Artist
> Has never been employed –
> Though his surpassing Merit
> Is freely certified
> (Fr1373; J1275)

48 Matt. 13.45–6.

CHAPTER 4

Quest

Boundary crossing remains a key theme in this chapter, which discusses the relevance of quest to Dickinson's sense of the poetic life. In Matthew's depiction of the garden of Gethsemane, Jesus draws attention to the path he must travel, praying: 'O my Father, if this cup may not pass away from me, except I drink it, thy will be done' (Matt. 26.42). Here there is a process to be undergone, a time to be lived through and a challenge to be accepted. These things are mortal and in theological terms they are transitory. That just makes them inescapably real for the lonely hero of the synoptic Gospels.

Dickinson used classical quest narratives to structure her appropriation of the Gethsemane story in order to convey the personal transition and loneliness that she felt as an inescapable part of the poet's life. This chapter explores the typological significance of Jacob's struggle at Peniel for Christ's struggle in Gethsemane, arguing that Dickinson was inspired by a biblical blurring of divine and diabolic power in both stories and that she drew parallels between this struggle and her own poetic project. The discussion also embraces phenomenological distinctions between space and place which are relevant both to Dickinson's poetics and to the geographical contours of religious experience. Old Testament and classical notions of 'wilderness', 'wandering' and journeying to the place of the dead had a central place in Dickinson's understanding of her own vocation.

THE POETIC AND RELIGIOUS QUEST:
FORMS OF CONVERGENCE

The sense of a life to be lived in the difficult knowledge of a goal beyond unites the poetic and religious quest. In *Emily Dickinson: Perception and the Poet's Quest*, Greg Johnson argues that Dickinson's career can be understood as a successful Romantic quest, which seeks to restore a lost or diminished spirituality. It is 'successful', he claims, not because of any optimistic resolution but because of the unflagging honesty and effort of her approach. For Johnson, the problem of quest is key to a deeper understanding of Dickinson's biography, which he conceives in terms of a myth of isolation and lyric voice: 'Dickinson's poetic canon comprises a drama whose theme is the adventure of consciousness, whose goal is a *visionary* (Dickinson's terms are clear) apprehension of spiritual reality, and whose implied heroine – appearing as the lyric "I" – is the poet herself'.[1] Johnson's argument is chronological, based on T. H. Johnson's 1955 dating of the poems, and dependent on a sense of Dickinson's progression from the presumptuous hope of the naïve quester to the 'confident despair' that is the poet's mature stance. This progression occurs through a growing dependence on perception as Dickinson realises a central tension in her poetry between the perceived and the unknown.

Greg Johnson's conception of Dickinson's poetic questing as a singular process of self-mythologisation appears somewhat dated now that work on Dickinson's manuscripts, fragments and letters (including letter-poems) have exposed her writings in their contingent relations to the outside world and Franklin's renumbering and redating has cast doubt on T. H. Johnson's chronology. But although the terms of the argument have changed, the scholarly emphasis on Dickinson's poetic questing has not diminished. For example: Marta Werner, who declares her project to be an undoing of former editing, focuses on the aesthetic of journey that she finds implicit in Dickinson's late letter fragments. She writes:

The biographical and textual conditions of a writer's life do not always act in collusion: in the 1870s Dickinson did cross her 'Father's ground' through her writing. She crossed outside quatrains and paragraphs and strayed beyond the resolution of sequences and series into rich and strange textual fields … the love letter (fragment, draft) celebrates diaspora, a refusal on the part of the subject to move to the center, perpetual marginality. Addressed to an absent other, lost in the moment it is sent, the love letter is a figure of the wanderer or the deviant. It may also be a figure for 'woman' herself, defined under the old patriarchal Law as the very principle of deviance, swerving extravagance.[2]

In this late period, Werner argues that Dickinson's refusal of literary destination (or final intentions) became an aesthetic in its own right.

The way in which Dickinson consciously worked and reworked her writings in every stage of her life – exploring variants, experimenting with audience and address in her letters and letter-poems, binding fair copies into fascicles and possibly scissoring the late fragments – suggests a mind that was never satisfied and a poetic quest whose object was its own process. This is hardly the rarefied 'pearl' that Johnson imagines to be the essential value of life and the symbol of her poetic existence and identity.[3]

That said, there are certain features of Johnson's work that remain highly relevant to my reading. The most important is the religious epistemology of the quest narrative he sees in Dickinson's poetry, the tension between her poetic reliance on perception and experience and her focus on an object that remains perpetually beyond her powers of expression. But where Johnson argues that the analogy between religious and artistic quest is forged in Dickinson's personal struggle towards spiritual fulfilment and fully developed selfhood, I will argue that the analogy brings specific notions of journey, place and presence into focus as the conditions for creativity and thus opens a new way of thinking about Dickinson's sense of her own vocation as a quest that is perhaps more in keeping with recent investigations into her working practice and more easily separable from arguments about her personal religiosity and self-mythologisation.

SOURCES

Quest is a particular kind of journey. The quest has purpose, hope and a solitary hero, whose personal journey often merges to become one with the movement of the quest, a quest of self-discovery as much as a search for something external.[4] Religious narratives gave Dickinson a rich vocabulary for this journey. She saw the classical rubric echoed in the Calvinist conversion experience, Jacob's struggle at Peniel and, perhaps most importantly for her, Christ's struggle in Gethsemane.[5] In the quest narrative the hero must face a challenge and survive the struggle. In the classical quest, this often takes the form of overcoming monsters. In *The Odyssey*, Odysseus and his men are trapped in the cave of the man-eating, one-eyed Giant Polyphemus.[6] Aeneus and his men fight the Harpies as do the Argonauts.[7] Christian encounters the dragon-like Apollyon and the Giant Despair.[8] In John Bunyan's *Pilgrim's Progress*, emotional states are allegorised into monsters and so 'overcoming the monster' becomes resisting the weakness of temptation. The hero of the classical quest may be tempted by a beautiful woman, as Odysseus is by Calypso, so that he will be lulled into forgetting his mission: Odysseus stays seven years in Calypso's cave.[9]

Dickinson would have been familiar with Aeneus's fight with the harpies and Odysseus's encounter with Calypso from the accounts in Thomas Bulfinch's *The Age of Fable: Stories of Gods and Heroes*, which was in her family library.[10] She also had access to descriptions of all the proper names in classical mythology and the stories which surround them in J. Lempriere's *Classical Dictionary*, which was in her home library, and Charles Anthon's *Classical Dictionary*, which was a required reference book at Amherst Academy.[11] Dickinson certainly read *Pilgrim's Progress* because she recommended it to Austin on 27 March 1853: 'How long it is since you've been in this state of complacence towards God and your fellow men? I think it must be sudden, hope you are not deceived, would recommend "Pilgrim's Progress" and "Baxter upon the will"' (*L*, p. 234). In *Pilgrim's Progress* it is Despair, an allegorical figure of an emotional state, who tempts Christian to abandon his journey.

Christ's 'monster' is usually understood to be a temptation to abandon his divine purpose, a struggle with loneliness and a yearning for human life and companionship. His most important test comes in Gethsemane, which is portrayed as a stage in a physical and mental journey. The synoptic writers indicate the structure of the scene through a concentration on movement. In Mark and Matthew, Jesus moves into Gethsemane in three steps. First he takes forward three of his disciples and then he moves forward again and prays. In the second half, Jesus comes back to his disciples three times after praying. Mark and Matthew depict Jesus as increasingly isolated from effective support. The prayer is the central point in the scene. It helps articulate Jesus's reaction to his fate and that of his disciples. Significantly, Jesus receives no answer to his prayer and is betrayed by one of his own disciples. He is abandoned by both man and God. One theologian, A. C. Buchanan, suggests that Jesus must not simply endure suffering, he must provoke it. He must walk to his fate. He must walk up to the traitor Judas and give him his chance. This, Buchanan argues, is absolute submission to God, a humiliating experience of loss leading to an exalting experience of gain.[12]

Dickinson would have been doubly familiar with this paradigm from the process of religious conversion, which mirrors Christ's suffering and resurrection precisely because both narratives take the form of a quest. The Calvinist conversion experience was a search for salvation to be prefaced, in the dramatic conversions of the Revivalist church, with intense sorrow and fear – the emotions Christ suffers in Gethsemane. God had to break those he would save and the preparation of the heart for Christ was an aggressive and disturbing experience. In 1638, the Puritan Thomas Hooker, writing on conversion, said that the Lord was required to seize regenerates from their corruption by a 'Holy kind of violence'.[13] The humiliation of the soul simulates a kind of spiritual death that contrasts with the sinner's subsequent and intensely joyful recognition of the saving power of eternal life – a triumph that lies behind Paul's rhetoric of salvation: 'O grave, where is thy Victory?'[14] Like the crucifixion narrative, therefore, conversion involves a making ready, the utter abasement of the soul, the agony of the in-between.

There is, of course, a peculiarly American strain of the quest narrative. The story of discovery, already familiar from classical and Judeo-Christian literature and mythology, was reshaped into a highly resonant yet distinctive version of the quest narrative. The various causes of the New World journey, whether land hunger, commercial development, glory-seeking adventure or religious vision, were all subsumed by the myth of progress and expansion – the push westward and the retrospective vision of 'manifest destiny'.[15] Although the actual experience was far from an uncomplicated story of search or triumphant westward expansion, the pioneer enterprise took on a mythical significance apart from the realities of the struggle and became, in many respects, the goal in itself, an ever-expanding, ever-creating movement of space and time.

Dickinson evidently identified Christ with the hero of the American quest. He is, to her, a 'tender pioneer' (Fr727). She would also have been able to identify him with the heroically defeated Promethean quester who became a model for the Romantic poet. Romantic Promethean iconography frequently merged Christ's purpose with that of the demi-god who stole fire from Zeus to save mankind from extinction in order to evoke the daring and struggle of poetic enterprise. Dickinson was probably influenced in this respect by her reading of, and about, Shelley. Shelley's poetical works were in the Dickinson family library and, as Lois Cuddy notes, there is also a copy of E. J. Trelawney's *Recollections of the Last Days of Shelley and Byron*, published in 1859 and inscribed to Emily by Sue.[16] Trelawney presents Shelley as a lonely, strong and noble genius on a spiritual quest, paying tribute to Shelley's conviction that as a poet you should 'write nothing but what your conviction of its truth inspires you to write; you should give counsel to the wise, and not take it from the foolish'.[17] When taken with Trelawney's claim that 'the utter loneliness with which [Shelley] was condemned to pass the largest portion of his life would have paralysed any brains less subtilised by genius than his were',[18] this, as Cuddy argues, would have made Shelley a hugely sympathetic figure for Dickinson.

In Shelley's drama, the suffering Titan is described as 'a youth / With patient looks nailed to a Crucifix'.[19] He cries: 'No change, no pause, no hope! Yet I endure'.[20] Prometheus, as a Christ-like man of suffering, endures torment as a result of his saving act and struggle with divinity.

This Prometheus is also a figure of the inspired poet. In his preface, Shelley writes:

a number of writers possess the form, whilst they want the spirit of those whom, it is alleged, they imitate; because the former is the endowment of the age in which they live, and the latter must be the uncommunicated lightning of their own mind.[21]

The Prometheus-Christ man of suffering serves as a figure for the inspired poet because of his 'divine' creative spark.[22] As Gaston Bachelard puts it, 'our Promethean dreams are fuelled by half a conviction that the fire is in us, that our bodies hold their own reserves of inner fire'.[23]

The Romantic sense of the poet as a Prometheus-Christ quester must have influenced Dickinson. Calvary, as the locus of both suffering and struggle, forges the connection between the Greek demi-god and the Christian God incarnate and, as I will suggest more strongly in the following chapter, Dickinson often used Calvary to create a poetic space in which the human poet can triumph or rail against divinity. But Promethean iconography made the poet-quester a man-god and Dickinson paid only muted tribute to this divinisation of humanity. A short poem, written in pencil on a leaf of stationery about 1868, when Dickinson's productivity waned dramatically, reflects her sense of the limitations of the Promethean urge. According to Franklin, she wrote only eleven poems in that year and Johnson suggests she wrote only six letters.

> The smouldering embers blush –
> Oh Cheek within the Coal
> Hast thou survived so many nights?
> The smouldering embers smile –
>
> Soft stirs the news of Light
> The stolid Rafters glow
> One requisite has Fire that lasts
> Prometheus never knew –
>
> (Fr1143; J1132)

Perhaps we should see this poem as Dickinson's acknowledgment of the boundaries of her craft. The Promethean spark stands in contrast to the slow 'smouldering ... blush' of love and Dickinson prizes the stirring strength of sexual awakening above the fleeting power of stolen fire. Humanity's inner fire becomes grounded in emotional and physical feeling – a domestic rather than alien province. Dickinson's variants for 'Fire that lasts' are 'earthly Fire', 'mortal Fire' and 'thorough fire'. The date of this poem may lead us to conclude that Dickinson was exploring or experiencing feelings that did *not* lead her to write. The poem itself suggests a wry amusement that the pure passion of 'smouldering' love is able to outlast the divine spark of poetic inspiration.

Her poet-quester is not just one who paves a way to God-like triumph of the human imagination, reaching into the unknown territory of Hephaestos's forge, but a figure whose sacrifice is mortal and whose poetic drive comes from this intense duality. She takes her inspiration from the agony of separation and liminality as she wrestles with the idea that the space between the finite and the infinite cannot quite be closed. That Dickinson regularly fused classical and biblical allusions together with her observations of religious conversions to faith in order to understand the psychology of the questing hero will become apparent in this chapter. That she forged an analogy between this struggle and her own poetic project will follow, partly because of the anguish involved and partly because of the way she takes the liminal place of the quest to be the province – and perhaps the aim – of poetic writing.

DICKINSON'S INTERNAL LANDSCAPE

Dickinson was typically Romantic in the way in which she internalised the quest narrative, eliding the difference between the landscape of the quest and the domain of the self. In 'One Crucifixion is recorded – only' (1863), she narrows the preoccupation of the quest to the self. Although the landscape is internal, Dickinson does not abandon the spatio-temporal concerns of the archetypal narrative, where heroic self-realisation, an advance in the internal journey of the quester, often takes place in a particular location along the way. In the Gospel quest narrative, this place is Gethsemane and awarding Gethsemane a central place in her inner landscape, Dickinson situates loneliness, conversion and struggle at the very core of her being. The heart of Gethsemane is not only a place that Jesus must enter alone but also, as I will explain later, a place of otherworldly encounter. Invoking the metaphor of Gethsemane, Dickinson suggests that the innermost part of the self remains somewhat occluded; 'the Being's centre' is a hidden place of transition.

> One Crucifixion is recorded – only –
> How many be
> Is not affirmed of Mathematics –
> Or History –

One Calvary – exhibited to stranger –
As many be
As persons – or Peninsulas –
Gethsemane –

Is but a Province – in the Being's Centre –
Judea –
For Journey – or Crusade's Achieving –
Too near –

Our Lord – indeed – made Compound Witness –
And yet –
There's newer – nearer Crucifixion
Than That –

(Fr670; J553)

The first stanza acknowledges the inadequacy of external empirical method to assess individual experience. If the Romantic quest collapses physical and mental space together in a narrative of internal struggle and suffering, it also removes the pomp and circumstance of the heroic tradition. There are no witnesses to this personal suffering and the locations of the quest are too near for any sense of glorious public achievement. Unlike Christ's sacrifice, or the voyages and crusades of ancient and medieval times, this personal quest goes unrecognised. But 'newer' and 'nearer' than the original, the self's own struggle is a painfully acute reality.

As Harold Bloom has argued, the cost of Romantic internalisation tends to manifest itself in the arena of self-consciousness, creating problems with regard to the object of the quest. He suggests that 'the quest is to widen consciousness as well as intensify it but the quest is shadowed by a spirit that tends to narrow consciousness to an acute preoccupation with self'.[24] Bloom's insight is one way to understand Dickinson's paradoxical depiction of a quest that denies 'Journey', claustrophobically reconfiguring adventure as the suffering of the self in transition. But if there is little space for 'Journey', there is a very strong sense of place and, in a phenomenological sense, it is by means of 'Being' that we find ourselves in this place. The landscape of the internal quest is therefore constituted by the emotional struggle that is central to its narrative.

STRUGGLE

The personal struggle implied in 'One Crucifixion is recorded' is fleshed out in 'I should have been too glad, I see –' (1862/3). This poem marries the narratives of voyage, conversion and crucifixion in order to emphasise the structural paradigm of the quest. It shows Dickinson's empathic connection with the questing hero as she uses the relationship between 'circuit' and 'circumference' to suggest an analogy with her own poetic project. The poet's questing 'circuit' yearns towards a greater hidden 'circumference'. Similarly, the religious quester struggles towards an ultimate goal, which remains partly occluded. The struggle that results from this tension is the focus of the poem as Dickinson writes, with hindsight, of the emotions involved. Never one to take obediently to received wisdom or religious doctrine, she exploits the paradigm of conversion for its structural possibilities rather than its theological merits. She is sceptical about the moral necessity of suffering, but appreciates the aesthetic qualities of desire and the motivating, animating power of a lack of satisfaction:

> I should have been too glad, I see –
> Too lifted – for the scant degree
> Of Life's penurious Round –
> My little Circuit would have shamed
> This new Circumference – have blamed –
> The homelier time behind –
>
> I should have been too saved – I see –
> Too rescued – Fear too dim to me
> That I could spell the Prayer
> I knew so perfect – yesterday –
> That scalding One – Sabachthani –
> Recited fluent – here –
>
> Earth would have been too much – I see –
> And Heaven – not enough for me –
> I should have had the Joy
> Without the Fear – to justify –
> The Palm – without the Calvary –
> So Saviour – Crucify –
>
> Defeat whets Victory – they say –
> The Reefs in old Gethsemane
> Endear the shore beyond!
> 'Tis Beggars – Banquets best define –
> 'Tis Thirsting – vitalizes Wine –
> Faith bleats – to understand!
>
> (Fr283; J313)

The object of this quest elides the difference between death, salvation and Dickinson's vocational 'Circumference'. In the final stanza, 'Victory' (echoing the eternal life of 1 Corinthians 15.54 where 'Death is swallowed up in Victory'), is the longed-for rest of the weary traveller, the food craved by the starving and the wine desired by the thirsty. In early Puritan writing, the desire for grace was often represented in physical terms of hunger and thirst. Hooker preached that a 'spirituall thirst' was a special work of the Spirit in a 'humble and contrite heart' that points to 'future faith'.[25] In the letter to Sue, discussed at the start of the previous chapter, Dickinson's 'thirsty blossoms' display the same spiritual craving and desire for religious conversion.

The Puritans took their metaphor from the Bible where thirst is symbolic of spiritual dryness and hunger the yearning for salvation. Psalm 107, for example, tells of the suffering of the Israelites who travelled without guidance in the desert, alone and in need of redemption:

They wandered in the wilderness in a solitary way, they found no city to dwell in. Hungry and thirsty their soul fainted in them. Then they cried to the Lord in their trouble and he delivered them out of their distresses. And he led them forward by the right way, that they might go to a city of habitation.[26]

Psalm 63 begins similarly: 'O God, thou art my God, early will I seek thee: my soul thirsteth for thee, my flesh longeth for thee in a dry and thirsty land, where no water is'.[27] In these examples, spiritual longing and the liminal process of wandering in the wilderness (the dry desert land) are identical. This biblical quest lies behind Dickinson's rather sarcastic assertion: 'Defeat whets Victory – they say –'.

Dickinson's focus on the extremities of experience leaves the space between blanked out. With the very absence of any words, and using dashes to drive the narrative, Dickinson renders an inherently Protestant sense of the elusive moment of arrival. Bunyan's Christian, journeying through the allegorical 'wilderness of this world', miraculously finds a key in his pocket called 'Promise'. Bunyan never tells us how he came by it and nor does he suggest that the hero may know how to hold onto it. In the Protestant quest for salvation, grace always arrives unexpectedly and usually remains precarious until the final arrival in Heaven. This is one of the reasons why Dickinson appears to struggle with the tone of this poem. While she deals ironically with the surrender implicit in doctrinal 'Faith', she cannot help but find the quest narratives of conversion and crucifixion analogous to her own poetic project. The poet's power, her 'new Circumference', arrives as unexpectedly and undeservedly as Christian's key.

THE WILDERNESS OF TRANSITION

Dickinson was a poet of both the religious and Romantic traditions and this, at least partly, explains her ambivalent and changing tone in 'I should have been too glad'. In early religious narratives, wilderness was a great evil and so the biblical notion of paradise revolves around a 'garden' – a piece of organised land. In this respect, the Bible writers were close to the Greek poets, who celebrated the farming of land. When Lucretius, Homer and Virgil expressed their love of nature, they were talking about the pastoral rather than the wilderness. Lucretius lauded the efforts of rural workers who 'forced the forests more and more to climb the moun-tain-sides' in order to make room for cultivated land.[28] In classical myth-ology, the wilderness is inhabited by lesser gods and evil demons. The most notorious was Pan, who gave his name to the word 'panic' because of the fear that would seize travellers upon hearing strange cries in the wilderness which they thought signified the approaching demon.

In the Judeo-Christian tradition, wilderness is synonymous with dan-ger, difficulty and the arid darkness which precedes the homecoming of salvation. For the Israelites, wandering in the wilderness comprises the challenge of the quest for the holy land. Wandering feet long to return home as thirsty souls desire the draught of salvation. In Isaiah, redemp-tion takes the form of water in the wilderness,[29] and in John's Gospel, Jesus offers himself as the remedy for spiritual dryness: 'If any man thirst, let him come unto me and drink'.[30] A remedy, Jesus also has experience of the condition he seeks to abate. He, too, wanders in the wilderness amidst temptation for forty days and forty nights (biblical shorthand for a very long time). Matthew's Christ, echoing the Old Testament psalms, claims: 'Blessed are they which do hunger and thirst after righteousness; for they shall be filled'.[31] Christ is not only the quencher of thirst, he is also the 'way' home.[32] He offers 'rest' from toil – a symbolic end to spirit-ual struggle.[33]

However, the Romantic sublime offered some redemption of the wilderness motif. With the distinction that Edmund Burke made between the sublime and the beautiful, wild places acquired a kind of glamour. The beautiful was pleasing, but the sublime was paralysing. He writes: 'astonishment ... is the effect of the sublime in its highest degree; the inferior effects are admiration, reverence and respect'.[34] Kant, too, emphasised the pleasure implicit in the overwhelming and annihilating power of the sublime: '[in confronting the sublime the mind is] incited to abandon sensibility'.[35] The Romantic sublime made the wilderness – and wildness – into something exciting and erotic. It was not that the qual-ities of the wilderness had changed but in the new intellectual climate of the eighteenth and nineteenth centuries, the solitary, the mysterious and the chaotic were respected as sources of creative (rather than purely destructive) power. This new philosophy appealed readily to artists of the New World wilderness. In the paintings of Thomas Cole, Albert Bierstadt and Frederic Edwin Church, the American wilderness is a sublime landscape of enticing possibility.

Dickinson's sympathy for religious wanderers was most definitely framed in the lens of Romantic admiration. Her old friend, Moses, is a man of the wilderness, leading his people through the arid region of Sinai to the bountiful promised land, but condemned only to 'see – the Canaan – / Without the entering –' (Fr521). 'Old Moses', a type for Christ and the poet, experiences defeat at the point of entry into the land. Like the sinner who undergoes a religious conversion, the Israelites who wander in the wilderness and Christ who suffers the agony of Gethsemane and the death of the cross, the poet must embrace fear and defeat as part of the quest.

It is in this mood that Dickinson invites the suffering of her 'little Circuit', proclaiming:

> I should have been too saved – I see –
> Too rescued – Fear too dim to me
> That I could spell the Prayer
> I knew so perfect – yesterday –
> That scalding One – Sabachthani –
> Recited fluent – here –

'Sabachthani' refers to Christ's anguished cry on the cross: 'Eli Eli lama sabachthani', 'My God, My God why hast thou forsaken me'.[36] The suffering of abandonment, isolation and fear is the cup from which he must drink before his consciousness of something beyond – a dim awareness of sanctification – can be justified. The poet, whose questing 'circuit' yearns towards a greater 'Circumference', feels the reality of her future power as a tangible absence, the feeling of being forsaken.

LONELINESS

In 'I should have been too glad' Dickinson treats the suffering of her 'little circuit' with affection. Gethsemane is an 'old' friend, encouraging her with hope as well as pain, forming the illusion of arrival in the 'reefs' in order to spur her on to victory at the 'shore'. Paradoxically, the 'old' friend of Gethsemane draws attention to the loneliness she has suffered. Christ enters Gethsemane without the support of his disciples and 'I should have been too glad' is also a lonely quest narrative. Dickinson compounds the feeling of loneliness with the uncomprehending 'bleat' of Faith towards the end, invoking the typology of the scapegoat sent to bear Israel's sins 'unto a land not inhabited' and Abraham's near-sacrifice of Isaac on Mount Moriah to convey the predicament of the abandoned innocent wandering alone in the wilderness.[37]

Dickinson's speaker invites suffering, guarding it with affection in order to preserve the dark and lonely place of transition. This protective instinct is even stronger in 'It might be lonelier' (1863), where the loneliness and suffering familiar from 'old Gethsemane' replace salvation as a trusted friend and an object of devotion:

> It might be lonelier
> Without the Loneliness –
> I'm so accustomed to my Fate –
> Perhaps the Other – Peace –
>
> Would interrupt the Dark –
> And crowd the little Room –
> Too scant – by Cubits – to contain
> The Sacrament – of Him –
>
> I am not used to Hope –
> It might intrude opon –
> Its sweet parade – blaspheme the place –
> Ordained to Suffering –
>
> It might be easier
> To fail – with Land in Sight –
> Than gain – My Blue Peninsula –
> To Perish – of Delight –
>
> (Fr535; J405)

Here again is the maritime setting of the quest. The quester, like 'old Moses', fails in view of her goal. In a sense, this poem is a testament to the fear of disappointment. For this reason, perhaps, Dickinson draws attention away from the object of the quest towards its lonely process. Importantly, the speaker is not afraid of the disappointment which results from loss but that which may follow gain: the destruction of the ideal by its reification in the world of things. In this way, the poem reconfigures the tension between 'circuit' and 'circumference'. The object needs to remain out of reach in order to give meaning to the questing journey.

Guarding her 'little room', Dickinson's speaker guards her privacy, power and control. This emphasis on control subverts the meaning of the religious quest. The quest narratives of conversion and crucifixion require a relinquishing of control – a process by which the self is eventually lost in God. Far from relinquishing control, Dickinson's speaker seeks to retain it and preserve her selfhood. Throwing out 'Peace', 'Hope' and 'Delight', she abandons the final homecoming in favour of the difficult but familiar journey.

The way that Dickinson makes loneliness into a fetish as opposed to a challenge reconfigures the religious quest for poetry by irreverently asserting both the dominance of the self and the importance of process over arrival. The tone is important here. Dickinson makes a play of religious language with a mixed effect. On the one hand, this poem sets up a challenge to God by refusing to relinquish control of the journey. Yet, the second stanza is rather self-mocking as if Dickinson is embarrassed about the way she has idolised 'Suffering'. Not wanting to let go, she displays the same tinge of self-reproach that we saw her display in 'I reckon – when I count at all' when she implied that poets, absorbed in their own greatness, are in fact cowardly when faced with the beyond.

OTHERWORLDLY JOURNEYS AND CREATIVE PROCESS

'It might be lonelier' suggests that death is the end of the quest narrative as 'Delight' stops transitional process of 'Suffering'. But Dickinson was also familiar with the way death could become part of the quest narrative. In John Bunyan's *Pilgrim's Progress*, Christian must pass through the Valley of the Shadow of Death before he can reach his goal.[38] Similarly, Odysseus is guided by Circe to the gates of the netherworld which lies beyond the River of Fear and the City of Perpetual Mist. The netherworld is the most liminal of places, situated on the edge of the world.[39]

Christ descends into Hell in the three days between his crucifixion and resurrection. But the Gospel writers all imply that this is not the first time he has made the voyage below. Gethsemane, too, has an otherworldly quality. For John, it is the garden of Paradisial delights. The only writer to refer to Gethsemane as a 'garden', he describes it as if it is a new Eden. This paradisial place is still forbidden to ordinary men and so the disciples have to fall back and let Jesus carry on alone.[40] For John, Christ's divine nature is always at the fore. But for the synoptics, Gethsemane is a darker environment, a place in between life and death and Christ has to enter that place by himself because his struggle is friendless and human; he will die alone. The disciples cannot follow Jesus into the heart of the 'place called Gethsemane' because from this point in his journey, the challenge is his to bear. In Matthew, when Jesus enters the place, he becomes 'sorrowful and very heavy', and in Mark 'he began to be sore amazed, and to be very heavy'.[41] Luke symbolises the transition by anticipating Christ's crucifixion in his mental suffering: 'and his sweat was as it were great drops of blood'.[42]

In her elegy to Charlotte Brontë, dated to early 1860, Dickinson uses the otherworldly associations of Gethsemane to describe the strangeness of a writer's life. Brontë becomes a figure who has made otherworldly journeys before reaching her final resting place and whose literary achievements came at the cost of great suffering and loneliness. As Franklin notes, Dickinson composed five stanzas on this theme and copied them all into fascicle 7. But, she appears to have thought that stanzas 2–3 and 4–5 were variants of each other. Between stanzas 3 and 4, although no extra space is left, she wrote 'Or', which Franklin takes to indicate a choice in constructing, with stanza 1, a three-stanza poem. Johnson, too, seems to have reached this conclusion as he offers stanzas 2–3 as a variant version of 4–5.

> All overgrown by cunning moss,
> All interspersed with weed,
> The little cage of 'Currer Bell'
> In quiet 'Haworth' laid.
>
> This Bird – observing others
> When frosts too sharp became
> Retire to other latitudes –
> Quietly did the same –
>
> But differed in returning –
> Since Yorkshire hills are green –
> Yet not in all the nests I meet –
> Can Nightingale be seen –
> [or]
> Gathered from many wanderings –
> Gethsemane can tell
> Thro' what transporting anguish
> She reached the Asphodel!
>
> Soft fall the sounds of Eden
> Opon her puzzled ear –
> Oh what an afternoon for Heaven,
> When 'Brontë' entered there!
>   (Fr146; J148)

The asphodel is the flower said to fill the plains of Hades or the underworld. Considering it to be the favourite food of the dead, the ancients often planted it near graves. In this elegy, Dickinson evokes both the Christian idea of the afterlife and the Greek one. But while the final stanza is clearly a description of Brontë's arrival in heaven, the fourth stanza seems to refer to her life on earth. The line, 'Gathered from many wanderings' invokes the traditional Christian image of death as a final and longed-for rest after life's wilderness journey. More unusually, Dickinson depicts this journey as a trip to the underworld. Like a hero of Greek mythology Brontë has descended into Hades while still living.

Dickinson may also have been influenced here by her reading of Elizabeth Barrett Browning.[43] In *Sonnets from the Portugese*, XXVII, Browning uses the asphodel to equate the perfection achieved in death with that gained through love. She writes:

> My own, my own,
> Who camest to me when the world was gone,
> And I who looked for only God, found *thee*!
> I find thee; I am safe, strong, and glad
> As one who stands in dewless asphodel,
> Looks backward on the tedious time he had
> In the upper life ...[44]

'Dewless asphodel' emphasises the otherworldly quality of love. As well as signalling life, dew marks the changing of night to day. The speaker's reference to the time she had in the 'upper life' also suggests that she is now in the 'lower life' or underworld. In her elegy to Brontë, Dickinson implies that Gethsemane bears witness to this otherworldly journey, a journey that is fulfilled through 'transporting anguish'. Once again, suffering preserves the liminality of place. Unusually, for Dickinson, the stanza ends with a sense of arrival. From Browning, Dickinson would have been familiar with the asphodel as describing perfection. Reading this tribute to another of her literary role models, it seems that when Dickinson writes 'Gethsemane can tell / Through what transporting Anguish / She reached the Asphodel', she is referring to Brontë's achievement as a writer.[45]

Dickinson depicts Gethsemane as a journey to the underworld in order to suggest that the place of a writer's creativity is neither in this world nor out of it. In stanzas 2–3, the analogy for Brontë's life is the journey of a migrating bird. But this is also a strange kind of journey, one where the travelling bird undergoes a change which cannot be undone. Three years later, Dickinson used the same image in a poem included in a letter of consolation to her cousins, Louise and Frances Norcross. On the death of their father in 1863 she offered the following balm:

> It is not dying hurts us so, –
> 'Tis living hurts us more.
> But dying is a different way,

A kind behind the door –
The Southern custom of the bird
That soon as frosts are due
Adopts a better latitude.
We are the birds that stay
The shiverers round farmers' doors.
For whose reluctant crumb
We stipulate – till pitying snows
Persuade our feathers Home.
(Fr528; J335)

Here, the migrating bird is a figure for the spirit's return to a heavenly home, which provides an escape from the bitter cold of earthly pain and grief. Unsurprisingly, in this consolatory poem, the journey is singular and irreversible. But, in Dickinson's earlier elegy to Brontë, the pattern of death is copied and experienced as a strange and otherworldly journey of voyage and return. It suggests a life lived in between worlds. The nightingale is a songbird (a Dickinsonian figure for the poet) forging yet another connection between the otherworldly journey and the poetic life. Recalling Orpheus – the half-divine half-human 'warbling teller' who first made the trip to Hades – the traveller in both versions of Dickinson's elegy suggests that the writer must journey between the world of the living and the world of the dead.

OTHERWORLDLY ENCOUNTERS AND POETIC INSPIRATION

In the early books of the Old Testament, God and his messengers have an uncanny affinity with the powers of darkness. During Moses's return to Egypt, he is suddenly and inexplicably attacked by God: 'And it came to pass by the way in the inn, that the Lord met him, and sought to kill him'.[46] God, in Genesis and Exodus, has demonic attributes and Moses's life is saved by a method used to fend off evil assaults: 'Zip-po-rah took a sharp stone, and cut off the foreskin of her son, and cast it at his feet, and said, "surely a bloody husband thou art to me". So he let him go: then she said, "A bloody husband thou art", because of the circumcision'.[47] The text suggests that Moses's life is saved through an old superstitious practice which used blood to frighten demons away. The same superstition quite possibly influenced Luke's description of Christ's struggle in Gethsemane. Christ appears locked in combat with an ambiguous force of good and evil, an angelic messenger who encourages his strength and heightens his pain. Death is not beaten as easily as Pauline theology would have us believe.

The morally ambiguous force which Christ fights in Gethsemane is one of the reasons his 'agony' is often seen as the typological fulfilment of Jacob's struggle at Peniel. Like Christ and Moses, Jacob was one of Dickinson's figures for the poet.

In April 1886 (shortly before the end of her life) she wrote to Higginson: 'Audacity of Bliss, said Jacob to the Angel "I will not let thee go except I bless thee" – Pugilist and Poet, Jacob was correct' (*L*, p. 903). Casting herself as Jacob to Higginson's Angel, Dickinson's performance recalls her early depiction of Jacob's struggle with the Angel in 'A little East of Jordan'. The poem, a variant of which was sent to Sue in early 1860, was copied into fascicle 7 as follows:

> A little East of Jordan
> Evangelists record,
> A Gymnast and an Angel
> Did wrestle long and hard –
>
> Till morning touching mountain –
> And Jacob, waxing strong,
> The Angel begged permission
> To Breakfast – to return –
>
> Not so, said cunning Jacob!
> 'I will not let thee go
> Except thou bless me' – Stranger!
> The which acceded to –
>
> Light swung the silver fleeces
> 'Peniel' Hills beyond,
> And the bewildered Gymnast
> Found he had worsted God!
>
> (Fr145; J59)

In his reading of this poem, McIntosh argues that Dickinson liked the story of Jacob's struggle with the angel because she saw Jacob as a representative man who takes on divine authority to bring inspiration through his words. He also quotes Dickinson's letter to Higginson, suggesting that: 'Poetry requires pugilism, a struggle with the divine, in order to have the power to bless'.[48] So, McIntosh argues that Dickinson identifies with Jacob because she has a vocation of power.

To say that Dickinson had a 'vocation of power' is not controversial in nineteenth-century terms. The unspecific notion of power characterises many of the major literary and philosophical works of the time. Indeed, as Michael Lopez has written, 'we could map the entire century ... in terms of the search for that Protean essence Emerson celebrated as "elemental power".[49] This would include Edgar Allan Poe's quest for a universal *prima mobilia*, Herman Melville's vision of a buried human power to be regained, Margaret Fuller's hope to raise the power of women and Walt Whitman's persona as the bardic incarnation of American energy. This nineteenth-century fascination with power arguably had its roots in a Romantic sensibility. For William Blake, energy was 'eternal delight', for Samuel Taylor Coleridge, 'imagination' was an 'indestructible power', and for Edmund Burke nothing was sublime that was not at root 'some modification of power'.[50]

Bloom has argued that the internalisation of the quest romance brought poetic consciousness and nature into a new relationship. He notes that implicit in all Romantics (and explicit in Blake) is a difficult distinction between organic and creative energy. For Bloom, the Promethean poet-hero is just the first stage in the Romantic quest for Imagination's freedom. In the Promethean stage, organic energy, or nature, is allied to the libido's struggle against repressiveness. In the second, creative stage, for which Bloom adopts Blake's term, 'real Man, the Imagination', nature is the immediate, though not the ultimate antagonist, which is selfhood. Bloom writes:

Prometheus rises from the id, and can best be thought of as the force of libido, doomed to undergo a merely cyclic movement from appetite to repression and then back again ... it is within the ego itself that the quest must turn, to engage the antagonist proper, and to clarify the imaginative component in the ego by its strife of contraries with its dark brother.[51]

As Bloom argues, the key difference between the religious and Romantic quest lies in its object and domain: 'the widened consciousness of the poet did not give him intimations of a former union with nature or the Divine, but rather of his former selfless self'.

In Dickinson's depiction of Jacob's triumph, the sudden acquisition of power that McIntosh rightly observes is very much in harmony with the forces of nature. It is hard to believe that Dickinson was not influenced here by her reading of Emerson's essay 'Nature', in which he describes the emergence of literary genius:

At the call of a noble sentiment, again the woods wave, the pines murmur, the river rolls and shines, and the cattle low upon the mountains, as he saw and heard them in his infancy. And with these forms, the spells of persuasion, the keys of power are put into his hands.[52]

Dickinson's bursting through of light is a moment of poetic inspiration, a signal of Jacob's illuminated mind. The moment of inspiration does more than interrupt the wilderness of the pugilist-poet's struggle, it dissolves it as the dawning light dissolves the darkness of the night-journey. 'Bewildered' Jacob, like Christian discovering the key called 'Promise', does not fully understand his reprieve. The wandering confusion of the wilderness still hangs upon his mind, but the dawning light of day mirrors the growing power of his success. The parting clouds therefore reveal the location of the fight. Peniel and the hills beyond symbolise the end of the wilderness land and the beginning of Jacob's homecoming. In Genesis, Jacob only names the place 'Peniel' after he survives the struggle, as a testament to his new-found faith and respect for God: 'And Jacob called the name of the place Peniel: for I have seen God face to face and my life is preserved' (Gen. 32.30).

In one sense, Jacob's 'wrestle' suggests the rise of the Promethean poet-hero, who harnesses divine light (or fire) for his own ends. But Dickinson's poem also suggests a struggle with a force of darkness and here Bloom's interpretation of the second stage of the internalised Romantic quest provides a way of reading the Romantic application of the religious narrative she invokes. Jacob, like Christ and Moses, struck Dickinson as a figure for the poet because he meets God face to face and survives the encounter (as Christ is resurrected and Moses not consumed). But that is not the end of their shared experience. Jacob, Christ and Moses are types of the poet-quester not only because they face and survive the unknown, but because they face and survive a dangerous and morally ambiguous unknown. Moses survives an inexplicable attack on his life and Christ survives the test of a dark and potentially demonic figure in Gethsemane. In Genesis, the angel uses supernatural powers to incapacitate Jacob: 'And when he saw that he prevailed not against him, he touched the hollow of his thigh; and the hollow of Jacob's thigh was out of joint'.[53] When Jacob affirms his faith after the battle, the sun rises and miraculously halts at the damaged part of his thigh. Jacob, like Moses, does not survive unhurt and God leaves the mark of his test upon him and his descendants: 'the children of Israel eat not of the sinew which shrank, which is upon the hollow of the thigh, unto this day: because he touched the hollow of Jacob's thigh in the sinew that shrank'.[54]

If we read Dickinson's poem as an analogy for internal poetic questing, then the demonic aspects of divinity are a way of understanding inspiration as a struggle with the self's darkness as well as the triumph of its own light. In Dickinson's rendering of Peniel, the God with whom Jacob finds he has power has demonic characteristics. He thrives at night-time and seems afraid of the day, shrinking from the appearance of light on the mountain. 'Light swung the silver fleeces' reflects the illumination we know

Dickinson associated with divine presence and also suggests the tearing
of cosmic fabric, a specific indicator of the unfolding of divine providence.
Jacob's worsting of God is paradoxically portrayed as a divinely sanctioned
triumph. Nature is suddenly and inexplicably co-operative. Jacob's 'cunning' was to demand a blessing, but his victory usurps the power to bless.

Jacob is a quest hero (the 'silver fleeces' even recall the golden fleece of
Jason's quest) who arrives at an unexpected goal. One of the most pertinent parallels between Romantic and religious quest narratives can be
found in the inexplicable nature of the shift towards enlightenment – the
moment at which tense and painful wrestling turns to reconciliation with
the creative or divine principle. For Bloom, the most developed example
of the singular Romantic quest is Blake's *Jerusalem*, which begins with
despairing struggle, anger and solipsistic withdrawal until the poem
quietly and inexplicably moves towards reconciliation between Los, the
Imaginative principle, and his emanative portion, Enitharmon.[55] Like
Blake, Dickinson realised that the quester cannot control the outcome
of the quest and she too knew that the wandering wilderness journey of
the poetic life, an existence neither entirely in nor out of this world, could
bring the poet into a struggle with darkness as well as an encounter with
light.

THE AGONY OF THE IN-BETWEEN

Jacob wrestles 'long and hard' before he triumphs. As a figure for the
poet, this pugilist draws attention to the agony of the in-between. His
struggle finds an alternate expression in the way Dickinson associates
pain with the border-crossing and extremity of experience that provides
the common ground for both death and poetic inspiration. Of the words
in her lexicon, 'agony' is of particular importance. 'Agony' would have
had theological significance for Dickinson. Part of Webster's definition
for 'agony' reads: 'Extreme pain of body and mind; anguish; appropri-
ately the pangs of death, and the sufferings of our Saviour in the garden of Gethsemane'.[56] The definition of Gethsemane in Dickinson's *Bible
Dictionary* was: 'Gethsemane – a small village in the Mount of Olives,
and where it seems there was an *oil-press*. Hither our Saviour sometimes
retired from Jerusalem; and in a garden belonging to it he had his bitter
agony, and was apprehended by Judas and his band.'[57]

When Dickinson used the term 'agony' to suggest closeness to overwhelming power, she would have been aware of its theological resonance.
In 'I like a look of Agony' (1862) she subverts the deathbed traditions of

nineteenth-century literature to emphasise a final journey between two worlds. Instead of becoming beatific, in the sentimental style, and signalling an arrival in Heaven, the dying person's *transitus* draws attention to the world they are leaving. Agony emphasises mortality, human suffering and struggle at the point of death. This poem leaves us firmly in the mortal world as Dickinson observes 'The Beads upon the Forehead / By homely Anguish strung'. This depiction of the *transitus* therefore focuses on closeness to another realm and the agony of the in-between, as opposed to the arrival on the other side.

In 'A nearness to Tremendousness' (1864), Dickinson elides the difference between death, ecstasy and poetic inspiration as she describes the agony of being close to a goal that remains just out of reach:

> A nearness to Tremendousness –
> An Agony procures –
> Affliction ranges Boundlessness –
> Vicinity to Laws
>
> Contentment's quiet Suburb –
> Affliction cannot stay
> In Acres – Its Location
> Is Illocality –
>
> (Fr824; J963)

To come close to the quest's final goal is more than a profoundly disorienting and bewildering experience. This poem suggests that journeying between two worlds destroys the principle of containment that the very notion of 'two worlds' represents. In the moments closest to triumph, the poet-quester loses control of the quest, subject to the lawless ravagings of her own affliction. 'Contentment's quiet Suburb' is about as appealing as the dew to the scorched flowers in Dickinson's letter to Sue. Its mundane and prosaic safety is the victim of poetic inspiration.

Dickinson's sense of mental anguish is carried by a strong emphasis on place. Her descriptive play on words in the last two lines offers a definition of this place that negates its own definitive properties. A location that is illocality is no location at all and yet it carries the sense of a place given meaning by an infinitely greater reality which paradoxically becomes part of, and remains at a tantalising distance from, finite experience. The variant ending, 'In Acre – or Location – / It rents Immensity', dismisses the place defined by expanse or precision and suggests the tearing of cosmic fabric – an example of extreme border-crossing– as the best descriptor.

'A nearness to Tremendousness' repeats many of the themes that we have seen Dickinson use to describe both the poetic and religious quest: isolation and transition, the strangeness and struggle of otherworldly journeys and encounters. Christ's 'Agony' is part of an extended conceit which implies that the poetic quest brings the poet close to the edge of her own existence. The emotional experiences of Gethsemane are therefore reconfigured for poetry as Dickinson depicts the strange and agonisingly intense position of the poet in the grip of inspiration.

QUEST AND POETIC PROCESS

As opposed to reading Dickinson's poetic quest as a process of self-mythologisation that aspires towards a rarefied pearl of poetic achievement, we might better understand it as a version of internalised Romantic questing that taps religious sources in order to understand a process that is always in search of its own meaning and that finds its 'location' in 'illocality'. This bears a closer relation to what we now know about her compositional practices. These practices changed over time. In the period around 1876, she seems to have stopped making fair copies of her poems and organising them into fascicles and sets. The poems we have from this late stage in her life have been collected from scraps of paper and letters found after her death. As Martha Nell Smith, Ellen Louise Harte, Marta Werner and most recently Aliki Barnstone have argued, this change in Dickinson's compositional practice has major implications for students of her work, implying that Dickinson no longer categorised her writings into 'poems' and 'letters'.[58] Dickinson had always sent poems to people in letters but as she aged, this desire to write to (and perhaps for) a selected reader seems to have intensified.

As part of Dickinson's religious imagination, quest is an enduring preoccupation through which we can understand her aesthetic decisions and indecisions even as they change form over time. Marta Werner, for example, offers an interesting way of reading Dickinson's late letter fragments and her fascicles as different versions of the same incarnational poetics of quest. If the late letters and fragments suggest wandering, a sensuous process of being carried away, then the fair copies emphasise stillness, a gesture towards the direction, if not the fulfilment, of parousia – being carried up.[59] The extent to which we know other people, particularly Sue Gilbert, to have been vitally involved in the composition of many of Dickinson's poems is not at odds with her thematic interest in loneliness (one can have many friends and feel essentially alone) but it does contradict the myth of her isolation.[60] She asked Sue for help and advice on tone and effect, she dispatched

poems (and letter-poems) as questers to find a home in the consciousness of her chosen readers, increasingly reflecting the truth of the sentiment she expressed in the following short poem, sent in a letter to the
Norcross cousins in 1862:

> A word is dead, when it is said
> Some say –
> I say it just begins to live
> That day
>
> (Fr278; J1212)

Quest may also be a way of understanding Dickinson's aversion to conventional publication. She clearly wanted her poems to have life away from
her. Her first letter to Higginson coyly displayed this very concern: 'Are
you too deeply occupied to say if my Verse is alive?' She knew that writing
involved outcomes beyond her authorial control. And she was rarely – one
might go as far as to say never – satisfied with fixity. As Franklin observes
in his thoughts on editing Dickinson:

Multiplicity did not bother this poet, and she would without qualms change a
reading in order to make it appropriate for different people and different occasions. Each of these fair copies is 'final' for its person or occasion but that cannot
be equated with final intention for publication. Sending a poem to a friend is a
type of publishing, but it fixes the poem only for that person on that occasion;
sending a poem to a publisher is distinctly different and, in theory, fixes the
form of the poem for all people and all time.[61]

With persistence and intensity of experiment, Dickinson kept search-
ing, destroying the notions of place and containment that she found
comfortable.

The poetic quest undoes the poet's 'little room' (the quietly powerful domain of the self or the contained form of the poetic artefact) by
bringing it to the edge of its own existence. Like Moses, Jacob and Jesus,
the poet survives but she suffers in the process. The laws of space and
time were both a burden and a reassurance – a 'prison' that got to be a
'friend' (Fr456) – and by continually reaching beyond them, Dickinson
rent boundaries but she also drove the nails of suffering into the (albeit
comforting) cross of her own existence.

NOTES

1 Johnson, *Perception and the Poet's Quest*, p. 2.
2 Marta L. Werner, *Emily Dickinson's Open Folios: Scenes of Reading, Surfaces of
Writing* (Ann Arbor, Mich.: University of Michigan Press, 1995), p. 26.

3 Johnson, *Perception and the Poet's Quest*, p. 129. Werner suggests a parallel between the hand that carefully sewed the fascicles and the hand that mutilated the fragments, *Open Folios*, p. 31.

4 See Todd M. Lieber, *Endless Experiments: Essays on the Heroic Experience in American Romanticism* (Columbus, OH: Ohio State University Press, 1973) and Janis P. Stout, *The Journey Narrative in American Literature: Patterns and Departures* (London: Greenwood Press, 1983).

5 Peniel is the place of Jacob's wrestle with the angel.

6 Homer, *The Odyssey*, trans. Albert Cook (New York: W. W. Norton and Co., 1974), Book IX, pp. 119–28, lines 215–566.

7 Virgil, *The Aeneid*, trans C. Day Lewis, ed. Jasper Griffin (Oxford: Oxford University Press, 1952), Book III, pp. 71–3, Apollonius of Rhodes, *Jason and the Golden Fleece*, trans. Richard Hunter (Oxford: Clarendon Press, 1993), Book II, pp. 42–3.

8 John Bunyan, *The Pilgrim's Progress* (1678; Harmondsworth: Penguin, 1965), pp. 51–5, pp. 99–101.

9 Homer, *Odyssey*, Book V, pp. 65–75.

10 Thomas Bulfinch, *The Age of Fable: Stories of Gods and Heroes* (Boston, Mass.: Sanborn, Carter and Bazin, 1855), pp. 319–33, 346–56. Vincent Cleary and Ken Hiltner argue that not only were classical stories available to Dickinson but that she could have read them in the original and was definitely influenced by their themes and structure. Vincent J. Cleary, 'Emily Dickinson's Classical Education', *English Language Notes*, 18.2 (1980), pp. 119–29. Ken Hiltner, 'Because I, Persephone, Could Not Stop for Death: Emily Dickinson and the Goddess', *Emily Dickinson Journal*, 10.2 (2001), pp. 22–42.

11 J. Lempriere, *Classical Dictionary: Containing a Full Account of all the Proper Names mentioned in Ancient Authors with Tables of Coins, Wrights and Measures in Use among the Greeks and Romans* (London: T. Allman, 1847). Charles Anthon, *Classical Dictionary: Containing an Account of the Principal Proper Names mentioned in Ancient Authors and Intended to Elucidate all the Important Points connected with the Geography, History, Biography, Mythology, and Fine Arts of the Greeks and Romans, together with an Account of Coins, Weights, and Measures with Tabular Values of the Same* (New York: Harper and Brothers, 1841). For a list of the textbooks used during Dickinson's time at the Academy, see Frederick Tuckerman, *Amherst Academy 1814–1861* (Amherst, Mass., 1929).

12 A. C. Buchanan, *A Place Called Gethsemane* (London: Macmillan, 1927).

13 Thomas Hooker, *The Unbelievers Preparing for Christ* (1638), quoted in Cohen, *God's Caress*, p. 81.

14 1 Cor. 15.55.

15 The term was used by Jacksonian Democrats in the 1840s to promote the westward push.

16 Lois A. Cuddy, 'Shelley's Glorious Titan: Reflections on Emily Dickinson's Self-Image and Achievement', *Dickinson Studies, U.S. Poet*, 55.1 (1985), pp. 32–40, at p. 32.

17 E. J. Trelawney, *Recollections of the Last Days of Shelley and Byron* (Boston, Mass.: Ticknor and Fields, 1859), pp. 176–7.

18 *Ibid.*, p. 187.

19 Percy Bysshe Shelley, *Prometheus Unbound* (1820), ed. Lawrence John Zillman (Seattle, Wash.: University of Washington Press, 1959), p. 166, Act I, lines 584–5.

20 *Ibid.*, p. 132, Act I, line 24.

21 *Ibid.*, pp. 122–3.

22 Other examples of the Romantic poet as Prometheus-Christ can be found in William Blake's *America* (1793) and *The Book of Ahania* (1795), as well as Coleridge's essay on 'The Idea of the Prometheus of Aeschylus' (1825), but Dickinson is unlikely to have read these works as only Blake's *Songs of Innocence and Experience* were around in America at the time and although Higginson read them in 1842, we assume he never showed them to her as he always claimed she 'unconsciously' echoed Blake. Edward J. Rose, 'The 1839 Wilkinson Edition of Blake's *Songs* in Transcendental America', *Blake Newsletter*, 4.3 (1971), pp. 79–81. Higginson, 'Preface to the 1890 Edition', Willis J. Buckingham (ed.), *Emily Dickinson's Reception in the 1890s: A Documentary History* (Pittsburgh, Penn.: University of Pittsburgh Press, 1989), p. 14. Dickinson would have known Coleridge's poems from *Harper's New Monthly* but probably not his essays. Capps, *Dickinson's Reading*, p. 129. *Blake's Poetry and Designs*, ed. Mary Lynn Johnson and John E. Grant (London: W. W. Norton and Co., 1979), pp. 103–21 and 160–8. Samuel Taylor Coleridge, 'Idea of the Prometheus of Aeschylus', in *The Literary Remains of Samuel Taylor Coleridge*, 4 vols. (London: William Pickering, 1836–9), vol. 2, pp. 323–60.

23 Gaston Bachelard, *Fragments of a Poetics of Fire* (Dallas, Tex.: Dallas Institute Publications, 1990), pp. 84–5.

24 Harold Bloom, 'The Internalisation of Quest Romance', *The Yale Review: A National Quarterly*, 58 (Summer 1969), pp. 526–36, at p. 527.

25 Thomas Hooker, *Spiritual Thirst: A Sermon Preached upon John 7.37* (1638), quoted in Cohen, *God's Caress*, p. 83.

26 Psalm 107.4–5.

27 Psalm 63.1.

28 *Titus Lucretius Carus on the Nature of Things*, trans. Thomas Jackson (Oxford: Oxford University Press, 1929), pp. 198–9.

29 Isa. 16.9.

30 John 7.37.

31 Matt. 5.6.

32 'I am the way, the truth and the life: no man cometh unto the Father, but by me.' John 14.6.

33 Matt. 11.28–9.

34 Edmund Burke, *A Philosophical Enquiry into the Origin of our Ideas of the Sublime and Beautiful* (1757; Oxford: Oxford University Press, 1990), p. 53.

35 Immanuel Kant, *Critique of Aesthetic Judgment* (1790), trans. J. C. Meredith (Oxford: Clarendon Press, 1911), pp. 90–203, at p. 92.

36 Matt. 27.46, Mark 15.34.
37 Lev. 16.10 and Gen. 22.7–8.
38 Bunyan, *Pilgrim's Progress*, p. 224.
39 Homer, *Odyssey*, Book XI, pp. 145–61.
40 John 18.1.
41 Matt. 26.37, Mark 14.33.
42 Luke 22.44.
43 An 1851 edition including 'Sonnets from the Portugese' found in Dickinson's home library exhibits the light markings thought to be hers. Harvard University, Houghton Library, Harvard EDR525.
44 Humphrey Milford (ed.), *The Poetical Works of Elizabeth Barrett Browning with Two Prose Essays* (Oxford: Oxford University Press, 1920), pp. 323–4.
45 In 1849, after first reading *Jane Eyre*, Dickinson returned the loaned copy of the book to Elbridge Bowdoin with a note which read: 'Mr Bowdoin. If all these leaves were altars, and on every one a prayer that Currer Bell might be saved – and you were God – would you answer it?' Bowdoin comments that 'the leaves mentioned were box Leaves, sent to me in a little bouquet'. Dickinson cannot be alluding to an illness of Charlotte Brontë because the book had only been published in the previous year and Brontë's true identity was still unknown. Johnson therefore argues that, 'her plea simply expresses her hope that Currer Bell will live long and write many more books' (*L*, p. 77).
46 Exod. 4.24.
47 Exod. 4.25–6.
48 McIntosh, *Nimble Believing*, p. 96.
49 Lopez, *Emerson and Power*, p. 12.
50 *Ibid.*, p. 11.
51 Bloom, 'The Internalization of Quest Romance', pp. 534–5.
52 Emerson, 'Nature' (1836), in *The Collected Works of Ralph Waldo Emerson*, ed. Joseph Slater, Robert Spiller, Alfred R. Ferguson *et al.*, 6 vols. (Cambridge, Mass.: Harvard University Press, 1971–2003), vol. i, pp. 7–51, at p. 21.
53 Gen. 32.25.
54 Gen. 32.32.
55 Bloom, 'The Internalization of Quest Romance', p. 535.
56 Webster, *Dictionary*, vol. i, p. 29.
57 Archibald Alexander, *A Pocket Dictionary of the Holy Bible containing a historical and geographical account of the persons and places mentioned in the Old and New Testaments and also a description of other objects, natural, artificial, civil, religious and military: together with a copious reference to texts of scripture under each important word. Prepared for the American Sunday School Union and adapted to general use* (Philadephia: American Sunday School Union, 1831), p. 233.
58 See the Dickinson Electronic Archives at www.emilydickinson.org or Barnstone, 'Four Changes', in *Changing Rapture: Emily Dickinson's Poetic Development*.

59 Werner, *Open Folios*, p. 52.

60 See Martha Nell Smith and Ellen Louise Hart, *Open Me Carefully: Emily Dickinson's Intimate Letters to Susan Huntingdon Dickinson* (Ashfield, Mass.: Paris Press, 1998).

61 R. W. Franklin, *The Editing of Emily Dickinson: A Reconsideration* (Madison, Wisc.: University of Wisconsin Press, 1967), p. 132.

CHAPTER 5

Sacrifice

The narrative of crucifixion is one of journey and climax – the struggle in Gethsemane and the death on Calvary. Calvary, seen in the broader context of sacrificial narrative, was of thematic and structural importance to Dickinson's poetry. Thematically, Dickinson uses the crucifixion to express her ambivalent feelings about martyrdom and the poetic quest. She also relies on the love and grief of a man, whose humanity opens a path to divinity, to express her own emotional anguish in the face of an unknowable beyond. Structurally, the sacrificial giving of self allows Dickinson to explore the poetic relationship between the self's essence and its representation.

It has become a commonplace of Dickinson criticism to say that she turned to Christ as a representative man of suffering. This chapter takes that idea in a new direction by opening up the theological meaning of that suffering. Suffering on the cross draws attention to the narrative of finite infinity because it returns us to the problems of the Word made flesh. Dickinson inherited a concept that articulated both the unbridgeable difference and the compact union of humanity and divinity. Christ's sacrifice emphasises the condition of that union at the very moment it is about to be dissolved. His death is, by definition, an intensely mortal experience but it is also fundamental to his redemptive mission. Dickinson's Puritan ancestors approached the issue by focusing on God's condescension to be man; her more liberal contemporaries frequently emphasised a humanistic approach. Drawing from the twentieth-century theology of Jürgen Moltmann, this chapter explores the relationship between theological and poetic interpretations of Christ's death.

MARTYRDOM AND THE POET'S QUEST

Dickinson, like many nineteenth-century comparative theologians, saw the story of the crucifixion echoed across the ancient and modern world.

And, like these theologians, she hardly tried to hide her motive for comparison, often admitting, as in the following poem composed early in 1862, that, in the suffering and self-sacrifice of others, she wanted to find a 'like story' to her own:

> Unto like Story – Trouble has enticed me
> How Kinsmen fell –
> Brothers and Sisters – who preferred the Glory –
> And their young will
> Bent to the Scaffold, or in Dungeons – chanted –
> Till God's full time –
> When they let go the ignominy – smiling –
> And Shame went still –
>
> Unto guessed Crests, my moaning fancy, leads me,
> Worn fair
> By Heads rejected – in the lower country –
> Of honours there –
> Such spirit makes her perpetual mention,
> That I – grown bold –
> Step martial at my Crucifixion –
> As Trumpets – rolled –
>
> Feet, small as mine – have marched in Revolution
> Firm to the Drum –
> Hands – not so stout – hoisted them – in witness –
> When Speech went numb –
> Let me not shame their sublime deportments –
> Drilled bright –
> Beckoning – Etruscan invitation –
> Toward Light –
>
> (Fr300; J295)

This poem repeats the journey motif and the encounter with light familiar from the previous two chapters. Here the guiding force is determinedly erotic. Dickinson's speaker is led by 'moaning fancy', the pilot of sexual pleasure and the haunting voice of the imagination. The erotic was profoundly important to Dickinson's notion of sacrifice and its permutations in the Christian story of sacrifice will be discussed in more detail later. Dickinson overshadows the erotic journey with the triumph and climax of its ending. Each stanza retells the story in order to emphasise the result. The opening, 'Unto like Story' also draws attention to the act of retelling, to the comparison and substitution of similar narratives. The Christian story is layered onto the Roman one. This is the speaker's passion narrative, but 'step martial' implies that she may also be a Roman killing God.

As the poem progresses, the degree of military action intensifies. We move from a 'letting go' to a 'martial step' to a full-blown 'revolution'. As a retelling of the passion narrative, this is surprisingly active, and the growing intensity of the action contributes to the feeling of climax. However, climax is not to be confused with resolution. Dickinson ends with the 'Etruscan invitation – / Toward Light'. So the ending of the poem pushes the narrative on towards an encounter that elides the difference between death, poetic inspiration and the glory of eternal life. The movement towards light shapes the crucifixion narrative just as it shapes Dickinson's poetic quest because light symbolises a power of infinite strength – the enticing and elusive goal of finite struggle.

Light comes from fire as well as spirit. There is good reason to assume that the 'light' at the end of this poem is also the fire that burns the stake of martyrdom. The speaker's small hands and feet suggest that the persona, like Dickinson, is a woman. There is a historical specificity to the narrative that implies this woman is Joan of Arc, who, famous for leading an army against the English and Burgundians, also had visions and reportedly heard the voices of St Catherine and St Margaret. St Catherine's birthplace, Siena, was an old Etruscan city.[1] The 'Etruscan invitation – Towards Light' may be St Catherine calling Joan of Arc home to heaven through the fire in which she was burnt at the stake. The roll of trumpets mimics the fanfare of the British army, and Dickinson conflates the beat of the drum with the march of feet, uniting martyrdom and war. This atmosphere of revolutionary war in which the speaker hears a 'spirit [who] makes perpetual mention' and feels the 'shame' which Joan of Arc sought to avoid by keeping her visions private makes the famous martyr a likely persona for the speaker of this poem.

So Dickinson equates crucifixion with a notion of martyrdom where the pain of death is liberation. The speaker is only freed through her absorption into divinity, which is linked to the martyr's burning death in the image of light. Union with God is the emancipation of human life but that emancipation comes with a struggle. Choosing Joan of Arc as her persona in this poem, Dickinson draws attention to the martyr's struggle and submission to the divine plan, unfolding providentially in 'God's full time'.

This struggle between the infinite and the finite is reflected in the struggle of Dickinson's philosophical and tonal stance. She is drawn to Christ's sacrifice as by a lover, but she is nervous and sceptical about losing control. Control is not only associated with finity, or limit, it is also rhetorically reflected in irony. Irony delimits and disowns its subject. While

the most obvious readings of irony often expose the foolishness or inadequacy of that subject, it is often the case, and I think very often the case
with Dickinson, that irony functions as a guard against anguish, a way of
protecting and distancing oneself from the subjects one cares most about.
So it is probably because Dickinson is attracted to the exquisite pain of
martyrdom that she cannot help being ironic about its unthinking devotion. The following poem (composed 1862) is a good example:

> To put this World down, like a Bundle –
> And walk steady, away,
> Requires Energy – possibly Agony –
> 'Tis the Scarlet way
>
> Trodden with straight renunciation
> By the Son of God –
> Later, his faint Confederates
> Justify the Road –
>
> Flavours of that Old Crucifixion –
> Filaments of Bloom, Pontius Pilate sowed –
> Strong Clusters, from Barabbas' Tomb –
>
> Sacrament, Saints partook before us –
> Patent, every drop,
> With the Brand of the Gentile Drinker
> Who indorsed the Cup –
>
> (Fr404; J527)

In religious colour symbolism, scarlet represents strength and the blood
of martyrs.[2] Dickinson conflates martyrdom with the sacrament of the
Eucharist and feeds it back into the narrative of Christ's suffering and saving power, alluding to both the cup of Gethsemane and the cup of eternal
life.[3] Sacrifice is not a path into the unknown but a path heavy with precedent. The smell of death guides the martyrs' journey as they savour the
pain and suffering of 'that Old Crucifixion'. As with Joan of Arc's passion
narrative, martyrdom forms a sensual relationship with the crucifixion.

Yet Dickinson cannot help but turn her ironic wit on their sacrifice.
Quite apart from the implication that martyrs romanticise their journey,
absurdly tasting the 'flavours' of their pain, she makes the crucifixion into
a 'Brand' of suffering. 'Patent' refers to patent medicine, a practice which
reached its height in the nineteenth century in America and became
renowned for its sham qualities. Inventors of patent medicine would, for
example, mix substances like alcohol and morphine into treatments for
colicky babies often with disastrous effects. These medicines would be

patented or branded so the inventor would reap the financial benefits. 'Patent', 'brand' and 'indorsed' tie the sacramental and saving power of Christ's body and blood in with this infamous practice of 'saving' medicine. The martyrs, their struggle echoed by the 'faint Confederates' of the Southern Army, like the gullible purchasers of 'patent' medicine, have been duped into believing their struggle is a noble one. The hope of their sacrifice becomes the con of a well-established industry (the doctrinal teaching of the church perhaps or the pro-slavery fervour of the South)[4] as Dickinson undercuts the integrity of Christ's 'straight renunciation'.

'To put this World down, like a Bundle' implies that life is a burden and a clumsy one at that. It also implies that this is all there is. The traveller's 'bundle' comprises all their worldly possessions, so it bears the imprint of their journey in the world. In Dickinson's simile, the martyr must fall for the lie that worldliness is all there is to this world – the doctrine of Christian 'renunciation'. But as she implies in the following poem on martyrdom, this renunciation has the effect of dulling the very human qualities that make Christ's sacrifice so important:

> Through the straight pass of suffering,
> The martyrs – even – trod.
> Their feet – opon Temptation –
> Their faces – opon God –
>
> A stately – shriven – Company –
> Convulsion – playing round –
> Harmless – as streaks of meteor –
> Opon a Planet's Bond –
>
> Their faith – the everlasting troth –
> Their expectation – fair –
> The Needle – to the North Degree –
> Wades – so – thro' polar Air!
>
> (Fr187; J792)

Interestingly, this poem exists in three versions. This one was included in a letter to Samuel Bowles in early 1862 with the following introduction:

Dear Friend,
   If you doubted my Snow – for a moment – you never will again – I know – Because I could not say it – I fixed it in the Verse – for you to read – when your thought wavers, for such a foot as mine –

(*L*, p. 394)

Likening her personal and metrical 'foot' to the martyr's tread, Dickinson forges another connection between sacrifice and her own story of poetic struggle. The image of 'Snow' is used two years later to represent both her poetic gift and the sacrifice of the virgin martyr.[5] Here it participates in a similar play on poetry and pure affection.[6] But Dickinson makes any exalted idea of her own vocation and devotion ironic in the 'Polar air' of the poem in which she 'fixe[s]' her poetic gift of self. 'Polar' clearly indicates extremity, an act of reaching beyond.[7] Dickinson mixes her metaphor, pouring water (and cold water at that) on the martyrs' airy hopes and her own sacrificial gift.

The degree to which she fixes her gift beyond 'doubt' and 'waver' is reflected in the fixed metrical feet of the poem, which remain constrained as the feet of the martyrs. In his note on this poem, Johnson suggests that its inclusion in the letter to Bowles is 'an attempt to make her position clear' (*L*, p. 395). But in fact the poem subverts the introductory assertion of clarity, and her claims cannot belie the sense in which she relishes Bowles's wavering doubt as to her own position. The doctrinally sound 'strait pass of suffering' (echoing the 'strait gate' that leads to eternal life and reflected in the poem's metrical constraint) requires an insensitivity to pain and grief. 'Convulsion – playing round –' is no convulsion at all. The agony that Dickinson deems essential to the bursting of finite experience does not touch the martyrs' inner cores and this heavy metrical treading of doctrinal faith makes the world a sinful 'Temptation' to be renounced in the narrow and airy focus of their hope in God. What Dickinson really leaves beyond doubt is the necessity and value of doubt itself.

STAGING THE SACRIFICIAL GIFT

The 'like story' of sacrificial dying was pursued rather more obliquely and suggestively in the connections Dickinson forged between the sacrificial gift of the martyr's death and the sacrificial gift staged by her performative poetics. In the wake of late twentieth-century philosophy we now have a substantial vocabulary with which to understand sacrificial dying as a gift of self for other.[8] Derrida, for example, takes inspiration from Heidegger's notion that death's dative is not substitution.[9] He writes: 'the sameness of the self, what remains irreplaceable in dying only becomes what it is, in the sense of an identity as a relation of the self to itself, by means of this idea of mortality as irreplaceability'.[10] It is only in the context of this uniqueness of self that dying for the other can make sense; so for Derrida the sacrificial gift is ultimately a gift of self. The theological turn of Derrida's philosophy of the gift derives from a notion with which Dickinson would have been very familiar. In Hebrews, Christ becomes the mediator of the covenant of grace (which replaced the covenant of works, broken by Adam's sin of disobedience):

[Christ] is the mediator of the new testament, that by means of death, for the redemption of the transgressions that were under the first testament, they which are called might receive the promise of eternal inheritance. For where a testament is, there must also of necessity be the death of the testator.[11]

Entry to the covenant of grace is therefore by means of Christ's sacrificial gift of self.

The connection that Dickinson forged between sacrificial narrative and performative poetics has its basis in the Baptismal imagery I discussed in Chapter 2 and Dickinson's concurrent concerns about self-representation. In religious terms, sacrifice connects Baptism and crucifixion. Christian Baptism realises Christ's sacrifice anew, as Dickinson would have known from Pauline theology: 'know ye not, that so many of us as were baptised into Jesus Christ were baptised into his death? Therefore we are buried with him by Baptism into death.'[12] The connection between immersion and burial is more than metaphoric. One event sacramentally realises the other. In Pauline theology, the baptised are sacramentally crucified and resurrected. In this way, they are bonded into Christ's sacrifice and allowed into the covenant of grace.

But the bond into Christ's sacrifice depends on a renaming of self – an 'ingrafting' into Christ. As I discussed in Chapter 2, Dickinson's Baptismal imagery exploits the way in which this renaming of self calls authenticity into question and helps to develop an aesthetic that comes to rely on the enabling constraint which performance or the persona provides. In this chapter I want to pursue the idea that sacrificial narrative bears an integral relation to Dickinson's performative poetics because it goes to the heart of the self's manner of representation.

In Dickinson's 'A Visitor in Marl –' (1863) the sacrificial narrative takes the form of a Baptism into death and the poem turns on a radical re-representation of 'Flowers'. 'Flowers' recur throughout Dickinson's career as avatars of herself. They were the means by which she expressed her passionate longing for transfigurative experience to Sue in 1852. When Higginson came to see her in August 1870, she kept him waiting downstairs for a long time until she finally appeared clothed in her habitual white dress and carrying two lilies. Higginson wrote to his wife: 'She came to me with two day lilies which she put in a sort of childlike way into my hand and said "These are my introduction"' (*L*, p. 473). As St Armand has noted, Dickinson particularly relishes identifying herself with wayside wild flowers, to the point of calling herself 'Daisy' in her love poems to 'Master'.[13] The language of flowers, then, would seem to be intimately bound up with Dickinson's self-presentation, the poses she adopted and the personas she inhabited, the kind of enabling constraint that I have argued is central to Dickinson's aesthetic of Baptism.[14] In this poem, her 'flowers' are baptised and bonded into death.

> A Visitor in Marl –
> Who influences Flowers –
> Till they are orderly as Busts –
> And Elegant – as Glass –
>
> Who visits in the Night –
> And just before the Sun –
> Concludes his glistening interview –
> Caresses – and is gone –
>
> But whom his fingers touched –
> And where his feet have run –
> And whatsoever Mouth he kissed –
> Is as it had not been –
>
> (Fr558; J391)

As Marl is a sediment found in glacial lakes, Judith Farr insists that the 'Visitor in Marl –' is frost, and that to read this as a poem about dew as, she notes, at least two other critics have done, 'drastically distorts the poem's meaning'.[15] Farr is right, of course, in emphasising that Dickinson sees a distinction between the two. She cites 'There is an arid Pleasure –' (1864) to make her case:

> As Frost is different from Dew –
> Like Element – are they –
>
> Yet one – rejoices Flowers –
> And one – the Flowers abhor –

Her partial citation, however, glosses over the parallel Dickinson draws between them. Frost, in this poem, is a corruption of dew. The full poem reads:

> There is an arid Pleasure –
> As different from Joy –
> As Frost is different from Dew –
> Like Element   are they –
>
> Yet one – rejoices Flowers –
> And one – the Flowers abhor –
> The finest Honey – curdled –
> Is worthless – to the Bee –
>
> (Fr885; J782)

If 'Dew' is 'Honey', 'Frost' is 'Honey – curdled –'. This poem focuses on the relationship between 'Frost' and 'Dew' – their deceptive and dangerous similarity in order to emphasise the cruel difference of their realities. The comparison between this poem and 'A Visitor in Marl' is found in the connection between 'Frost' and 'Dew'. Yet, Farr writes: 'the … visitor of [the] poem [Visitor in Marl –] is obviously not dew but death in the guise of frost, and the poem's eroticism is not merely ominous but deadly'.[16] There can be little doubt that this is a killing frost, but the poem exploits the connection between frost and dew in order to emphasise the closeness between death and life. Night-frost begins its life as dew; the frost is only formed when temperatures drop and this poem describes the transformation from dew to frost by 'Influence' – a change over time.

Dew is a natural symbol for the waters of Baptism. Dew comes from above. It comes, according to the biblical worldview, from heaven. In Isaiah, dew is a symbol of the resurrection: 'awake and sing, ye that dwell in dust: for thy dew is as the dew of herbs'.[17] Dew is a fitting reminder of the Christian's Baptism into Christ's death and resurrection; the renewal of the earth depicts the washing of regeneration. The biblical connection between dew and Baptism is strengthened when we remember that dew is associated with the anointing of priests:

It is like the precious ointment upon the head, that ran down upon the beard, even Aaron's beard: that went down to the skirts of his garments; As the dew of Her-mon, and as the dew that descended upon the mountains of Zion: for there the Lord commanded the blessing, even life for evermore.[18]

The psalm connects dew with Baptism in two ways. First: the mountain is like the priest and the dew that falls is parallel to ordination. Second: as oil is symbolic of the Holy Spirit throughout the scriptures and as mountains are frequently places where the divine and human meet, dew is associated with the outpouring of spirit, which is in turn symbolised by the pouring of water in Baptism. As anointing the head is an induction into priesthood, Baptism is an induction into the body of Christ, his death and resurrection.

Dickinson exploits the ambiguity of 'marl', symbolic of frost *and* dew, to create a sense of being baptised into death. The chalky grey colour of marl and its association with cold suggests a corpse-like creature, made even more vivid by the lifelessness of 'Busts' and 'Glass'. As Farr notices, 'Marl' is also a contraction of 'marble'. This may well be the sense with which Dickinson was more familiar. In a letter to Elizabeth Holland in January 1875, Dickinson wrote: 'Mother is asleep in the Library – Vinnie – in the

Dining Room – Father – in the Masked Bed – in the Marl House' (*L*, p. 537). As Farr explains, the masked bed is a coffin, whose interior might be covered in silk or satin, and the marble house is a grave with its marble headstone. The effect of the visitor seems to be to freeze and kill. But 'Influence' also suggests a relationship in which the flowers are being cast in the image of their visitor. The brittle texture and cold colourless appearance of 'Busts' (busts are often made of marble) and 'Glass' may remind the reader of 'Marl'. The flowers are not just killed; they are bonded into death personified, and made again in his image. The words 'orderly' and 'Elegant' imply, together with the rigidity of 'Busts' and 'Glass', that this bond can also be understood as the constraint of propriety.

So, the idea of being baptised into death, or the narrative of sacrificial dying, is part of Dickinson's concern with the self and its representation. The speaker describes the visitor's 'Influence' in unquestionably erotic terms – 'Caresses', 'touched', 'kissed'. This tenderness, which Farr notices is 'not merely ominous but deadly', is a violation. It recalls the kiss by which Judas betrayed Jesus and sent him to his death (Matt. 26.48–9). The erotic, in this poem, is the means of intrusion upon the very essence of self and a betrayal of that self. This eroticism, however, remains secret: it happens during the night and in the day 'Is as it had not been –'. If there is an element of masochistic pleasure in the annihilation of self in the presence of the visitor, it is expressed in the pleasure of forbidden sexual encounter. The final line suggests the absence of any trace of touch (dissolved as the sun melts the frost) and an undoing of the subject through erotic encounter. Not only the trace of touch, but those who have been touched are 'as [they] had not been –'. Being baptised into death re-creates the self in death's image (the imposed identity *is* death), and in doing so it negates the value of the self's former existence. However, this negation relies on there being something to undo. 'Is *as* it had not been – ' (emphasis added) uses the simile to suggest that the rebirth of self is equivalent to its own erasure, which is not the same as saying that it has been erased. Some part of an original self is left but it has been *almost* annihilated.

THEATRICALITY AND SELF-PRESERVATION

Sacrifice, connected through Baptism to Dickinson's fictions of naming, goes to the heart of the theatrical nature of Dickinson's verse, the poses she adopted, and the personas she inhabited. In 'A Visitor in Marl –' the simile performs, in miniature, the theatricality that she made so important to her poetics. The self that is 'as it had not been' preserves some part of itself through repeated sacrifice. As the Baptism into death retains an element of masquerade or staging, some part of the flower survives the frost.

In 'What would I give to see his face?' (1861) a reference to *The Merchant of Venice* further exemplifies Dickinson's staging of the sacrificial gift. In this poem, as in 'A Visitor in Marl', performing her sacrifice is a means of self-preservation:

> What would I give to see His face?
> I'd give – I'd give my life – of course –
> But *that* is not enough!
> Stop just a minute – let me think!
> I'd give my biggest Bobolink!
> That makes *two – Him –* and *Life!*
> You know who '*June*' is –
> I'd give *her –*
> Roses a day from Zinzebar –
> And Lily tubes – like wells –
> Bees – by the furlong –
> Straits of Blue –
> Navies of Butterflies – sailed thro' –
> And dappled Cowslip Dells –
> Then I have 'shares' in Primrose 'Banks' –
> Daffodil Dowries – spicy 'stocks' –
> Dominions – broad as Dew –
> Bags of Doubloons – adventurous Bees
> Brought me – from firmamental seas –
> And Purple – from Peru –
>
> *Now –* have I bought it –
> 'Shylock'? Say!
> Sign me the Bond!
> 'I vow to pay
> To Her – who pledges *this –*
> *One hour –* of her Sovreign's face'!
> *Extatic* Contract!
> *Niggard* Grace!
> My *Kingdom's worth* of Bliss!
>
> (Fr266; J247)

The reference to Shylock's demand for a 'pound of flesh' makes a physical giving of self central to the economy of the gift in this poem. In the opening stanzas, giving equates with buying. There is a heavy irony to the 'banks' of primroses, 'daffodil dowries' and 'spicy "stocks"'. Far from an act of benevolence, it is part of a contract, a method of exchange. Dickinson, like Emerson, anticipated the twentieth-century debate over the economy of giving. Where Emerson begins his essay, 'Gifts', with an economic metaphor – 'it is said that the world is in a state of bankruptcy, that the world owes the world more than the world can pay, and ought to go into chancery, and be sold' – Dickinson begins 'What would I give to see His face?' by weighing gains and losses.[19] Moreover, Dickinson, like Emerson, moves quickly to an excess of giving and finally, through the Shakespearean reference, to a giving of self, echoing Emerson's thought that, 'The only gift is a portion of thyself. Thou must bleed for me.'[20]

Shakespeare is commonly thought to have used Alexander Silvayn's *The Orator* as one of his sources for the play. In the English translation of this play, the Jew says: 'what a matter were it then if I should cut off his privy members supposing that the same would altogether weigh a pound'.[21] In the late sixteenth century, the word 'flesh' was frequently used, especially in the Bible, instead of 'penis'. The discussions of sexuality and disease in Leviticus repeatedly refer to 'flesh' in this sense. The 'pound of flesh' conflates sexual and religious violence. Genesis of the King James Bible dictates: 'circumcise the flesh of your foreskin' (17.11). The Geneva Bible, with which Shakespeare would have been familiar, is even more explicit: 'circumcise the foreskin of your flesh' (Gen. 17.11).

Shylock's demand that Antonio be circumcised is significant, because, as Baptism can be seen to be that which makes a Christian, circumcision can be seen to be that which makes a Jew. The Christian sacrament of Baptism replaced the Jewish tradition of circumcision as the sign of the covenant God made with Abraham, a sign of God's grace or God's gift. Circumcision is instituted in Genesis 17 at the same time as Abram's name is changed to Abraham. God's naming of Abraham is also a sign of the covenantal bond: 'Neither shall thy name any more be called Abram, but thy name shall be Abraham; for a father of many nations I have made thee'.[22] In Pauline and Calvinist theology, Baptism is, in many ways, a continuation of the essence and purpose of circumcision. Paul writes: 'in [Christ] also ye are circumcised with the circumcision made without hands, in putting off the body of the sins of the flesh by the circumcision of Christ. Buried with him in Baptism, wherein also ye are risen with him through faith.'[23] Calvin's interpretation of this passage consequently emphasises the connection between circumcision and Baptism: 'what do these words mean, but just that the truth and completion of Baptism is the truth and completion of circumcision, since they represent one thing? For it is his object to show that Baptism is the same thing to Christians that circumcision formerly was to the Jews.'[24]

Only near the end of *The Merchant of Venice* do we discover that Shylock intends to cut the flesh from close to Antonio's heart, parodying Paul's assertion that physical circumcision should be replaced by a spiritual circumcision of the heart.[25] The logic of Shylock's contract is to exact revenge on Antonio's body by forcing it into a likeness of his own. Shylock's emotion desires physical resolution: 'Hates any man the thing he would not kill?' he asks.[26] In a defence of Baptism as a replacement of circumcision, Sir Philippe de Mornay, echoing Calvin and sounding uncannily like a modern critic, wrote: 'the thing which doth always deceive ... [the Jews is that] ... they take the sign for the thing signified'.[27] Shakespeare's characterisation of Shylock participates in this common sixteenth-century prejudice which not only aligned Jews with idolaters but also equated this idolatry with an obsessive literality of the mind.

One might expect Dickinson's shift from the language of financial balancing to that of a giving of self ('*Extatic* Contract!') to mirror the conflation of the sign with the thing signified that is Shylock's revenge. Yet Dickinson's speaker willingly offers herself. The tone remains dramatic and the stance one of performance. She gives herself in the currency of flowers and bees whereas Antonio's Christian identity is literally extracted from him. Thus, Dickinson's take on the ecstatic contract retains a sense of *representative* value that Shylock destroys in Antonio. Dickinson's speaker holds Shylock in her grasp: 'Sign me the Bond!' She remains able to move within the linguistic world of signification and worth that Shylock seeks to conflate with the physical world. Dickinson's speaker represents herself in her offering. Her construction of herself through giving therefore turns on its head Shylock's deconstruction of Antonio's self through taking. Ecstasy, rather than robbing the speaker of her sense of self, becomes the condition of empowerment.

However, Dickinson, like Shakespeare, uses Shylock's logic of bonds to parody the covenant of which Baptism is a sign and seal. Hers is a covenant of 'Niggard Grace!'. The bond is not to be treated reverently but with contempt. Moreover, it is a covenant which compromises the categories of sacred and profane. The very act of quantification, even if that quantification did not overtly measure and ridicule it, destroys the absolute quality of the divine gift. In this poem it is the speaker, not the divine other, who gives. 'What would I give to see his face?' recalls Abram falling on his face in the presence of God before the covenant which institutes circumcision and renames him Abraham. Abram hides his face partly out of respect and partly because the divine presence over-whelms the mortal eye. The speaker's careless 'I'd give my life of course' mocks the seriousness associated with divine presence. As in so many of her poems, Dickinson elides the difference between the divine other and the human lover, partly defrauding her 'sovereign' of his transcend-ence, an action emphasised by the monetary pun. Staging the gift of self, Dickinson's speaker preserves her own power and turns an ironic and withering eye on the dynamic of the Puritan conversion experience and the Christian's humble participation in Christ's sacrifice.

SUFFERING

The performative nature of Dickinson's verse often made a staged ver-sion of sacrifice into a process by which she could explore the dissonance between the self's essence and its representation. But she was also intensely moved by the suffering implicit in sacrifice and she did not always treat the narrative of sacrificial dying with such ironic self-awareness.

The idea of Christ as the 'man of sorrows' is derived from Isaiah 53.3: 'He is despised and rejected of men; a man of sorrows, and acquainted with grief'. Two years from the end of her own life Dickinson invoked this passage in a letter to her bereaved friend, Mrs Henry Hills:

When Jesus tells us about his Father, we distrust him. When he shows us his Home, we turn away, but when he confides to us that he is 'acquainted with Grief', we listen, for that also is an Acquaintance of our own. (*L*, p. 837)

Dickinson evokes a common bond of human suffering as opposed to a doctrine of incarnation or salvation and it is no coincidence that to do this she draws on the tender and atmospheric narration of Isaiah. In this letter the lack of specificity clearly met her need for empathy and condolence.

Dickinson had available to her a wider vocabulary for suffering, derived as much from New Testament notions of agony and subservience as from Old Testament mystery. She was only nineteen when she concluded her remarks on the death of another friend's father with words indebted to a New Testament understanding of the cross:

What a beautiful mourner is her sister, looking so crushed and heart-broken, yet never complaining, or murmuring and waiting herself so patiently! She reminds me of suffering Christ, bowed down with her weight of agony, yet smiling at ter-rible will. (*L*, p. 100)

Her naïve and romanticised delight in the spectacle of Christ-like mourn-ing clearly gave way to a more personal and sorrowful identification as age brought her the experience rather than just the imagination of grief. Yet while the young and the old Dickinson differ remarkably in tone and bear testimony to the importance of experience in the personal under- standing of grief, this comment shows that she was beginning, even at nineteen, to comprehend the philosophical meaning of the cross and her imagination was struck by the idea that Calvary was a test of Christ's *humanity* – his patience, his agony, his suffering and his subservience to the divine will of the father.

The New Testament depictions of Christ's suffering partly have their foundation in Psalm 22 – David's Song of Lament – which is quoted nine times in the four crucifixion narratives. The Psalm opens with the words: 'My God, my God, why hast thou forsaken me?' The line is more famil- iar to us, perhaps, as Christ's anguished cry on the cross in the synoptic Gospels: 'Eli, Eli lama sabachthani', the lament that Dickinson echoes in 'I should have been too glad'. The crucial question in understanding the Gospel depiction of Calvary is whether suffering equals resistance and resistance, struggle.

The biblical scholar John R. Donahue notes that although commenta- tors often speak of Christ's cry of abandonment on the cross, Psalm 22 as a whole moves from the apparent despair of God's presence to a hope of vindication. Donahue claims that, if the writer refers to the larger con- text of a verse when quoting the Old Testament, readers of the Gospel are supposed to hear Christ's words as those of the suffering one who dies with the hope of vindication.[28] Psalm 22 focuses on David's dependence on God: 'He trusted on the Lord that he would deliver him'.[29] Christ's cry of pain and abandonment, often a key example of the separation between man and God on Calvary, can also be read as an indication of Christ's willing participation in the providential plan, something Dickinson may have inferred when she wrote of him 'smiling at terrible will'.

Dickinson's late admission that she 'distrust[s]' Christ's talk of his father affirms her sense of the importance of this world over any other but it cannot belie her interest in the relationship between the two. Her response is humanistic but not entirely secular. Some understanding of the passion narratives and their possible humanistic theological inter- pretations is therefore helpful if we are to take readings of crucifixion in Dickinson's poetry further. Hans Reudi Weber argues that the Gospels coincide most closely on the passion narrative precisely because of the emphasis they place on the relationship between the son and the father.[30] Dickinson's favourite Gospel writer, Matthew, makes the contrast between the powerful and righteous son of God with his godforsakenness central to his account. Shortly before he tells of the moment of Christ's death, Matthew echoes Psalm 22: 'He trusted in God; let him deliver him now'.[31] The rephrasing implies a test has been passed. It recalls Abraham's near sacrifice of Isaac and suggests that Christ's suffering is both an indication of struggle (the difficulty of the test) and of submission (it is God's will that he should suffer and trust).

Mark emphasises the eyewitness account of the crucifixion, drawing attention to the agony of the suffering messiah, and prophetic apocalyptic notions of Jesus's death. He gives vivid descriptions of Christ's humiliation: 'And they smote him on the head with a reed and did spit upon him'.[32] He tells how 'the scripture was fulfilled',[33] and ends with an account of how, 'Joseph of Arimathea, an honourable counsellor, which also waited for the kingdom of God, came, and went in boldly unto Pilate, and craved the body of Jesus'.[34] In Mark, the crucifixion becomes a call and encouragement to faith in God and Christ. In Mark's eye, the degradation of his human suffering makes Christ, in his divinity, an even greater object of admiration.

In the Lucan version, Christ appears primarily as the innocent sufferer who goes the way ordained by God: 'And there followed him a great company of people, and of women, which also bewailed and lamented him. But Jesus turning unto them said, Daughters of Jerusalem, weep not for me, but weep for yourselves and for your children.'[35] Suffering, here, appears as submission. Unsurprisingly, John's account of the crucifixion is very brief and prosaic. He makes no mention of abandonment or sacrifice. There is no emphasis on suffering. For John, who always puts Christ's divine nature at the fore, it is as if the son and the father are already united: 'Jesus, knowing that all things were now accomplished, that the scripture might be fulfilled, saith, "I thirst" … When Jesus had therefore received the vinegar, he said, It is finished: and he bowed his head, and gave up the ghost.'[36]

But, in all three of the synoptic Gospels, suffering draws attention to Christ's human body and his human will. The cry of abandonment may be an indication of his ultimate dependence on God and participation in the providential plan, but it is also an indication of mental and physical anguish. In drawing attention to Christ's humanity, pain marks the bursting of the finite on Calvary. Suffering, therefore, locates both submission to the divine plan and the final assertion of Christ's humanity. Christ's suffering is not simply his human resistance to God's plan, but a locus for both submission and resistance and so for struggle.

FINITE INFINITY

Christ's suffering on the cross is the narrative of finite infinity, a meeting of humanity and divinity that calls into question the nature and definition of both terms.

In a poem where Dickinson yearns to know 'just how he suffered' (1861), she explores this narrative in terms of two loves: 'love that was – and love too best to be –'. This poem does not name Christ, but the suffering and end of human nature evokes the death on Calvary:

> To know just how he suffered – would be dear –
> To know if any human eyes were near
> To whom he could entrust his wavering gaze –
> Until it settled broad – on Paradise –
>
> To know if He was patient – part content –
> Was Dying as He thought – or different –
> Was it a pleasant Day to die –
> And did the Sunshine face His way –
>
> What was his furthest mind – Of Home – or God –
> Or what the Distant say –
> At news that he ceased Human Nature
> Such a Day –
>
> And Wishes – Had he Any –
> Just His Sigh – accented –
> Had been legible – to Me –
> And was He Confident until
> Ill fluttered out – in Everlasting Well –
>
> And if He spoke – What name was Best –
> What last
> What One broke off with
> At the Drowsiest –
>
> Was he afraid – or tranquil –
> Might He know
> How Conscious Consciousness – could grow –
> Till Love that was – and Love too best to be –
> Meet – and the Junction be Eternity
>
> (Fr688; J622)

The poet in Dickinson wants to read Christ's emotions as she might read a work of literature – his expressions of grief 'accented' by the supreme Author and 'legible' to her human eyes. But an accurate reading of a legible script is impossible here and so she derives partial satisfaction from wondering and imagining what it would be like 'to know'.

Implicit in the speaker's longing 'To know if any human eyes were near' is an acknowledgment that only humanity, and not God, could offer support for this intensely mortal experience. 'Wavering gaze' refers back to 'human eyes'. 'Wavering' suggests fear and faltering; so the bond between 'wavering gaze' and 'human eyes' emphasises the vulnerable nature of humanity. The rhyme of 'dear' and 'near' suggests that, just as this knowledge would be precious to the speaker, that human bond would have been precious to the dying man. The safekeeping implied in 'entrust' implies that this 'wavering', his vulnerable and precious humanity, is not something that he can take with him to the world beyond. The contrast between 'wavering' and 'settled broad' compounds this. Change and movement are the conditions of mortality; stillness is the condition of death, even a divine death. Humanity is valuable *because* of its vulnerability, the shaky weakness of a 'wavering gaze' expresses the mutability and possibility of human existence.

The process of dying is an intensification of humanity – a consciousness of consciousness. The way in which the dying man's awareness of the world and people around him can be seen to *matter* at the point of his death is partly what gives the poem its poignant tone. The speaker's emphasis on the capacity of consciousness is another: 'suffered', 'entrust', 'wavering', 'patient – part content', 'thought', 'pleasant', 'wishes', 'sigh', 'confident', 'drowsiest', 'afraid', 'tranquil' and, perhaps most importantly, 'love', depict the dying man in terms of emotional (and therefore human) possibility. Reading this poem, one may be reminded of Auden's comment on the paintings in the Musée des Beaux Arts: 'About suffering they were never wrong / The Old Masters; how well they understood / It's human position; how it takes place / While someone else is eating or opening a window or just walking dully along.' 'Even the dreadful martyrdom' Auden wrote, 'must run its course / Anyhow in a corner, some untidy spot'.[37] Dickinson's speaker understands that your day to die may only be special for you. And, in this sense, the day of Christ's death seems to be a very human day, a day on which his humanity is intensified, but set quite possibly against the backdrop of human indifference.

But if this death is intensely human, it is also unquestionably divine. The doctrine of salvation, that lies behind the line 'Ill fluttered out – in Everlasting Well', states that Christ dies in order to redeem mankind. Dickinson's phrasing elides the difference between sin and life-blood. 'Fluttered', like 'wavering', implies the changing quality of the human life which flows in the blood of Christ's dying body, but it also describes the release of the 'ill', or sin, that his divine death undoes in the 'well' waters of eternal life. Through the blood of Christ, the sins of Adam are washed away. The redemption that Christ's suffering and death brings for humanity is only possible because he is the son of God and has a divine nature. Paradoxically, the God who sacrifices Christ for mankind must also be the God who dies with him on the cross and who is incapable of suffering and change.

This tension between movement and fixity is one expression of the narrative of finite infinity or temporal eternity. To read this poem in a theological context is illuminating. The twentieth-century theologian, Jürgen Moltmann, argues that the question that has preoccupied modern theologians of the cross is not simply whether God can be seen to have suffered, but whether God can be seen to have changed. Moltmann is a particularly interesting theologian to read alongside Dickinson because he helps frame Dickinson's individual relationship to the theologies of her time. The doctrine of two natures maintained by Puritan theologians was born out of the fundamental division between the transitory, changeable and suffering nature of mortal humanity and the incorruptible, unchangeable and indivisible nature of immortal divinity. As we have seen, Dickinson's poetic duality owed much to this theology. But, the liberal theology of men like Channing, Parker and Emerson developed an approach from below that focused on the human Jesus over and above the will of the Father. Moltmann argues that any theology of the cross must acknowledge that humanity and divinity encompass each other.

He reconciles the philosophical dilemma by arguing that Christ's intervention can be seen not only as mediation ('an emergency measure on the part of God, because of the distress that mankind has brought upon itself by sin') but also as creative action, a continuous making of possibilities.[38] In other words, the concept of God must be continually corrected by the God who is present in Jesus. Christ is God's representative on earth and Moltmann suggests that representation, or the representative, must keep the place of the original open. It must represent *something* or *someone*. However, if the place occupied by the real occupant is either not there yet or not there in its full and free form, then the representative has the effect of making the original. Therefore, for Moltmann, the incarnation not only represents divinity to man, but in the unfolding of Christ's life, and in his death and resurrection, it creates a new kind of God.

So, to return with these ideas to the final stanza of Dickinson's poem:

> Was he afraid – or tranquil –
> Might He know
> How Conscious Consciousness – could grow –

Till Love that was – and Love too best to be –
Meet – and the Junction be Eternity

Something new is born here and born from the union of two impossibilities. 'Love that was', Christ's human affection, dies with him on the
cross, 'and Love too best to be –' derives its superlative meaning from its
experiential hopelessness. The meeting point of these two impossibilities
is a departure, a 'Junction' whose possibility is impossibility, an 'Eternity'
that is new, that we cannot know or experience and that is born from the
creative potential of Christ's death.

LOVE

For Moltmann, as for many theologians, divine love becomes a tool for
reasoning the impossibility of a divine death:

God allows himself to be forced out. God suffers, God allows himself to be crucified and is crucified, and in this consummates his unconditional love that is so full
of hope. But this means that in the cross he becomes the condition of this love.[39]

In other words: the making possible of the impossible, the suffering God,
is the means by which we are able to know God's love. By this logic,
Christ's suffering is more than an expression of God's love; it is its supreme
manifestation. And wondering 'just how he suffered', Dickinson's speaker
describes Christ's death in terms of both human and divine love.

In both the theology of the cross and in Dickinson's reworking of that
theology, love is crucial to the relationship between man and God on
Calvary. Joan of Arc's passion narrative is framed in terms of a human
love affair. She is 'enticed' by 'trouble' as by an illicit lover and follows
him with a 'moaning fancy'. Calvary holds the allure of romance; in the
retelling of Christ's suffering there is an erotic urge. The draw she feels
is indicative of the sacrificial experience itself. By turning to the passion
narrative, she experiences it as her own intimate love affair. The poet, like
Christ on Calvary, loses control as if she is falling in love.

The sacrificial gift performed on Calvary was not only philosophically
important to Dickinson's notion of poetic self-representation but also per-
sonally important to her understanding of suffering and sacrifice as part
of her own life. So, Calvary is frequently depicted as an experience of
grief and love, of mutable and moving humanity far from the rigidity of
doctrinal conviction. Grief is, in one poem, explicitly a cross to bear. In
another, the 'crucifixal clef' and 'key of Calvary' are the tunes best suited
to the 'Morning after Woe'. All too often, Calvary is in some sense a

'letting go', a relinquishing of human ties and connections; the suffering that doctrines of martyrdom name but do not understand.

Sacrifice asks for trust not certainty. Dickinson deals ironically with the hope of martyrdom precisely because of its doctrinal surety – the way in which it tries to remove doubt. Martyrs who buy into a 'Brand' of faith get nothing. But those who surrender to 'Calvaries of love' hold the promise of poetic fulfilment, the election that Dickinson held supreme as a 'Day – at Summer's full' (1862):

> There came a Day – at Summer's full,
> Entirely for me –
> I thought that such were for the Saints,
> Where Resurrections – be –
>
> The Sun – as common – went abroad –
> The Flowers – accustomed – blew –
> As if no soul – that solstice passed –
> Which maketh all things – new –
>
> The time was scarce profaned – by speech –
> The symbol of a word
> Was needless – as at Sacrament,
> The *Wardrobe* – of Our Lord!
>
> Each was to each – the sealed Church,
> Permitted to commune – *this* time –
> Lest we too awkward show
> At Supper of 'the Lamb'.
>
> The hours slid fast – as hours will,
> Clutched tight – by greedy hands –
> So – faces on two Decks – look back,
> Bound to *opposing* – lands –
>
> And so when all the time had leaked,
> Without external sound
> Each bound the other's Crucifix –
> We gave no other Bond –
>
> Sufficient Troth – that we shall *rise* –
> Deposed – at length, the Grave –
> To that new – Marriage –
> Justified – through Calvaries of Love!
>
> (Fr325; J322)

This poem has an interesting genesis. The earliest version of the final stanza, sent in a letter of consolation to the Reverend Edward S. Dwight on the death of his wife, reads:

> Sufficient troth – that she will rise –
> Deposed – at last – the Grave –
> To that *new* fondness –
> Justified – by Calvaries of love –

In this consolatory mode, 'Calvaries of love' appears as a tribute to the tenderness of marital affection – an earthly 'fondness' mirrored in the Heavenly resurrection. But in a copy made about the same time and kept in her possession, and in all later versions of the poem, Dickinson replaced the gentle and ephemeral 'fondness' with the specifically contractual 'Marriage'. What began as sympathy with another's grief, emerged as an erotic and personal meditation on election. The change from 'fondness' to 'Marriage' is not incidental here. The marriage day is familiar from Dickinson's poems of Baptism as a day exalted above any other. As William Shurr argues in his reading of this poem, the major movement in this poem is from marriage here on earth to the New Marriage in Heaven. The formal word 'troth' appears in nearly every marriage service in the ceremony of the exchange of rings. But here, the lovers exchange crucifixes instead of rings, needing no other bond to signify their love.

The poem's Calvary is the pivotal point in a triptych that includes transfiguration and resurrection. The solstice could be considered the 'noon of the year' and 'Summer's full' seems to suggest a day pregnant with light. This is another poem which invokes the archetypal sun-god. The solstice 'maketh all things new' is a powerful god of light and echoes the words of Christ in Revelation:

Behold, I make all things new … Write: for these things are true and faithful. And he said unto me, It is done. I am Alpha and Omega, the beginning and the end. I will give unto him that is athirst of the fountain of the water of life freely.[40]

The reference implicates writing as the act which unifies cosmic and personal time – the narrative of finite infinity that is expressed in the love shown on Calvary. In this sense, the fulfilment Dickinson explores is poetic as well as personal. Returning again to the maritime setting of the quest, Dickinson exposes the agony and grief of separation. Time keeps the lovers together and time cannot last. The 'greedy hands' of the clock clutch every passing minute, allowing the lovers no respite from the inexorable movement towards death and the end of time. Reduced to 'faces' staring across the growing chasm of separation, the lovers are powerless to resist the inevitable leaking of time. One ship will sink and 'bound to opposing lands', one will die and one will live.

The reciprocal binding of crucifixes functions as a last gesture of love that is both human and divine. Their 'troth' in divine love is especially poignant because of their desperate longing to remain united in this world. 'Parting', Dickinson wrote in a manuscript that remains undated because the original was lost, 'is all we know of Heaven / And all we need of Hell' (Fr1773).[41] The lovers' parting grief is the truest rendering of faith because in the pain of separation they feel the hope of eternal life. Like Christ on the cross, they mourn the end of human nature even as they acknowledge their pain to be the condition of divine love and the hope of resurrection. The parting of the lovers, like the death on Calvary, is a moment of finite infinity and, like the communion of sacrament and the profound glorification of a saint's day, an experience of human-divine encounter.

There is an odd similarity between the scene of separation on the boats and the image of Christ on the cross who, in a poem thought to be composed at a similar time in early 1862, is desperate to maintain his 'single Screw of Flesh':

> A single Screw of Flesh
> Is all that pins the Soul
> That Stands for Deity, to mine,
> Opon my side the Vail –
>
> Once witnessed of the Gauze –
> Its name is put away
> As far from mine, as if no plight
> Had printed yesterday,
>
> In tender – solemn Alphabet,
> My eyes just turned to see –
> When it was smuggled by my sight
> Into Eternity –
>
> More Hands – to hold – These are but Two –
> One more new-mailed Nerve
> Just granted, for the Peril's sake –
> Some striding – Giant – Love –
>
> So greater than the Gods can show,
> They slink before the Clay,
> That not for all their Heaven can boast
> Will let its Keepsake – go
>
> (Fr293; J263)

Critics agree on the centrality of love to this poem. Virginia Oliver suggests that it explores the soul as a link between the human and divine and the tenuous association of soul and body – the soul is contained in the body by a 'single Screw of Flesh'.[42] Oliver argues that Dickinson sees finitude and infinitude, or mortality and immortality, joined proleptically in the human soul through love, both human and divine.[43] William Shurr posits the idea that the poem memorialises an imagined child who has been prematurely lost. He notes that in Virgil's *Aeneid* Dido appeals to Aeneus for a 'keepsake' – a child to remind her of him after he has gone. Also, he comments on the nineteenth-century household use of 'screw' to mean 'small package' – a screw of tobacco or spices. Shurr points out that the subject is described as having a 'name', as now 'put away' and 'smuggled … Into Eternity' as offering her 'More Hands – to hold' as 'clay', and that all these require a human being.[44]

And as Barton Levi St Armand goes some way towards arguing, there is good reason to assume that the human being is Christ, or an avatar of Christ. He suggests the poem is about a beloved who, like Christ, has passed beyond the veil of flesh. Dickinson, he argues, can only represent the life that he has seen by the symbol of the 'gauze', which she associates with her own poetic ability. St Armand writes: 'For the initiated soul, a totally new kind of seeing as well as a new name and a new order of being are in force, while those who remain "this side of the veil" … can only await their own swift summons to the realm of unimpeded vision'.[45]

But St Armand is too eager to do away with the finite in favour of the infinite and his celebration of poetic vision misses the speaker's desire to remain on the mortal side of the veil of flesh. The 'striding – Giant – Love –' is egocentric, reaching outwards and desiring 'More Hands – to hold'. This passion overwhelms the gods – they 'shrink' before the mighty feelings of the 'clay' of human flesh. Human love, in this poem, is power; it has strength and capability. The poem that begins on a note of abandonment and suffering ends with a challenge to God. Humanity's 'keepsake' of heaven is the God-man, in which humanity and divinity touch. The poem's lament is that the two natures, joined in the 'single Screw of Flesh' will be severed. These poems expose the meeting of egocentric and theocentric love and mourn the end of a duality which marks Christ out as an avatar for the poet, negotiating a reach into the 'beyond' through the fleshy realities of life.

DICKINSON'S QUARREL

Dickinson was certainly capable of imagining the divine demand for sacrifice as a brute force able to be overpowered by human cunning. A

relatively late satirical poem (*c*.1874) on Abraham's near-sacrifice of Isaac
figures God as a 'Mastiff' 'Flattered by Obeisance' (Fr1332). And it was
not just the Old Testament God who lent himself to such a characterisation. In 'They put us far apart –' (1863), Dickinson integrates Old and
New Testament references in a poem that makes the association between
sacrifice, grief and love an explicit source of her quarrel with God:

> They put us far apart –
> As separate as Sea
> And Her unsown Peninsula –
> We signified 'These see' –
>
> They took away our eyes –
> They thwarted Us with Guns –
> 'I see Thee' each responded straight
> Through Telegraphic Signs –
>
> With Dungeons – They devised –
> But through their thickest skill –
> And their opaquest Adamant –
> Our Souls saw – just as well –
>
> They summoned Us to die –
> With sweet alacrity
> We stood upon our stapled feet –
> Condemned – but just – to see –
>
> Permission to recant –
> Permission to forget –
> We turned our backs upon the Sun
> For perjury of that –
>
> Not Either – noticed Death –
> Of Paradise – aware –
> Each other's Face – was all the Disc
> Each other's setting – saw –
>   (Fr708; J474)

The lovers' 'stapled feet' suggests the Calvary motif governs this poem.
The familiar themes of love, death and grief are here tied to the omnipotence of God. 'These see' is a reference to Psalm 107.24: 'These see the
works of the Lord and his wonders in the deep'. The psalm celebrates
God's omnipotence and his ability to perform miracles and control the
natural world. The line immediately following Dickinson's quotation
reads: 'For he commandeth and raiseth the stormy wind, which lifted
up the waves thereof'.[46] But here God's power has caused the suffering

and separation of the lovers. The miracle of creation (separating the earth from the sea) becomes an act of cruel manipulation.

Divine strength manifests itself as boorish thuggery. Guns and blinding have little power against 'Telegraphic Signs' and in the speaker's juxtaposition of divine power and human love, the former becomes dependent on a brute show of strength while the latter survives through a kind of spiritual communion. So, 'I see Thee' mirrors 'These see' and Dickinson emphasises the reversal of power by punning on 'thickest' in the third stanza. God's minions are both devious and stupid. Death holds no threat for the speaker – she goes to meet it with 'sweet alacrity'. The real danger comes in the glimpse she has of the beyond. Dickinson deliberately leaves the subject of the beyond to our imaginations, implying that knowledge is beyond the reach of the poem but the begging desperation of 'Permission to recant – Permission to forget –' implies its awfulness. It is at this moment of extremity that the speaker and her lover turn their backs on light, life and, implicit in the image of the sun, divinity. Dying usurps the sun's power; their faces eclipse its light as divine brutality palls beside the pain of human separation and the power of human love. Calvary therefore becomes a way of knowing human pain and not divine goodness.

'They put us far apart –' makes Dickinson's quarrel one of quiet strength. But she could fight a noisier fight, celebrating the obscene triumph of the flesh at Calvary over the weaker hope of spiritual resurrection. 'Rearrange a "Wife's" affection!' is a violent example of anger and defiance (late 1861):

> Rearrange a 'Wife's' affection!
> When they dislocate my brain!
> Amputate my freckled Bosom!
> Make me bearded like a man!
>
> Blush, my spirit in thy Fastness –
> Blush my unacknowledged clay –
> Seven years of troth have taught thee
> More than Wifehood ever may!
>
> Love that never leaped its socket –
> Trust entrenched in narrow pain –
> Constancy thro' fire awarded –
> Anguish – bare of anodyne!
>
> Burden – borne so far triumphant –
> None suspect me of the crown,
> For I wear the 'Thorns' till *Sunset* –
> Then – my Diadem put on.

Big my Secret but it's *bandaged* –
It will never get away
Till the Day its Weary Keeper
Leads it through the Grave to thee.
(Fr267; J1737)

Pushing everything that should remain secret or taboo centre-stage, Dickinson's speaker delights in her vulgarity with exclamatory zeal. The first stanza revels in its own unnaturalness, echoing Lady Macbeth's violent desire to 'unsex me here'. But the masculine changes stand in contrast to the speaker's true state of mental and physical female desire. She lays her femininity bare like her naked bosom– 'freckled' suggests exposure to sunlight – and the heart, head and body are forcefully united. To alter her affection is tantamount to removing her brain and surgically changing her woman's body into a man's.

As the first stanza removes any opposition between head, heart and body, so the second stanza destroys the binary of spirit and flesh. The spirit blushes like the clay. Yet the body, the speaker tells us, is 'unacknowledged'. Here, perhaps, we are given a clue as to the reason for Dickinson's quotation marks around 'Wife'. This is a poem about betrothal ('Seven years of troth') not marriage. So the speaker's flesh is 'unacknowledged' by her lover. Seven years was the length of service required of Jacob by Laban for his daughter's hand in marriage. Seven is a number of cosmic as well as personal significance. The Sabbath on the seventh day,[47] the seven years of plenty and the seven years of famine in Egypt,[48] and the seven priests and seven trumpets marching round Jerusalem are all examples of the cosmic significance of the number.[49] The number seven is particularly prominent in Revelation. There are seven churches, seven seals, seven trumpets, seven bowls and seven stars.[50] The number seven makes its final appearance in the Bible at the presentation of the bride of Christ: 'And there came unto me one of the seven angels which had the seven vials full of the seven last plagues, and talked with me, saying, Come hither, I will show thee the bride, the Lamb's wife'.[51]

So, in biblical terms, 'Seven years of troth' gestures towards a time of cosmic fulfilment. But Dickinson makes this a poem about sexual gratification. One can easily read a metaphor of male and female virginity into the first two lines of the third stanza: 'Love that never leaped its socket – / Trust entrenched in narrow pain'. Her poetic identification with Calvary through the burden and the crown of thorns is conflated with the agony of unfulfilled sexual desire and the queenly 'diadem' of sexual fulfilment. Christ's crown of thorns is replaced at night by a queen's diadem and the poem seems deliberately ambiguous as to whether this is the sunset of each day or the sunset of life. Writing her poetry at night, Dickinson may well have imagined herself elected every evening as the bride of Christ with a 'Rearranged Affection', a masturbatory self-love turned towards her own poetic greatness rather than a wifely devotion to God.

This, perhaps, is the speaker's big secret. 'Bandaged' implies a swollen body part, a suggestion which is helped by 'big'. It may be crippled, severed or bleeding because it is incomplete or unfulfilled. It is certainly restrained, trapped inside the speaker until death. Leading her animal lust to its rightful owner, Dickinson makes the grave an instance of carnal satisfaction rather than spiritual elevation. However, even that satisfaction is lukewarm. 'Weary' has none of the poem's opening passion. Tired out, neither the speaker nor her secret will be much good to the 'thee' of the final stanza. Dickinson's moment of election has arrived so many times before that this final homecoming seems jaded and the goods worn out.

SACRIFICIAL NARRATIVE AND THE POETIC VENTURE

Sacrificial narrative opens a space between humanity and divinity and it provokes a mutable response in Dickinson as she explores the contours of that space. She is both sceptical and trusting of the martyr's journey; she expresses semi-ironic faith in the narrative of finite infinity; and she feels a mixture of anguish and anger at the brutish God who she sometimes beats at his own game. The self's process of becoming has at its centre a fundamental indeterminacy, preserved through a dramatic staging of the sacrificial gift and defined by the paradox of a divine death.

The death of the God-man suggests a point of departure for poetry because the inadequacies of religious revelation or poetic representation become the genesis of creative action. If we return to 'Life – is what we make it –', first discussed in Chapter 1, we can see how Dickinson's poetry uses the death of Christ to compass the unknown:

> Life – is what we make it –
> Death – We do not know –
> Christ's acquaintance with Him
> Justify Him – though –

He – would trust no stranger –
Other – could betray –
Just his own endorsement –
That – sufficeth Me –

All the other Distance
He hath traversed first –
No New Mile remaineth –
Far as Paradise –

His sure foot preceding –
Tender Pioneer –
Base must be the Coward
Dare not venture – now –
(Fr727; J698)

I take Dickinson's focus on embodiment in this and other poems to be a modern, poetic reconfiguration of the older theological concept of incarnation. From the fact of being in a body and subject to the temporal conditions of a 'life', she writes poetry driven by the unseen and the intangible. In 'Life – is what we make it –', death is this driving force and the poem's emphasis on corporeal experience in the description of an infinitely unknowable reality mirrors the paradox of the hypostatic union. If Christ reveals the Word of God because he is flesh, this poem traces the route of an impossible discovery through very possible terrain. But if Dickinson goes some way towards inverting the familiar rubric of the bourne from which no traveller returns (suggesting by 'No New Mile remaineth –' that there is no 'undiscovered country') she also ends the poem at the start of a new and strangely uncertain 'venture'. Even in Dickinson's experiential typology, whereby the death of Christ finds its fulfilment in every individual death, there is a void that can only be filled by actual experience. Her imperfect typology reflects the fundamental problem of American incarnation theology and of the narrative of finite infinity. Dickinson's words made flesh still leave something to be discovered, something to be understood. Dickinson's poetry, like the incarnation and the crucifixion, takes human understanding of the incomprehensible to a new 'venture' but that is just a beginning; it cannot complete the quest.

'The other Distance', which recalls the space of separation that makes 'distant' the voices in 'To know just how he suffered' and the growing chasm between boats bound to opposing lands, is the terrain of possibility opened by sacrificial narrative. What is lost on the cross also gestures towards what is gained and, as 'Must be a Wo –' suggests, it was in this vital space of possibility Dickinson found her angle of vision:

Must be a Wo –
A loss or so –
To bend the eye –
Best Beauty's way –

But – once aslant
It notes Delight
As difficult
As Stalactite –

A Common Bliss
Were had for less –
The price – is
Even as the Grace –

Our lord – thought no
Extravagance
To pay – a Cross –
(Fr538; J571)

This change in vision is not a Blakean cleansing of the doors of perception but the result of a twist, an unnatural bend brought about by suffering.[52] This is an unnatural position, a delight that defies happiness in the
same way a stalactite seems to defy gravity. But from this angle 'aslant',
which recalls the 'slant' angle of poetic truth-telling, the poet has a perspective on the superlative 'Best Beauty' which, like a 'Love too best to
be', suggests an over-extended reach of the mind. Sacrificial narrative
forges a poetic way through pain and the peculiar advantage of that way
is that it exists on the cusp of the finite and the infinite. The stark simplicity of this verse mirrors the stark simplicity of the poet's choice. 'Wo[e]'
is not too high a price to pay. The death of the God-man opens a space
between two distinct natures. Dickinson's poetry voyages further into
that space.

NOTES

1 The Etruscans were members of an ancient civilisation who survived into
   Roman times. See Charles G. Leland, *Etruscan Roman Remains and the Old
   Religion* (London: Kegan Paul, 2002).
2 John Taylor, *Icon Painting* (Oxford: Phaidon, 1979), p. 7.
3 'If this cup may not pass away from me except I drink it' (Matt. 26.42). 'If any
   man thirst, let him come unto me and drink' (John 7.37).
4 The poem is dated to autumn 1862, when the civil war would no doubt have
   been on Dickinson's mind.
5 Fr788.

6　It may be significant that 'snow' recalls the gown from the Marcan transfiguration story. 'And his raiment became shining, exceeding white as snow; so as no fuller on earth can whiten them' (Mark 9.3).

7　It also recalls the narrative of the soul's process of becoming in 'There is a solitude of space' (Fr1696).

8　Since the publication of Marcel Mauss's anthropological study of the gift in 1950, there has been a substantial amount of literature on the connections between sacrifice and gifts. See Marcel Mauss, *The Gift* (1950; London: Routledge, 2002); Lewis Hyde, *The Gift: Imagination and the Erotic Life of Property* (New York: Vintage, 1979); Jacques Derrida, *The Gift of Death*, trans. David Wills (Chicago and London: University of Chicago Press, 1992).

9　Martin Heidegger, *Being and Time* (1927), trans. John Maquarrie and Edward Robinson (New York: Harper and Row, 1962), p. 284.

10　Derrida, *Gift of Death*, p. 45.

11　Heb. 9.15–16.

12　Rom. 6.3–4.

13　St Armand, *Dickinson and Her Culture*, p. 8.

14　See also variant versions of 'I hide myself within my flower' (Fr80) and 'I send you a decrepit flower' (Fr1346). The first, dated around 1859, and the second, dated around 1874, suggest that the image together with the practice of sending flowers with poems remained relevant to Dickinson's concern with self-presentation throughout her life.

15　Judith Farr, *The Gardens of Emily Dickinson* (Cambridge, Mass., and London: Harvard University Press, 2004), p. 9.

16　*Ibid.*, p. 10.

17　Isa. 26.19.

18　Psalm 133.

19　Emerson, 'Gifts' (1844), in *The Collected Works of Ralph Waldo Emerson*, ed. Joseph Slater, Robert Spiller, Alfred R. Ferguson *et al.*, 6 vols. (Cambridge, Mass.: Harvard University Press, 1971–2003), vol. 3, pp. 92–6, at p. 93.

20　*Ibid.*, p. 94. Emerson may have also been influenced by Shakespeare.

21　James Shapiro, *Shakespeare and the Jews* (New York: Columbia University Press, 1997), p. 113.

22　Gen. 17.5.

23　Col. 2.11–12.

24　Calvin, *The Institutes of the Christian Religion*, trans. Henry Beveridge, 2 vols. (Edinburgh: T & T Clark, 1895), vol. 2, p. 536.

25　'Neither is that circumcision, which is outward in the flesh ... circumcision is that of the heart, in the spirit' (Rom. 2.28–9).

26　4.1.66.

27　Shapiro, *Shakespeare and the Jews*, p. 118.

28　This, he argues, is particularly true of Mark's Gospel. John R. Donahue, 'Mark', *Harper's Bible Commentary*, ed. James L. Mays (San Francisco: Harper and Row, 1988), pp. 983–1009, at pp. 1007–8.

29　Psalm 22.8.

30 Hans Reudi Weber, *The Cross: Tradition and Interpretation* (London: SPCK, 1979), pp. 97–132.
31 Matt. 28.43.
32 Mark 15.19.
33 Mark 15.28.
34 Mark 15.43.
35 Luke 23.27–8.
36 John 19.28–30.
37 W. H. Auden, 'Musée des Beaux Arts', *Collected Shorter Poems 1927–1957* (London: Faber, 2003), pp. 123–4.
38 Jürgen Moltmann, *The Crucified God: The Cross of Christ as the Foundation and Criticism of Christian Theology* (London: SCM Press, 1974), p. 260.
39 *Ibid.*, p. 248.
40 Rev. 21.5.
41 The manuscript was transcribed by Mabel Loomis Todd.
42 Virginia Oliver, *Apocalypse of Green: A Study of Emily Dickinson's Eschatology* (New York: Peter Lang, 1989), p. 208.
43 *Ibid.*, p. 211.
44 Shurr, *Marriage of Emily Dickinson*, p. 177.
45 St Armand, 'Veiled Ladies', p. 27.
46 Psalm 107.25.
47 Lev. 23.3.
48 Gen. 41.1–22.
49 Josh. 6.4.
50 Rev. 1.1–6.
51 Rev. 21.9.
52 'If the doors of perception were cleansed, everything would appear to man as it is: infinite.' Blake, 'The Marriage of Heaven and Hell' (1793), *Blake's Poetry and Designs*, ed. Johnson and Grant, pp. 81–102, at p. 93. Dickinson could not have known this text. The comparison is to define the particular nature of her visionary poetry.

CHAPTER 6

Resurrection

As we saw in the previous chapter, Christ's death is often viewed as the corollary of his love, and in Paul's account of resurrection we see life subsist on this death, 'But now is Christ risen from the dead and become the firstfruits of them that slept',[1] and dissolve back into life at the cost of life, 'And that he was buried and that he rose again the third day'.[2] For Paul, Christ's resurrected body is not the same as the one that dies on the cross. He talks of the resurrection of both Christ and man in terms of an incorruptible body: 'all flesh is not one flesh ... there are also celestial bodies and bodies terrestrial ... So also is the resurrection of the dead. It is sown in corruption and raised in incorruption.'[3] Paul insists on an 'incorruptible body' as the sign of spiritual resurrection for a number of reasons, the most obvious being his desire to construct the church as a body of Christ. Another that is particularly relevant here is the importance of the body as a point of continuity between the old and the new. Paul prefaces his doctrine with an account of how the resurrected Christ was witnessed in his human form, not only by him, but by many other people.[4] It is Christ's corporeal presence that assures Paul of his resurrection because a body can be witnessed; it is able to be known and recognised.

The philosophical and aesthetic implications of this doctrine are important to understanding the kind of artistic inspiration resurrection provided for Dickinson. She found a vocabulary with which to question the bodies in which her own poems came. She asks how and if poems can be finished as she thinks about the forms in which they might be renewed or said to live again. Resurrection also brings us back to the relationship between incarnation and poetic representation because of the central role of the body. But it provides a new point of departure for this discussion because the body it brings into play is 'incorruptible'. The very notion of an 'incorruptible body' seems oxymoronic; a body that cannot decay or die challenges the essential concept of corporeality.

The kind of personal continuity that a body provides was a source of perennial fascination for Dickinson. But she also understood that there was a difference between the body known in life and the body resurrected in death. The resurrected body therefore becomes part of the semiotics of loss, gesturing towards something which cannot be fully regained. For this reason, perhaps, resurrection focuses Dickinson's attention on the epistemic absence at the heart of her own poetic vision, the experiences which her experiential verse can only imagine and which the poetic gesture of the simile and the narrative gestures of allegory or vision can only begin to enact.

In its peculiar concepts of the incorruptible body, rebirth, initiation and return, Dickinson found resurrection to be a locus for philosophical, religious and aesthetic engagement. It is hard to separate these notions for Dickinson in the way her contemporary, Kierkegaard, managed to do, for example, in *Stages on Life's Way* (1845). Unlike Kierkegaard, Dickinson is not concerned with delineating progressive categories of experience but with the power of poetry to move between them and question their essential validity. Resurrection allows for what is quite possibly the clearest expression of the 'Compound Vision' of Dickinson's religious imagination as it engenders a mutually enriching discussion between religious and aesthetic forms of rebirth and renewal.

MIRACLES, RATIONALITY AND THE CALL TO FAITH

In the eighteenth century, David Hume had placed faith in miracles such as resurrection outside of the domain of rational thought, saying that, 'no testimony for any kind of miracle has ever amounted to a probability, much less to a proof'.[5] This statement is part of a wider argument in which Hume claims that the evidence against the occurrence of any purported miracle is typically going to be so strong as to overwhelm the evidence in favour of it. Thus, Hume suggests the epistemological principle that wise people proportion their belief to the evidence. In Hume's eighteenth-century discussion, faith in miracles like resurrection can be seen as part of a larger epistemological problem of what it means to know.[6]

Late eighteenth- and early nineteenth-century German writers often sought to explain the resurrection in terms of hallucination, swoon theory, a stolen body or the wrong tomb. In 1778, the German scholar H. M. Reimarus published *The Goal of Jesus and his Disciples*, in which he argued that the disciples stole the body of Jesus in order to continue living the kind of life they had led with him. In 1828 another German scholar by the name of Heinrich Paulus wrote a *Life of Christ* in which he argued that Christ had not actually died on the cross but had been taken down alive.

In nineteenth-century New England, the idea of resurrection was arguably made more accessible and believable by the emphasis ministers like Amherst's own Reverend Colton and Dickinson's close friend, the Reverend Charles Wadsworth, placed on regeneration of spirit in *this* life. Wadsworth preached: 'earnestness will come too late if it come only to baptise with its spirit the coming generation'.[7] Wadsworth draws his metaphor from the notion that Christians are baptised into Christ's death and resurrection, echoing John the Baptist's claim that after him will come one who will baptise with spirit and with fire.[8] Earnestness, participation in *this* life, is therefore figured as resurrection.

In addition, natural theology often sought to find evidence for miracles such as resurrection in the observable world. Dickinson's teacher Hitchcock extracted the following explanation from the theory of conversion of matter: the incorruptible (immortal) body was like the corruptible (mortal) body in composition and proportion but made up of different particles because the particles of earthly bodies were bound to decay and find new forms. But Dickinson was sceptical of the kind of exegesis that replaced trust, or faith, with certainty. 'The Chemical conviction' (1865) shows Dickinson's response to Hitchcock's teaching. This poem is interesting because of the playful and subversive way in which it handles diction derived from science, aesthetics and theology to assess the epistemological context for resurrection:

> The Chemical conviction
> That Nought be lost
> Enable in Disaster
> My fractured Trust –
>
> The Faces of the Atoms
> If I shall see
> How more the finished Creatures
> Departed me!
>
> (Fr1070; J954)

While Hitchcock looked to science to make faith a more empirically verifiable position, Dickinson uses his method to expose the hubris of science that claims 'Conviction' or knowledge in place of 'Trust' or faith. Dickinson bears comparison with Emerson who writes in 'Self-Reliance': 'Trust Thyself'.[9] The reference to 'Know Thyself', the motto on the Temple of Apollo at Delphi, replaces knowledge with trust. It is clear that

Emerson's understanding of consciousness, at this point, is still working with the notion of divine possession, the Oracle at Delphi, and the idea that in 'great men ... the absolutely trustworthy was seated at their heart'.[10] Implicit is the question of whether we are able to 'know' anything with the absolute certainty historically attributed to the divine. Emerson's substitution of trust for knowledge allows the dynamic of faith and doubt to frame the question of what is knowable.

The strength of Dickinson's poem turns on a comparable contrast between the wholeness of certainty and the fragmentation associated with 'Trust'. In the first stanza, the contrast is forged quite obviously through the solidity of 'conviction' (named elsewhere by Dickinson as that 'Granitic Pillar') and the fragility of a damaged or 'fractured Trust'. The idea of a body disintegrating upon death echoes in the state of that 'Trust' as it suffers the trauma more commonly associated with bodily breakage. Even as the second stanza closely echoes Hitchcock's teaching, drawing a parallel between corruptible 'Atoms' and incorruptible 'finish', it reconfigures it within the dynamic of faith and doubt as scientific assurance takes on the 'fractured' quality of 'Trust' and atomised matter becomes eclipsed by the enduring wholeness of 'finished Creatures'.

There is a caveat here too. 'Finished Creatures' suggests the dual perfection of death and aesthetic completion, but it is also heavily ironic if the 'Trust' in the poem relies on their return and continuity. The assertion of wholeness and completion is therefore haunted by a sensation of doubt. In this sense, the poem reconfigures the central paradox of Paul's doctrine of resurrection through its subversive rendering of natural theology. The 'finished Creatures' have become signs of their departure, their meaning constituted by the loss occasioned by it. But, by the same token, the word 'Creature' carries a distinctly animate meaning; as a term of endearment it also emphasises the speaker's attachment to the 'Departed' and so resists abstract interpretation. The departed creatures are both incorruptible in the sense that they are finished or perfected and undeniably corporeal as the speaker's 'Trust' in resurrection is born from a personal desire for reunion with their animate bodies.

Dickinson introduces an ambiguity between God's 'Creatures', biological 'Creatures' and her own 'Creatures' or creations.[11] The recent critical trend to see Dickinson as editor, reviser and compiler of her own work makes 'finished' an intriguing adjective here. The 'finished Creatures' achieve perfection that still leaves the possibility of change. There is a tempting parallel to be drawn between the sentiment of this poem and Dickinson's clearest expression of faith in resurrected creations – 'A word

is dead, when it is said, / some say. / I say it just begins to live / that day'
(Fr278). Throughout this book we have seen Dickinson draw subtle but
not infrequent analogies between her understanding of religion and her
understanding of poetry as the two endlessly fed off each other in the fertile grounds of her imagination. Resurrection gave her a powerful stimulus to question the bodies in which her poems came and, often, came
again.

By the time she wrote 'The Chemical conviction' in 1865, Dickinson
had become sceptical about the 'Conviction' of both science and religion,
describing 'Faith' in a poem dated to the same year as

> a Pierless Bridge
> Supporting what We see
> Unto the Scene that We do not –
> Too slender for the eye
>   (Fr978; J915)

But we know that Dickinson drew some comfort from Hitchcock's thinking in her early years. In 1877 she confessed to Higginson: 'When Flowers
annually died and I was a child, I used to read Dr Hitchcock's Book on
the Flowers of North America. This comforted their Absence – assur-
ing me they lived' (*L*, p. 573). The connection between spring and resurrection finds obvious expression in the festival of Easter, which grafted
the Christian story of resurrection onto the existent pagan celebration
of renewed natural life. To see 'evidence' of divine design in the fabric of
the natural world was also the founding principle of natural theology. As
Dickinson's comment to Higginson implies, an anxiety of temporality is
part of the narrative of spring or resurrection – one must live through a
period of uncertainty in need of 'comfort' and 'assur[ance]'.

Dickinson also emphasises that the narrative structure of resurrection
is founded in 'Absence'. In any notion of resurrection there is a space of
loss in between death and the rebirth of life – a period of time and a narrative of journey. In the Christian story, this takes the form of the three
days between Good Friday and Easter Sunday, during which time Christ
is supposed to descend into Hell. In the pagan narrative onto which this
story was layered, it takes the form of the long winter or, as I will discuss later, certain instances of journey and return to the Underworld.
The 'Absence' then is both a lacuna, accompanied by feelings of loss
and bereavement, and a space filled with meaning and the possibility
of change. The body that returns functions in some sense as a representational sign of the one that has been. Living through the long winter
months as a child, Dickinson drew comfort from the symbolic revival

of spring in books. In her recollection of childhood trust, she not only recognises the pivotal experience of 'Absence' or loss to the resurrection narrative of spring, she also reveals something of the preoccupation with body and sign that I will suggest formed an essential part of her later meditations on the relationship between resurrection and representation.

'When they come back', also dated to 1865, shows a more mature anxiety about the nature of return and resurrection she witnessed in the natural world:

> When they come back – if Blossoms do –
> I always feel a doubt
> If Blossoms can be born again
> When once the Art is out –
>
> When they begin, if Robins may,
> I always had a fear
> I did not tell, it was their last Experiment
> Last Year,
>
> When it is May, if May return,
> Had nobody a pang
> Lest in a face so beautiful
> He might not look again?
>
> If I am there – One does not know
> What Party – One may be
> Tomorrow, but if I am there
> I take back all I say –
>
> (Fr1042; J1080)

Her anxiety, here, is founded in the fallacy of causality. She does not trust that the cyclical pattern will continue as precedent could simply be 'experiment' (the manipulations of science) or 'Art' (the deceptions of poetry). And if spring is no guarantee of its own return, neither, the speaker implies, is life. So, the beauty of spring and renewed life remind this speaker of death. Her fear that spring may not come again is inextricable from the realisation that she may not live to see it. The world is only important as long as the speaker can experience it, but the transitory nature of her encounter with the beauty of spring makes her aware how easily this experience of the world could be lost. The other if, 'if I am not there', remains unspoken, implied but unexplored. Dickinson's observations of the natural world, far from providing assurance of a world beyond, or a 'Chemical conviction That Nought be lost', force her to confront the anxiety of temporality, the troubling assurance that life may be all there is.

TIME AND ETERNITY

Dickinson's most famous poem on the theme of resurrection mixes such observations of the natural world with references to Christian doctrine, creating a deliberate and somewhat uncomfortable juxtaposition between time passing and the suspension of movement beyond it. This tension between time and eternity is another way of expressing the difference between that which is knowable and that which is not. 'Safe in their Alabaster Chambers' exists in seven versions and many variants. The earliest extant holograph of the poem (1859) reads:[12]

> Safe in their Alabaster Chambers –
> Untouched by Morning
> And untouched by Noon –
> Sleep the meek members of the Resurrection –
> Rafter of satin,
> And Roof of stone.
>
> Light laughs the breeze
> In her Castle above them –
> Babbles the Bee in a stolid Ear,
> Pipe the sweet Birds in ignorant cadence –
> Ah, what sagacity perished here!
>
> (Fr124; J1243)

Critics disagree on the tone of this poem. Inder Nath Kher suggests that death, for Dickinson, is a release from existential suffering and the 'alabaster chambers' seem safe.[13] By contrast, McIntosh reads it as part of Dickinson's quarrel with God. He writes: '"The meek members of the Resurrection" simply moulder in their alabaster chambers'.[14] While I do not think this poem displays much hope of an afterlife, McIntosh's sense that the 'meek members ... simply moulder' also seems to miss the crucial point of the 'Alabaster Chambers'. The members of this resurrection are preserved out of time: 'Untouched by Morning / And untouched by Noon –'. 'Sleep' suggests a state of suspense, of waiting. The dead do not participate in the world but the euphemism, 'sleep', relies on continuity with the living. Sleep is not frightening because it is part of our earthly experience and therefore within our realm of comprehension.

The platitudes echo Matthew 5.5: 'the meek shall inherit the earth'. But, Dickinson inverts the teleological force of Matthew's prophecy; the meek lie trapped in between time and eternity, while the earth continues without them. They sleep in a gilded but impenetrable prison. The dead who lie inside the 'Alabaster Chambers' are as still and cold as the stone from

which their dwelling place is made. Earth is defined by time, movement
and decay. The carefree ease of 'light laughs ... Babbles ... Pipe ... sweet
[and] ... ignorant' contrasts strongly with the heavy stone of the tomb.
Her faith in time as opposed to fixity is compounded in the subtle twist
of the last line. In the guise of praise for the wisdom of those who hold
faith in resurrection, her final lament also suggests that such faith is the
death of wisdom and level-headedness. Dickinson implies that the extension beyond time is a fool's pipe dream.

This version of the poem instigated one of the poet's many literary cor-
respondences with her sister-in-law Sue. In response to Sue's criticisms
of the second stanza, she sent the following altered version with the line,
'Perhaps this verse would please you better – Sue –':

> Safe in their Alabaster Chambers –
> Untouched by Morning –
> And untouched by Noon –
> Lie the meek members of the Resurrection –
> Rafter of Satin – And Roof of Stone!
>
> Grand go the Years – in the Crescent – above them –
> Worlds scoop their Arcs –
> And Firmaments – row –
> Diadems – drop – and Doges – surrender –
> Soundless as dots – on a Disc of Snow –[15]

Gone is the light ticking over of time as the resurrected lie deprived of
their happy passing. Here, instead, is a sense of scale and importance.
But even the grand sweep of time and narrative is soundless, invisible and
minuscule against the eternity on which it is enacted. Dickinson uses circular forms to represent both time and eternity. But the 'Arc', unlike the
'Disc', is an incomplete circle; time is an incomplete form of eternity. And
'Worlds scoop their Arcs – ' makes this incomplete reach towards eternity
a figure for time-bound human reaching and, as a variation of 'circumference', one that recalls the reach of poetry itself.

Sue, however, liked this version even less and responded:

I am not suited dear Emily with the second verse – It is remarkable as the chain
lightning that blinds us hot nights in the Southern sky but it does not go with
the ghostly shimmer of the first verse as well as the other one – It just occurs
to me that the first verse is complete in itself it needs no other, and can't be
coupled – Strange things always go alone – as there is only one Gabriel and one
Sun – You never made a peer for that verse, and I *guess* you[r] kingdom doesn't
hold one – I always go to the fire and get warm after thinking of it, but I never
can again. (Fr161)

Yet Dickinson clearly was not satisfied with a single verse and tried her hand at two other variations of the second stanza, sending the next one to Sue with the somewhat wry question: 'Is this frostier?' Cold, winter images abound, no doubt generated by Sue's comment. But, clearly unsatisfied with Sue's opinion that 'Strange things always go alone', she is still concerned to set her meditation in the context of the narrative of time and eternity:

> Springs – shake the Sills –
> But – the Echoes – stiffen –
> Hoar – is the Window – and numb – the Door –
> Tribes of Eclipse – in Tents of Marble –
> Staples of Ages – have buckled – there –

Here the temporal narrative is expressed in the tension between movement and fixity, the shake of new life and the stiffening of death, the transience of the tent and the permanence of the marble tomb. Her reluctance to give up on a second stanza to this poem and the way in which all her variations concentrate on the time-bound tensions of a world outside of the 'Alabaster Chambers' suggests that the force of Dickinson's intention turned on some kind of juxtaposition between the preserved, timeless members of the resurrection and the worldly narrative which gives that preservation meaning.

RENEWAL AND REBIRTH

The 'Alabaster Chambers' cut off knowledge – a reflection, perhaps, on the potentially limiting nature of doctrinal faith. This stasis finds its opposite in the feeling of initiation manifest in certain poems that treat resurrection as a process of rebirth, not just of spirit but more broadly of self. It is in the notion of rebirth that the Christian resurrection trope circles back to the idea of Baptism. Peter talks of: 'being born again, not of corruptible seed, but of incorruptible, by the word of God, which liveth and abideth forever'.[16] In the Gospel narratives, the resurrection is anticipated in Christ's own Baptism. Matthew's account of the conversation between John and Jesus before the Baptism indicates that Jesus's Baptism was different to the others that John administered because it was the first time the gift of the spirit had been associated with Baptism:

But John forbad him, saying, I have need to be baptised of thee, and comest thou to me?

　　And Jesus answering said unto him, Suffer it to be so now: for thus it becometh us to fulfil all righteousness. Then he suffered him.[17]

In Luke, John the Baptist's assertion that Christ 'shall baptise you with the Holy Ghost and with fire' links Baptism, transfiguration and resurrection in an image of transformative spirit and light.[18]

Christ's resurrection is closely associated with his ascent to heaven. Luke separates the resurrection and ascension by forty days but elsewhere they are not distinguished. Paul describes resurrection as ascension: 'Then we which are alive and remain shall be caught up together with them in the clouds, to meet the Lord in the air'.[19] This rebirth of spirit is, on the one hand, a passing beyond the constraints of time and space and, on the other, a phenomenon that exists in a distinct relation to creaturely reality. Dickinson's 'My Cocoon tightens' (1865) explores the related ideas of ascension and resurrection as processes of rebirth and tests of knowledge and experience. It describes a process of initiation, beyond earthly womanhood into a sphere characterised by poetic qualities of gesture and reach. Importantly, though, this poem is not governed by a sense of arrival. Resurrection, here, is a process of beginning, not an acknowledgment of an end:

> My Cocoon tightens – Colors teaze –
> I'm feeling for the Air –
> A dim capacity for Wings
> Demeans the Dress I wear –
>
> A power of Butterfly must be –
> The Aptitude to fly
> Meadows of Majesty implies
> And easy Sweeps of Sky –
>
> So I must baffle at the Hint
> And cipher at the Sign
> And make much blunder, if at last
> I take the clue divine –
>
> (Fr1107; J1099)

As an image of rebirth, the metamorphic transition in this poem conveys the change brought about by Baptism as well as resurrection and ascension. This is hardly surprising considering the intrinsic relation of one to the other in the Gospel narratives and Christian theology. In the Pauline writings, Baptism signals a passage from death to life, from slavery to freedom, from ungodliness to righteousness, and Calvin owed much to Paul. For Calvin, Baptism marks the purging of the old life through mortification, which is accompanied by the forgiveness of sins, and thus the creation of a new life in Christ. The words 'capacity', 'Aptitude', and the projected but uncertain future of Dickinson's phrase 'if at last' construct a narrative of possibility that is governed by the Baptismal dynamic of freedom and constraint. 'Meadows of Majesty' evokes the coronation imagery central to the ritualism of New England Baptism, and the juxtaposition of 'Wings' and 'Dress' emphasises the oppositions of air and earth, angel and human, spirit and body. The speaker's 'Dress' also symbolises her propriety, her womanhood and her social role. There is a clear implication that these forms of identity are a mask or a heavy constraint and it is easy to see the transformation of woman to poet expressed as freedom from the earthly husk in the image of the meta-morphic caterpillar.

Yet, the very fact of earthly constraint suggests the cocoon's enab-ling strength. The cocoon 'tightens', focusing the speaker's attention on her body and simultaneously awakening her awareness of her possible 'power'. At least part of the 'power' the speaker imagines lies in her abil-ity to attach herself to the power of suggestion and possibility which the 'Cocoon' and 'Dress' define partly by their opposition to it and partly by their role in its realisation. From the earthbound position of the 'Cocoon' or 'Dress', the lines, 'Meadows of Majesty implies / And easy Sweeps of Sky –', bring to mind both the free movement of the butter-fly and the gestural qualities of writing – the transformation, in other words, from woman to poet. But the power of the butterfly does not just stand for the ability to write, 'The Aptitude to fly', but also for the move-ment between different narratives and images, the movement between a plurality of 'Meadows' with a number of 'Sweeps'. This poem looks for-ward to release but it has not arrived there. It focuses on the process of becoming rather than on fixed states of being, and that is the enabling power of the constraining cocoon.

The metamorphic transition does not denote a narrative which is known, but one which must be felt out and sensed as a butterfly feels for the air or a priestess receives divine inspiration in bafflement. Dickinson plays on the difficulty of human–divine communication ('Hint', 'Sign' and 'clue'), focusing our attention on the mystery, the space between sig-nifier and signified. The final movement, an entry into the secret sacred, an acceptance of the 'clue divine –', hangs on an 'if', which the last dash leaves unresolved. If we read the caterpillar's metamorphosis as a metaphor for the speaker's poetic capability, this sacred and secret place becomes the domain of poetic activity. Although other poems allow for little doubt that Dickinson accepted the responsibility and privilege she associated with poetic life, this poem hangs in the balance. She may be about to be born anew, but that such rebirth is possible rests on trust as opposed to certainty.

THE CORPOREAL MEDIUM

The 'Cocoon' is another version of the veil that stood, among other things, as a symbol for the corporeal medium. The caterpillar's metamorphosis seems particularly appropriate to a poem that deals with resurrection partly because it implies a rending of the veil and progression into the world of spirit and partly because it suggests a transformation from one body to another. As the caterpillar sheds its cocoon and ascends as a butterfly, the resurrected shed their corporeal bodies and assume incorporeal ones. Embodiment was so important to Dickinson's verse and so connected to the pain and suffering of mortal existence that the notion of a body that could not feel pain or suffering, but that was somehow continuous with mortal existence, intrigued her.

It seems to have continued to intrigue her. In '"And with what body do they come?"', composed as late as 1880, she used Pauline theology as a starting point to explore the idea of the incorruptible body:

> 'And with what body do they come?'
> Then they do 'come.' Rejoice!
> What door – What hour? Run, run, My Soul!
> Illuminate the house.
>
> 'Body'! Then real! A face and eyes!
> Conviction it is them! –
> Paul knew the man that knew the news,
> He passed through Bethlehem.
>
> (Fr1537; J1492)

The opening quotation is from 1 Corinthians 15.35. This part of Corinthians proclaims the certainty of the resurrection and Paul uses Christ's resurrection as proof of the resurrection of humanity: 'if there be no resurrection of the dead, then Christ is not risen'.[20] The line that Dickinson quotes is attributed to the sceptic who does not understand *how* the dead undergo a bodily resurrection. Paul's answer is the incorruptible body. Dickinson's speaker's excitement, conveyed through the exclamatory statements in the first stanza, arises from the idea that she will recognise the resurrected and that they will find her. It rests, in other words, on a belief in continuity between this world and the next, a reality she can understand: '"Body!" Then real! A face and eyes.' At the same time, 'then' implies a change of state, movement and possibly alteration. Despite, or perhaps partly due to, the opening excitement, which Dickinson can't help making a little ironic, the tone of this poem is ambiguous.

The sense of distance in the second-hand relation of knowledge, 'Paul knew the man who knew the news', which is underlined by the apparent pun on 'news', may be seen to lend it an incredulous tone. The speaker does not claim that she knows anything for herself. But there is also a sense in which she sweeps aside the scepticism inherent in the quotation from Corinthians and seizes on the notion of bodily resurrection with almost childlike delight. If the punctuation in the third line (rendered variously as dashes or commas) can be seen to stagger the poem, it could also encourage a breathless and eager reading of it. The repetition of 'knew' and the hammering out of the same sound in 'News' at least leaves the reader wondering what it might be like to know. Dickinson is concerned with states of knowing and unknowing in this poem, positioning herself on the edge of faith in the resurrection and playing semi-ironically with the notion of a corporeal spirit by telling her soul to 'run'.

The poem was originally included in the following letter of consolation on the death of a child:

Dear Cousin –
  The sweet Book found me on my Pillow, where I was detained or I should
   have thanked you immediately –
  The little Creature must have been priceless – Your's, and not your's, how
   hallowed –
  It may have been she came to show you Immortality – Her startling little
   flight would imply she did –
  May I remind you what Paul said, or do you think of nothing else, these October
   nights, without her Crib to visit? The little Furniture of Loss has Lips of Dirks
   to stab us – I hope Heaven is warm – There are so many Barefoot ones –
   I hope it is near – the little Tourist was so small – I hope it is not unlike
   Earth that we shall miss the peculiar form – the Mold of the Bird –
     'And with what body do they come?' –
     Then they *do* come – Rejoice!
     What Door – What Hour – Run – run – My Soul!
     Illuminate the House!

     'Body!' Then real – a Face and Eyes –
     To know that it is them! –
     Paul knew the man that knew the News –
     He passed through Bethlehem –
  With love for you and your sweet wife, 'whom seeing not, we' trust.
                                              Cousin Emily –
                                              (*L*, pp. 678–9)

The letter was written in October 1880 to Perez Cowan whose daughter, Margaret, had died the previous year. Thanking him for a memorial of the child, Dickinson pictures the infant as a minute revelation of

'Immortality'. But her mode of consolation focuses on matters of the body rather than the spirit – her hopes are for warmth, nearness and familiarity. Both the departed and the bereaved draw comfort from their continuity with the other side. If this poem situates itself on the edge of faith in the resurrection, it does so because that peripheral position, acknowledging scepticism as well as trust, is a consolatory mode. Dickinson's words of consolation do not ask for the surrender of humanity but emphasise, through the body, a sense of continuity between this world and the next. Her final regards to his wife, '"whom seeing not, we" trust', echoes the trial of faith described in 1 Peter 1.7–8:

That the trial of your faith, being much more precious than of gold that perisheth, though it be tried with fire, might be found unto praise and honour and glory at the appearing of Jesus Christ. Whom, having not seen, ye love; in whom, though now ye see him not, yet believing, ye rejoice with joy unspeakable and full of glory.

Trust without proof is the natural condition of the faith Dickinson espouses in her final line of consolation. Trusting in them, she makes faith integral to human love and comfort, implying that it is not too difficult a trial to manage.

This is one of several poems in which Dickinson quotes 1 Corinthians 1.15. There is a particularly interesting early piece (1860) which brings the notion of embodied form to bear on the writing of poetry itself:

'Sown in dishonour'!
Ah! Indeed!
May *this* 'dishonour' be?
If I were half so fine myself
I'd notice nobody!

'Sown in corruption'!
Not so fast!
Apostle is askew!
Corinthians 1.15 narrates
A circumstance or two!
(Fr153; J62)

The manner in which Dickinson cites the biblical text raises questions as to its status as a text that finds itself incarnated in the corrupt body of poetry. The third line points to the poem itself; '*this* "dishonour"' suggests the corruptive act of writing. Dickinson's familiarity with liberal and comparative theology would certainly have influenced her ideas about the way a biblical text should be read. Strauss and Feuerbach, Parker and Channing emphasised the historical and narrative qualities of the Bible and Dickinson often displays an interest in the Bible as an 'Antique Volume', as she put it in a late poem written about 1882 (Fr1577). Her interest in the Bible as a sacred text or the vehicle of the revealed Word was tempered by a disregard for piety which made it primarily a literary interest in the representational qualities of revelation. Here, she draws the reader's attention to 'circumstance' and perspective: 'Apostle is askew'. Her tone is decidedly irreverent, making a play of doctrine for poetry. For, if the Word made flesh expresses the corruptive act of writing, what, she asks, is the status of a poem which comes in the form of a resurrected body?

'The Bone that has no Marrow' (*c*.1871) again poses that very question:

> The Bone that has no Marrow,
> What Ultimate for that?
> It is not fit for Table
> For Beggar or for Cat –
>
> A Bone has obligations –
> A Being has the same –
> A Marrowless Assembly
> Is culpabler than shame.
>
> But how shall finished Creatures
> A function fresh obtain?
> Old Nicodemus' Phantom
> Confronting us again!
>   (Fr1218; 1274)

Nicodemus asks: 'How can a man be born again when he is old?'[21] Christ answers: 'Except a man be born of water, and of spirit, he cannot enter into the kingdom of God'.[22] Dickinson's twist on Nicodemus's words elides the difference between 'old', 'dead' and 'resurrected'. She exploits Nicodemus's doubt in regeneration. The question is not 'why' but 'how': 'how can these things be?'[23] The first two stanzas build up a sense of precedent and parallel: 'A Bone has obligations – / A Being has the same –'. Our purpose in this world has a comprehensible frame of reference and that reference is the 'marrow' of our understanding as it is essential to the core of our being. Understanding resurrection as regeneration requires a different set of references. So, Dickinson invokes Nicodemus to ask what the future resurrected body is *for*. The question: 'But how shall finished Creatures / A function fresh obtain?' also puns on 'Creatures' to imply a desire for writing that is continually relevant and continually renewed, again recalling Dickinson's assertion that words begin to take on new life when they are uttered.

READING THE CORPOREAL SIGN

The best example of the narrative possibilities of the resurrected body is the story of doubting Thomas. Thomas is not convinced of Christ's resurrection until he has physically touched his wounds: John writes: 'But he [Thomas] said unto them, except I shall see in his hands the print of the nails, and thrust my hand into his side, I will not believe'.[24] It is the reality of these flesh wounds which convince him the man is Jesus. Christ's willingness to allow Thomas to push his fingers into his wounds suggests that he feels no pain: 'Then saith he to Thomas, Reach hither thy finger, and behold my hands; and reach hither thy hand, and thrust *it* into my side'.[25] The wounds convince because they are real and yet they do not have the attributes of real wounds; they do not hurt. They encapsulate the paradox of the resurrected body, at once real and representational, literal and allegorical, a corporeal sign.

'Split the Lark' (1865) is Dickinson's take on the incident. She maps the aesthetic contours of poetic experience in the corporeal sign of Christ's resurrected body, teasing the rationalist who, like the religious sceptic, destroys the god of the unknown by bringing it too close to his understanding through an analytic as opposed to sensual approach to meaning and interpretation. The play on doubt, and by implication faith, redefines the familiar religious debate in aesthetic terms. 'Split the Lark' satirises a failure of faith in poetic experience. The ironic politeness of its tone mocks the gentility of those who would cling assiduously to that which they can understand:

> Split the Lark – and you'll find the Music –
> Bulb after Bulb, in Silver rolled –
> Scantily dealt to the Summer Morning
> Saved for your Ear when Lutes be old –
>
> Loose the Flood – you shall find it patent –
> Gush after Gush, reserved for you –
> Scarlet Experiment! Sceptic Thomas!
> Now, do you doubt that your Bird was true?
> (Fr905; J861)

The violence of release inherent in 'Bulb after Bulb' as in 'Gush after Gush' mimics the force and movement of uncontrolled and inexhaustible bleeding – recalling the 'Everlasting Well' of sin in 'To know just how he suffered'. These lines are shocking because of their intense physicality. There is even a play on the fear of menstrual bleeding in 'Gush after Gush' and 'Loose the Flood'. This is a taboo subject, Dickinson implies,

a grotesque rendering of the body's involuntary seepages. Yet the pro-
tected delicacy of 'in Silver rolled' suggests that what is being released is
pure idea, or ideal. This uneasy juxtaposition reflects Dickinson's search
for a language which can describe the paradox of the resurrected body,
a state which, as the songbird image suggests, appeals as a metaphor for
Dickinson's poetic project. But 'patent' (recalling the 'patent' doctrines of
the church) makes mock of the analyst, who dissects a poem in the manner of a religious sceptic, and needs a personal assurance or proof that
their reasoning was correct.

It is helpful to position Dickinson's engagement with the resurrected
body in the context of the American nineteenth-century literary engagement with corporeality that was discussed in Chapter 1. When Sharon
Cameron explores the relationship between body and spirit in Melville
and Hawthorne, she argues that Hawthorne's tales interrogate that relationship through dismemberment. She writes:

While Hawthorne's allegory is most frequently predicated on the severing of one
part of the human body from another, this mutilation is accompanied by the
implicit directive that we not read mutilation in terms of physical dismemberment, that we not read it by the very terms in which it has predicated itself.[26]

She points out that the allegorical mode is predicated on doubleness not
just because it has more than one level of significance but also because it
often asks you to read violence done to the human body in non-bodily
terms. Hawthorne, she suggests, asks whether the distinction between the
allegorical and the literal blurs when the subject is not only the human
body but the taking of the body apart. His characters wish to be distilled
to their representative essences. Thus Hawthorne tries to replace human
bodies with aesthetic emblems: all that remains of Fanshawe, she points
out, is a monument and *The House of the Seven Gables* tries to match
human beings to portraits whose moulds they barely fit.[27] Cameron concludes that Hawthorne's allegory makes visible divisions that would be
internal. In *The Scarlet Letter*, Hester's moral trespass is visibly displayed
on her dress. In externalising the split between body and soul he attempts
to unify the outside of the body with what cannot be unified within.[28]

Dickinson is fond of asking us to believe in corporeal signs, to read
spiritual, emotional and mental states in strongly physical, and often violent, terms. 'The Soul', she wrote in 1862, 'has Bandaged moments –' and
those moments test the limits of consciousness.

> The Soul has Bandaged moments –
> When too appalled to stir –

She feels some ghastly Fright come up
And stop to look at her –

Salute her – with long fingers –
Caress her freezing hair –
Sip, Goblin, from the very lips
The Lover, – hovered – o'er –
Unworthy, that a thought so mean
Accost a Theme – so – fair –

The soul has moments of escape –
When bursting all the doors –
She dances like a Bomb, abroad,
And swings opon the Hours,

As do the Bee – delirious borne –
Long Dungeoned from his Rose –
Touch Liberty – then know no more,
But Noon, and Paradise –

The Soul's retaken moments –
When, Felon led along,
With shackles on the plumed feet,
And staples, in the Song,

The Horror welcomes her, again,
These, are not brayed of Tongue –
(Fr360; J512)

Dickinson's poem lends itself to a similar kind of analysis to the one Cameron undertakes with Hawthorne. These are emotional states allegorised into physical conditions. The second stanza is strongly reminiscent of Johann Heinrich Fuseli's 'Nightmare' (1781) where a demon crouches on the exposed and sleeping body of a young girl, whose physical attitude suggests both sexual and mental disturbance. There is no direct evidence that Dickinson saw this painting but it was extremely famous and generally well known that she could have been familiar with it. Whether or not there is a conscious echo, her poem carries a similar sense of discomfort because she shares Fuseli's practice of using physical states to allegorise the non-physical. At the same time as we are being asked to read violence in non-physical terms our imagination turns on bodily experience. 'Bandaged', though it allegorises a state of emotional hurt and constraint, forces us to think about physical restriction, swelling and bleeding.

Most obviously, perhaps, the poem gains strength from the initial gendering of the soul as female. Dickinson represents the soul's vulnerability in particularly sexual terms and the interaction between the soul and her 'fright' gains its power from physical intimacy and detail. Fright is not only personified, it has 'long fingers'. There is a vampire-like quality to this goblin, who drinks of the soul from lips a lover should kiss. Tenderness, here, is a violation. Fright has no right to take what should only be given in, and to, love. In moments of escape the soul becomes male, violating the helpless rose. So the soul's moments of escape become physical revenge – a deliberate assumption of male sexual power. The soul's reach beyond the body, its explosion from the limits of consciousness are described as a profoundly physical reality. Dickinson's verbs and adjectives convey the reckless energy and abandon of its movements: 'bursting ... dances ... swings ...delirious'. The imaginative coherence of this poem lies in sensuous bodily experience.

Cameron identifies the tension between body and spirit as a wider issue in nineteenth-century American literature and it is an area in which Dickinson has a clear voice. Cameron elucidates the way in which American fiction is concerned not simply with notions of self but with problems of human identity predicated in terms of the body. For Dickinson – and one might well extend this enquiry to her literary contemporaries – the terms of the body bear the print of incarnation and resurrection theology. Cameron's work helps us understand the way in which Dickinson's concerns about the self, expressed through allegories of the body, are related to her sense of the resurrected body as a corporeal sign. This is because allegories of the body have the narrative status of a corporeal sign. 'The Soul has Bandaged moments' not only forces us to consider the way the physical and the non-physical interact, it forces us to question the validity of the body–soul dichotomy, the founding principle of dualism.

POETIC PERSPECTIVE

The resurrection narratives begin with an open tomb which no longer conceals the body of Jesus. In Matthew (Dickinson's favourite Gospel account) the open tomb is revealed by an angel whose 'Countenance was like lightning, and his raiment white as snow'.[29] Matthew narrates:

And for fear of him, the keepers [of the tomb] did shake and become as dead men. And the angel answered and said unto the women, Fear not ye: for I know that ye seek Jesus, which was crucified. He is not here: for he is risen, as he said. Come, see the place where the Lord lay.[30]

The angel heralds mortal death and eternal life. In Hebraic tradition, to look upon the face of God is a death sentence (something Dickinson acknowledges in the ending to Fr1353, 'For none see God and live'). So, to look on the face of an angel of the Lord is to 'become *as* dead'. The keeper's reaction is a simulacrum of an encounter with God as the messenger is a simulacrum of God's presence. Pointing them towards the open tomb, and referring to the corpse in the past tense, the angel makes the absent body a signal of future life.

The open tomb is the reification of the space in between life and death, humanity and divinity or the corruptible and incorruptible body. 'The Admirations – and Contempts – of time –' (1864) uses the narrative of the open tomb to explore the unusual perspective of poetic vision. The working of this poem suggests a visionary process, a reorganisation of thought that can only be a suggestive 'estimate' of the truth. Like the incarnation and resurrection of Christ, the compounding movement of Dickinson's poem hinges on an absence or loss. This hiatus is the poet's vantage point:

> The Admirations – and Contempts – of time –
> Show justest – through an Open Tomb –
> The Dying – as it were a Height
> Reorganises Estimate
> And what we saw not
> We distinguish clear –
> And mostly – see not
> What We saw before –
>
> 'Tis Compound Vision –
> Light – enabling Light –
> The Finite – furnished
> With the Infinite –
> Convex – and Concave Witness –
> Back – toward Time –
> And forward –
> Toward the God of Him –
>
> (Fr830; J906)

In this poem, a funeral is not only a time when what we know is 'Reorganise[d]', but when our attitude towards knowledge shifts with perspective. The speaker balances admiration with contempt and clarity with obfuscation, pivoting on the imperfect 'Estimate' that changes when a confrontation with 'Dying' begins to open a path of reconciliation between the temporal world of finity and the infinite sense of beyond.

The speaker's perspective is from both sides of the tomb or lens, both sides of the dying. So, the second stanza pushes back and forth, the poetic movement supporting the opening claim, ''Tis Compound Vision –'.

The 'as it were' of the first stanza is a proposition; the gesture of the simile not only allows for a gap, it depends on one for its meaning and function. The simile is Dickinson's most common poetic hinge, repeatedly drawing our attention to the experiences her experiential verse can only 'estimate' or 'infer'. In this case, her poetic structure actually thinks through the meaning of this 'estimate'. Dickinson almost rhymes the words 'forward' and 'toward'. Their sense is also very similar, but there is a slight jarring in sound, an imperfection in the rhyme, which mimics the absence at the heart of the poem.

And that which is gained gestures towards that which is lost:

> And what we saw not
> We distinguish clear –
> And mostly – see not
> What We saw before –

Dying correlates visually with the lens and linguistically with the simile. It also correlates with the narrative gesture of allegory; all are motivated by the absence that lies at the heart of the substitution of one narrative for another. Dickinson's 'lens' preserves the distinction between time and eternity while enabling their interaction. The image of 'Light – enabling Light –' hints at the old sun and moon dichotomy again. The finite moon of artistic endeavour (recalling the 'lunacy of light' in 'I thought I was enchanted') is 'furnished' with the infinite light of the symbolic sun of divine presence. Out of this stereoscopic vision Dickinson breeds multiplying possibilities, expressed in the endless refraction of light. Writing her letter of consolation to Perez Cowan, Dickinson emphasised the continuity between life and resurrection with the tacit acknowledgment that there must also have been an unfathomable difference. In this meditation on the open tomb, she draws attention to the loss that shadows resurrection and the peculiar sense of mourning that is the inspiration for visionary poetics.

Another example of this absence can be found in 'Those not live yet' (*c.*1879) where Dickinson's treatment of resurrection is again concerned as much with space and distancing as it is with fusion.

> Those not live yet
> Who doubt to live again –
> 'Again' is of a twice
> But this – is one –

> The Ship beneath the Draw
> Aground – is he?
> Death – so – the Hyphen of the Sea –
> Deep is the Schedule
> Of the Disk to be –
> Costumeless Consciousness,
> That is he –
>
> (Fr1486; J1454)

Suzanne Juhasz notes that the original of this poem is signed in pencil, 'Easter'.[31] This is a meditation on resurrection in terms of doubling and difference, repetition and singularity of experience. The 'Hyphen of the Sea –' recalls the simile and the altered perspective of 'The Admirations – and Contempts – of time', forming a bridge that is also a fissure between the 'one' and the 'twice'. As in Dickinson's letter of consolation to Cowan, the resurrected will be both familiar and different. The contrast between the shallow draw of death and the deep disk of eternity confirms that doubling is not duplication, just as resurrection is not resuscitation.

The 'disk', or circle, is an image of eternity and perfection – no doubt one of the reasons for Dickinson's appropriation of 'circumference' as a metaphor for her own 'business'. Dickinson reconfigures the classical notion that to complete the quest is to come full circle and also to have survived a transformative experience. Here the end conflates the beginning with something altogether new, a state of being that is both concrete and abstract; 'Costumeless Consciousness' returns to the relation between body and spirit, simultaneously disembodying the self and personifying it as a figure able to be clothed. As Juhasz argues in her reading of this poem, the images are all informed by the literal phrase which introduces them – 'this – is one –' – and the figurative phrase which closes them – 'Costumeless Consciousness'.[32] So the poem moves in the direction of the conflation of the literal and the abstract, reaching beyond the self from the very foundations of individual experience. Bringing together life, death and eternity in the unity of consciousness, Dickinson emphasises the reach of the self. However, Juhasz's elucidation of the unity of consciousness understates the disruption at its core. Resurrection conflates literal and figurative, concrete and abstract meanings, but it has at its centre the irreversible loss of death which is, simultaneously, the enabling 'Hyphen of the sea'. The resurrection of Easter implies compound vision which has, at its centre, a lack of certainty, a space generated by the tender beauty of loss.

DISTANCE AND FUSION

Informally titled 'Easter', 'Those not live yet' acknowledges the origins of
resurrection in the pagan spring festival devoted both to the god of death
and the god of fertility. As a result of the way in which pagan rituals
conflated the god of fertility with the god of death, the resurrection of
Christ has come to symbolise decay and regeneration as much as perfection and incorruptibility. On the one hand, Christianity was born into
a world where its central claim was known to be false. Resurrection was
very often not a way of describing what death consisted of but a way of
describing what everyone knew could not happen: the undoing of death.[33]
In Homer's *Iliad*, Achilles says to Priam: 'You will be dead yourself before
you bring him back to life'.[34] Apollo, in Aeschylus's *Eumenides*, claims:
'Once a man has died, and the dust has soaked up his blood, there is
no resurrection'.[35] Virgil in the *Aeneid* allows that some 'sons of God'
especially beloved by Jupiter be allowed back but for the others the door
remains shut.[36] The dead, in the classical world, are shadows and Hades is
a dark, gloomy place not fit for human habitation.

  Not far away from her own death in 1881, Dickinson certainly experimented with these ideas:

> The Things that never can come back, are several –
> Childhood – some forms of Hope – the Dead –
> Bur Joys like men may sometimes make a Journey
> And still abide –
>
> We do not mourn for Traveler, or Sailor,
> Their Routes are fair –
> But think – enlarged – of all that they will tell us –
> Returning here –
>
> 'Here!' There are typic 'Heres' –
> Foretold Locations –
> The Spirit does not stand –
> Himself – at whatsoever Fathom
> His Native Land –
>
>   (Fr1564; J1515)

It is easy to see a classical influence on the kind of journey this poem
presents – circular journeys of voyage and return, quest and triumph. But
death, Dickinson writes, is a narrative of a linear sort. The familiarity of
the world's perimeter, 'typic "Heres" – / Foretold Locations –', makes the
classical circular journey a narrative of contrast rather than analogy for
the spirit. The spirit will not return to life as the sailor returns from the

sea because life and death are not part of the same compass. Dickinson puns on 'Fathom', suggesting its distance is beyond both nautical measurements and understanding.

But, despite a rather large emphasis on the finality of death, the ancient world did provide several very strong precedents for resurrection. The myth of Osiris was one. James Frazer, whose seminal work, *The Golden Bough*, followed immediately upon the nineteenth-century interest in comparative religion, explained that, as a personification of the corn, which died and came back to life every year, the Egyptian god Osiris was also a god of death and resurrection.[37] The annual festival of Osiris was essentially a festival of sowing. Frazer commented that in one of the chambers dedicated to Osiris in the temple of Isis at Philae the dead body of Osiris is represented with stalks of corn springing from it and a priest is watering the corn. Next to it an inscription reads: 'This is the form of him whom one may not name, Osiris of the mysteries, who springs from the returning waters'.[38]

Persephone, too, was a figure for the resurrected. Persephone, kidnapped by Pluto, the god of the dead, is taken to the underworld to be his wife. Her mother, Demeter, swore that no seeds should grow in the earth and no corn should sprout until her lost daughter was returned to her. Finally, Zeus, in order to stop the starvation of mankind and to ensure the continuation of the sacrifices made to the gods, persuaded Pluto to return her. Pluto agreed but gave Persephone the seed of a pomegranate to eat, which would force her to return to him. From that day on Persephone spent two-thirds of the year with her mother, who renewed the fertility of the earth, and one-third with her husband in the netherworld. Thus, Persephone returned each year from the dead and her return heralded the renewal of spring.[39] The oldest literary source for this story is the Homeric *Hymn to Demeter* and if Dickinson did not know this version, she would have been familiar with the tale from Bulfinch's *Age of Fable*.[40]

She also read Shakespeare's *A Winter's Tale*, which was strongly influenced by this myth and probably also by the myth of Alcestis.[41] Alcestis was the wife of Admetus, King of Pherae, to whom Apollo has been enslaved as punishment. In return for Admetus's hospitality, Apollo tricks the Fates into granting Admetus the privilege of escaping death should someone else die in his place. Alcestis volunteers. She is brought back to life by Persephone or Hercules (who physically fights with Death) and is restored to Admetus. In Euripides's play Alcestis does not speak for three days because she is still consecrated to the gods and it will take three days to purify her. Obviously, this is interesting as a potential source for the

Gospel claims to the three days in between Christ's death and resurrection. It is also a very likely influence on the theme of resurrection and return in *The Winter's Tale*.

The play is particularly relevant to notions of revival and reawakening and Shakespeare exploits the sense of trickery inherent in the classical myth of Demeter and Persephone. From the very first act, the characters seem detached from their appearance. Hermione says to Leontes: 'You look / As if you held a brow of much distraction. / Are you moved my lord?'[42] Moreover, there is a danger in the questioning of origins. Camillo speculates: 'I am sure 'tis safer to / Avoid what's grown than question how 'tis born'.[43] Leontes's reaction to what he supposes is his wife's bastard child is to destroy it at the start: 'Better burn it now than curse it then'.[44] The final scene plays on the relationship between the double and the resurrected body. Shakespeare repeatedly uses the verb 'mock' to describe the effect of likeness. Paulina introduces Hermione, 'Prepare / To see the life as lively mocked as ever / Still sleep mocked death',[45] and Leontes later exclaims, 'The fixture of her eye has motion in't, / As we are mock'd with art'.[46] Doubling and resurrection are cruel because they make a fool of reason. They ask us for a particular kind of faith, a faith in recognition to replace loss, to elide the difference between old and new.

So, loss shadows resurrection. Hermione preserves herself for her lost daughter and Dickinson's poems on resurrection return to images of loss and mourning – the open tomb and the lost ship floating on the sea of death. In *The Winter's Tale*, loss denies the simple linear progression of time. The sheep-shearing feast is a midsummer event. But at the feast, Florizel's address to Perdita, 'she who has been lost', sets the time at April: 'These your unusual weeds to each part of you / Does give a life; no shepherdess but Flora / Peering in April's front'.[47] It is impossible to take this address literally. We know the feast takes place in midsummer and Perdita cannot be decked in the flowers of spring because they would not last that long. We must concede that Perdita is being emblematised as spring, the season of rebirth and renewal. She represents the fusion of spring and summer. Perdita's address to Camillo and Polixenes also points towards winter: 'For you there's rosemary and rue. These keep / Seeming and savour all the winter long.'[48] Yet we know we are still in midsummer. Several lines later, the literal and symbolic merge in the 'flowers / Of middle summer ... given / To men of middle age'.[49] What Perdita (she who has been lost) forces us to accept is the fusion of the literal and the allegorical, the world of actuality and the world of the symbol.

These themes of classical and Shakespearean resurrection surface in a poem Dickinson wrote in response to a topical incident. On 23 March 1864, the Springfield Republican reported the shooting of Susan Dickinson's friend, Mrs Gertrude Vanderbilt, who ran to the assistance of one of her maids when she came under attack from her spurned lover. Mrs Vanderbilt had not been expected to survive, but Sue wrote to Emily in September with news of her recovery. Clearly captivated by the heroine's return from the brink of death, Dickinson replied: 'I am glad Mrs – Gertrude lived – I believed she would – Those that are worthy of Life are of Miracle, for Life is Miracle, and Death, as harmless as a Bee, except to those who run –'. She also included the following lines in a letter to the recovering victim, later transcribing them onto the bifolium sheets she had formerly bound into fascicles.[50] The poem describes the return of a bride which may well have been influenced both by the classical myths of Alcestis and Persephone and Shakespeare's rewriting of them in *The Winter's Tale*:

> To this world she returned.
> But with a tinge of that –
> A compound manner,
> As a Sod
> Espoused a Violet,
> That chiefer to the Skies
> Than to Himself, allied,
> Dwelt hesitating, half of Dust,
> And half of Day, the Bride.
> (Fr815; J830)

The bride is both woman and a symbol of womanhood, of the delicacy implied in 'Violet' and the modesty suggested in 'hesitating'. The bride *inhabits* the symbol – an idea which Dickinson suggests in 'Dwelt'. The contrast between day and dust, like sod and violet, earth and sky, is the contrast between the clarity of the literal and the gesture implied in the allegorical, the woman and the bride. 'Tinge' implies something which almost eludes us. The bride with her 'compound manner', like Alcestis, Persephone, Perdita or, perhaps more accurately in this poem, Hermione, represents both the conflation of these two worlds and the space between them. 'Hesitatingly' implies the bride is unsure about the world in which she wants to live.

In *The Winter's Tale*, the theme of resurrection occurs in the context of a confrontation with loss, which is also a confrontation with a figure who is both representative and actual – a figure like the bride of 'To this world'. Dickinson's resurrection trope establishes loss as an emotional, poetic and religious stimulus. Shadowing resurrection, loss creates an absence that allows for gesture, suggestion, imagination and the interrogation of faith.

NOTES

1　1 Cor. 15.20.
2　1 Cor. 15.4.
3　1 Cor 15.39–42.
4　1 Cor. 15.5–8.
5　David Hume, 'An Inquiry Concerning Human Understanding' (1748), *The Philosophical Works of David Hume* (Edinburgh: Port, 1826), vol. 4, §10, p. 150.
6　*Ibid.*, vol. 4, §10, pp. 127–54.
7　Charles Wadsworth, *A Sermon preached in the Arch Street Presbyterian Church, Philadelphia, on Thanksgiving Day, November 25, 1852* (Philadelphia: Moran and Sickels, 1852), p. 24.
8　Luke 3.16.
9　'Self-Reliance' (1841), in *The Collected Works*, ed. Slater, Spiller, Ferguson *et al.*, vol. 2, pp. 25–53, at p. 28.
10　*Ibid.*
11　Among the definitions in Webster's dictionary are: '1. That which is created; every being beside the Creator, or every thing not self-existent. The sun, moon and stars; the earth, animals, plants, light, darkness, air and water etc are the creatures of God. 2. In a restricted sense an animal of any kind; a living being; a beast. In a more restricted sense, man (…) 5. That which is produced, formed or imagined; as, a creature of the imagination.' Webster, *Dictionary*, vol. 1, pp. 415–16.
12　Franklin dates the latest variant to 1883 suggesting that Dickinson did not give up on the theme.
13　Inder Nath Kher, *The Landscape of Absence: Emily Dickinson's Poetry* (New Haven and London: Yale University Press, 1974), p. 192.
14　McIntosh, *Nimble Believing*, p. 42.
15　Johnson (ed.), *Collected Poems*, p. 152. He notes that the new version was included in a note to Sue and then copied into packet 37 of the fascicles.
16　1 Peter 1.23.
17　Matt. 3.14–15.
18　Luke 3.16.
19　1 Thess. 4.17.
20　1 Cor 15.15.
21　John 3.4.
22　John 3.5.
23　John 3.9.
24　John 20.25.
25　John 20.27.
26　Cameron, *Corporeal Self*, p. 78.
27　*Ibid.*, p. 80.

28 *Ibid.*, pp. 131–3.
29 Matt. 28.3. The same phrase is used to describe Christ's appearance during his transfiguration. The shining light is clearly associated with divine presence.
30 Matt. 28.4–6.
31 Suzanne Juhasz, *The Undiscovered Continent: Emily Dickinson and the Space of the Mind* (Bloomington, Ind.: Indiana University Press, 1983), p. 164.
32 *Ibid.*, pp. 164–5.
33 N. T. Wright, *The Resurrection of the Son of God* (London: SPCK, 2003), p. 35.
34 *Iliad*, 24.594–51, cited in *ibid.*, p. 33.
35 *Eumenides*, line 674, cited in *ibid.*, p. 33.
36 *Aeneid*, 6.127–31, cited in *ibid.*, p. 33.
37 James Frazer, *The Golden Bough*, 2 vols. (London: Macmillan 1890), vol. 1, pp. 301–10.
38 *Ibid.*, vol. 1, pp. 330–1. The story is told in Bulfinch, *The Age of Fable*, pp. 389–94.
39 Frazer, *The Golden Bough*, vol. 1, pp. 393–4.
40 Bulfinch, *The Age of Fable*, pp. 78–86.
41 The myth of Alcestis is described in Bulfinch, *The Age of Fable*, pp. 246–9.
42 1.1.150–2.
43 1.2.432–3.
44 2.3.156–7.
45 5.3.18–20.
46 5.3.67–8.
47 4.4.1–3.
48 4.4.74–5.
49 4.4.106–8.
50 Franklin, *Poems*, pp. 769–70.

Compound vision

The compound vision of Dickinson's religious imagination emerges most strongly through the interplay of poetic and religious ideas in four major and interdependent themes: body, mediation, journey and gesture. In Chapter 1, we saw how Dickinson's poetic concern with embodiment reconfigures the problem of the Word made flesh – the difficulty of holding humanity and divinity together in one relationship. As aesthetic and religious ideas converge in the body long before the nineteenth century, she can be seen to be writing within an informed New England tradition that continued to impact upon the theological and literary terrain she inhabited. Revelation influenced notions of representation and human language from the Mathers through to Edwards, Emerson and Channing at least partly because the incarnation was perceived to be a corporeal signifier of incorporeal meaning.

Dickinson's Christological reworking of corporeality as a way of understanding the medium of poetry and poetic experience not only provides a foundation for the compound vision of her religious imagination, it also suggests that the nineteenth-century literary obsession with corporeality has a theological component that has been largely overlooked. Dickinson's strategies of verbal condensation, her depiction of duality as an unexpected and questionable gift, and her sense of the body as both the enabling condition and the limiting constraint of her vision are indebted to the conceptual vocabulary of the hypostatic union and the Word made flesh. Through the conceit of the veil, Dickinson also drew a parallel between incarnation and imagination and in this sense she bridged religious and Romantic poetics. The veil, a religious symbol of the last barrier between man and God and a type for the body of Christ, is also a Romantic symbol for the sublime quality of the imagination. The veil is both a barrier signalling distance and an invitation to enter, somewhat imperfectly, into the presence of an absolute. It is a manifestly corporeal symbol and central to understanding the way religion fed Dickinson's imagination of poetry as a fleshy form of communication.

The flexibility that Dickinson establishes between incarnation and embodiment helps to explain the poetic relevance of many of the themes discussed in this book. Dickinson's fictions of naming, and to a greater extent her explorations of sacrifice, gain from a complicated aesthetic of Baptism at least partly derived from the doctrine of rebirth into the body of Christ. The enabling power of temporality, implicit in bodily constraint, and the sensual or sexual potential of embodied experience are similarly essential to the intensification of life by death and the experience of eternity within time that Dickinson explores through transfiguring encounters with light. These encounters with light express the desire for, and frequent distrust of, poetic inspiration and posterity and recall, through the lens of comparative religion, the incarnational revelations of Christ's transfiguration as the moment when eternity is given face in time.

As a signifier of the laws of time and space, the body also has a religious and poetic significance that extends beyond incarnation and comes into focus as a border-crossing at the point of death. This Dickinson exposes when she renders 'agony' as a 'Nearness to Tremendousness' and through a phenomenological poetic that brings out the importance of the body to Dickinson's notion of Gethsemane as a liminal place from which to write. It is also essential to understanding the way Dickinson's depictions of Calvary throw the hypostatic union into relief at the very moment of its dissolution. Finally, in the paradoxical quality of the resurrected body, the 'incorruptible flesh', Dickinson understood a challenge to notions of corporeality. The idea of a body that could function as a corporeal sign – at once literal and allegorical – intrigued her, especially as her own poems frequently indulged in allegories of the body. Moreover, Dickinson liked to draw parallels between resurrected bodies and her own 'finished Creatures' or creations. Resurrection therefore provided a powerful stimulus for Dickinson's interest in corporeality, and in her sensitive explorations of theological problems her poems were as imaginatively exegetical as they were indebted to the theology they questioned.

Just as Christ's role as mediator is central to the incarnation, the question of mediation emerges as a central feature of Dickinson's concern with embodiment. Nowhere is this clearer than in the extended conceit of the veil. Dickinson compares the disembodied or unmediated forces of poetry and love to the consuming fires of the Old Testament. By contrast, through ideas derived from Christian tradition, poetry finds a more honest, if compromised, manifestation for Dickinson as a point of orientation towards an absolute rather than a state of being identical with it. So, she admits that through such mediated experiences 'We both and neither Prove'. In this paradoxical vision, encounter is possible only by means of separation and distance. Dickinson may desire the privilege of unmediated access, the elevated stance of those who 'walk within the veil', but such access is incompatible with human nature and to claim it strikes her as dangerously hubristic.

So her performative poetics developed at least partly from her sense of the 'name' as a veil or symbol of mediation. Within Dickinson's fictions of naming, personae and theatrical performances retain a sense of orientation towards a 'supremest name', a notional absolute or essential state of being. For Dickinson, names signify roles that can be easily taken on and thrown off again when desired. Her performative poetics are both delightfully playful and rooted in a fundamentally serious post-lapsarian distinction between essence and representation. Dickinson's playfulness and occasional silliness derive from a delight in subversive fictions which deny both Puritan piety and Transcendentalist earnestness. This playfulness is a huge part of her (and my) poetic enjoyment and it should not be sidelined. But there is also a serious purpose to the self that can only be staged or mediated by another. Dickinson draws a connection between the sacrificial gift of martyrdom (realised anew through the sacrament of Baptism) and the sacrificial gift staged by her performative poetics. Her poems repeatedly enact a sacrifice of self, drawing from the related theologies of Baptism and crucifixion. But *enacting* that sacrifice allows her to preserve some part of an original self from extinction. Like the veil or the naming event of Baptism, performance allows Dickinson a necessary shield. Performance and personae are enabling constraints; they allow encounter precisely because they engender distance and separation.

Mediation is also at issue in Dickinson's encounters with light. As she plays with ideas of possession and origin, she acknowledges the difference between mediated and unmediated inspiration and also interrogates the origins of creativity in divine or dark forces. Here Dickinson's religious and Romantic strains cannot be disentangled. She is deeply indebted to the Romantic oracular tradition and she wonders what it would be like to inhabit passively the medium of light, finally concluding that such passivity lacks the Promethean urge. She also suggests that to be conscious of poetic inspiration, as to come face-to-face with God, is dangerous. Her ambivalent feelings towards poetry as a medium through which poets secure themselves some measure of immortality or fame are also integrally related to her doubts about Heaven. Attractive as the prospect seems, Dickinson cannot help but fall into irony as she wonders whether fame is any more real or satisfying a prospect than the Heaven that tests her faith.

Through the rebirth of spirit Dickinson explores the related ideas of resurrection and ascension as a way of passing beyond the mediatory veil. While the veil, or cocoon, intensifies her awareness of a power beyond, the resurrected body intrigues her as a new form of mediation. In the consolatory mode found in many of Dickinson's poems on resurrection the resurrected body functions as a point of personal continuity and connection between the dead and the living. But resurrection also encouraged a philosophical enquiry into the status of a poem that comes in the form of a resurrected body. From the strange paradox of Paul's 'incorruptible body' Dickinson derived a challenge to her incarnational aesthetic, an idea of essential rather than representative flesh.

As they narrate the life of Christ, a sense of journey pervades the Gospels. In Dickinson's reworking of this life as a series of aesthetic positions, that sense of journey can be found in the emphasis she places on process and growth in consciousness. Her encounters with light are juxtaposed with experiences of dark wandering pregnant with creative potential. The journeys she describes here are sensual and groping, celebrating the touch of the unknown and displaying a desire to return to its dangers. Dickinson's appetite for danger is, in many respects, an endorsement of the Romantic sublime. But here too the religious and Romantic strains of her imagination are hard to separate. Dickinson's renderings of numinous experience as fluid creative potential are modified by notions of darkness derived from tales of religious encounters with light. So the shapeless dark of the sublime often takes the form of a divine other, which is sometimes indistinguishable in Dickinson from the erotic pull towards a lover.

Dickinson's encounters with light also implicate the transitus, a period of all eternity compressed into time, in the experience of poetic inspiration. This essentially religious invocation of death's border-crossing was commonly used by many of Dickinson's American and British contemporaries, including Tennyson. However, Dickinson used it in a rather unorthodox and sometimes parodic way, emphasising the relevance of the temporal and mortal world over the final homecoming in Heaven. As a result she focuses on the process of journey and privileges the importance of liminality over the sensation of arrival. Encounters with light prove fleeting but journey remains the condition of her existence.

Journey is most important to understanding the compound vision of Dickinson's religious imagination through its particular manifestation as a quest. Dickinson mixes biblical and classical allusions in poems that demonstrate a typically Romantic internalisation of the quest narrative as a journey of artistic struggle and triumph. She aligns the poet-quester with the Prometheus-Christ man of suffering, focusing her attention on the intensely painful consciousness of transition and the violent emotions of crucifixion and conversion. The quester also finds parallels in Odysseus and Orpheus who, like Jesus, journey to the place of the dead while still alive. The lonely struggle of the quest hero is essential to their story and Dickinson makes it a fetish, luxuriating in the difficulty of her journey. So, in her version of internal poetic questing, inspiration becomes a struggle with the self's darkness as well as the triumph of its own light. The lonely struggle takes place at the centre of consciousness and the shift towards enlightenment shares in the unexpected and inexplicable sense of arrival common to the creative or divine principle of the Romantic or religious quest.

The quest that makes journey its object has a parallel in Dickinson's own sense of poetic process. The scholarship of the last two decades has encouraged a reassessment of Dickinson's intention in authorial composition. This does not mean that we need to abandon a long-held sense of the parallels between the religious and artistic quest. Both share the same epistemology through a life lived in the sense of something beyond. But it is as problematic to identify Dickinson's vocation with a progressive journey towards a rarefied pearl of poetic achievement as it is to assume that this is the way in which she interpreted the religious quest. The nuance that Dickinson brings to her depictions of religious quest narratives arises out of a fascination with the conditions of process – struggle, loneliness and border-crossings. Her analogy between the religious and poetic quest therefore brings such notions into focus as the conditions for creativity.

The quest narrative recurs in Dickinson's engagement with sacrifice. In these instances she again forges her sense of journey through an emphasis on struggle, particularly the struggle between human submission and resistance to the divine plan. The conflict between humanity and divinity finds its most forceful expression in the context of human love which emerges as an amazingly powerful challenge to the gods. As a pull towards something greater than the self, the erotic movement is also an experience of journey. For Dickinson, this is both its attraction and its threat. She is drawn towards the impulse of sacrifice as by a lover but, as she is nervous about losing control of the journey, she often falls into irony as a way of guarding against anguish. The journey suggested by Dickinson's poems on sacrifice is one that negotiates a reach into the beyond through the painful realities of human suffering. The shared epistemology of the religious and poetic quest is profoundly relevant here. As Calvary stimulates the poetic experience of struggle and journey, Dickinson implies that her poetry, like the incarnation and crucifixion, takes human understanding of the unknown to a new 'venture' but it cannot complete the quest.

So it is through this sense of journey into the beyond that we arrive at the last of the four themes: gesture. In every chapter the space between the divine and the human or the eternal and the temporal has been a key theme. The compound vision of Dickinson's religious imagination relies on the paradoxical preservation of such a space and the gesture towards closing it. So it exploits the absence which is at the heart of analogy, the substitution of one experience for another evident in the similes and metaphors on which Dickinson's poems so often rely, her painful absorption with the 'fashions – of the Cross / And how they're mostly worn – Still fascinated to presume / That Some – are like [her] Own'. Her refusal to admit of finite ending and her frequently displayed desire to push past the end of the poem with a dash and/or an incomplete meaning are part of this gestural poetic movement that hinges on an absence, the 'as it were' that is essential to understanding Dickinson's creative interplay of poetic and religious ideas.

In both Puritan and liberal Christian thought the gap between divinity and humanity defined the shared aesthetic and theological vocabulary of the Word made flesh. The absence implicit in revelation informed the gesture implicit in representation. The space between God and humanity therefore became a matter of theological and poetic concern. Dickinson's position in this terrain helps situate her unique reworking of the Word made flesh. While indebted to the humanistic freedom of liberal thought that encouraged her to see the Bible as a literary work, her imagination was fundamentally of an older cast than Emerson's or Channing's. Where Emerson's 'priest or poet' desired illimitability, blurring the distinction between divinity and humanity, Dickinson's theological poetics exploited that distinction for its tensions. Though persistently unworried by Puritan preaching of sin and damnation, she loved the poetry of Edwardsian sermons that enabled people to experience ideas and so brought the distinction between divinity and humanity into the arena of consciousness. Her own typology depends on interior space, on experience and judgment rather than verification and, in withholding typological fulfilment, she frequently gestures towards an unknown beyond that experience, a realm into which poetry can only begin to 'venture'.

This gesture is the basis of the incarnational aesthetic that I have suggested Dickinson reconfigured through embodiment. Dickinson's focus on corporeality and mediation is therefore intrinsically linked to her emphasis on gesture. As a way of rendering 'distance' accessible, the incarnational basis of her embodied poetics relies on a space that can never be fully bridged. It is the same space denoted by the veil, the space that creates a distinction between the post-lapsarian 'name' and the namelessness of the beyond and the space that Dickinson exploits through performative poetics that rest on the dissonance between essence and representation. Most importantly, perhaps, it informs the religious epistemology of a poetic quest rooted in the gesture beyond. As Dickinson writes about liminality and illocality, she also makes such an in-between space the province of poetry and inspiration.

In Dickinson's depictions of sacrifice the space in between humanity and divinity not only lends meaning to the nature of suffering, it also lays the ground for her quarrel with God. In poetic terms, the inadequacies of revelation and representation become the genesis of creative action as the death of Christ becomes analogous to a poetic compassing of the unknown. In the final chapter I explored the idea that resurrection allows Dickinson to experiment with the possibilities of closing this space. Beginning with Paul's notion of the 'incorruptible flesh', I suggested that the resurrected body asks to be read both as a literal reality and a representational sign. The space between death and resurrection asks for a faith and is haunted by a loss that allows for poetic gesture.

It is by no means coincidental that this arises out of the fusion of opposites, life and death, which is central to Paul's account of the risen Christ. It is important also that a duality of vision was part of Dickinson's Puritan heritage and essential to the philosophy of Transcendentalism. Dickinson's poetic exploration of body and spirit in resurrection, rather than eliding the difference between them, focuses in the end on that sense of gesture which was the enabling possibility of her religious imagination.

Bibliography

DICKINSON EDITIONS

Franklin, Ralph William (ed.), *The Manuscript Books of Emily Dickinson*, 2 vols. Cambridge, Mass.: Belknap Press, 1981.
The Poems of Emily Dickinson: Reading Edition. Cambridge, Mass.: Belknap Press, 1999.
The Poems of Emily Dickinson: Variorum Edition, 3 vols. Cambridge, Mass.: Belknap Press, 1998. All references are to this edition unless otherwise stated.
Johnson, Thomas Herbert (ed.), *The Poems of Emily Dickinson: Including Variant Readings Critically Compared with all Known Manuscripts*, 3 vols. Cambridge, Mass.: Belknap Press, 1955.

LETTERS

Bianchi, Martha Dickinson (ed.), *Emily Dickinson Face to Face: Unpublished Letters with Notes and Reminiscences*. Boston, Mass.: Houghton Mifflin Co., 1932.
Bingham, Millicent Todd, *Ancestor's Brocades: The Literary Discovery of Emily Dickinson and the Editing and Publication of her Letters and Poems*. New York: Dover, 1967.
Bingham, Millicent Todd (ed.), *Emily Dickinson's Home: Letters of Emily Dickinson and her Family*. New York: Harper, 1955.
Franklin, Ralph William (ed.), *The Master Letters of Emily Dickinson*. Amherst, Mass.: Amherst College Press, 1986.
Hart, Ellen Louise, and Martha Smith, *Nell, Open Me Carefully: Emily Dickinson's Intimate Letters to Susan Dickinson*. Paris: Paris Press, 1998.
Johnson, Thomas Herbert, and Theodora Ward (eds.), *The Letters of Emily Dickinson*, 3 vols. Cambridge, Mass.: Belknap Press, 1958. All references are to this edition unless otherwise stated.
Todd, Mabel Loomis (ed.), *Letters of Emily Dickinson*. Boston, Mass.: Roberts Brothers, 1894.

SECONDARY WORKS

Ackerman, Robert, *The Myth and Ritual School: J. G. Frazer and the Cambridge Ritualists*. London: Garland, 1991.

Affrey, Shawn, 'Against Calvary: Emily Dickinson and the Sublime', *Emily Dickinson Journal*, 7.2 (1998), pp. 48–64.

Akli, Lawrence Perry, *The Pauline Concept of Baptism and New Life in Christ: The dynamics of Christian Life according to St. Paul.* Rome: printed by N. Domenci-Pecheux, 1992.

Aquinas, Thomas, *Summa Theologiae: A Concise Translation*, ed. Timothy McDermott. London: Eyre and Spottiswoode, 1989.

Alexander, Archibald, *A Pocket Dictionary of the Holy Bible containing a historical and geographical account of the persons and places mentioned in the Old and New Testaments and also a description of other objects, natural, artificial, civil, religious and military: together with a copious reference to texts of scripture under each important word. Prepared for the American Sunday School Union and adapted to general use.* Philadelphia: American Sunday School Union, 1831.

Allan, Archibald, *The Transfiguration.* London: Oliver and Boyd, 1923.

Ambruster, Carl J., 'The Messianic Significance of the Agony in the Garden', *Scripture: The Quarterly of the Catholic Biblical Association*, 16.36 (1964), pp. 111–19.

Anderson, Douglas, 'Presence and Place in Emily Dickinson's Poetry', *New England Quarterly*, 57.2 (1984), pp. 205–24.

Anderson, Peggy, 'The Bride of the White Election: A New Look at Biblical Influence on Emily Dickinson', *Nineteenth-Century Women Writers of the English-Speaking World*, ed. Rhoda B. Nathan. London: Greenwood Press, 1986: pp. 1–11.

Anderson, Vincent P., 'Emily Dickinson and the Disappearance of God', *Christian Scholar's Review*, 11.1 (1981), pp. 3–17.

Anthon, Charles, *Classical Dictionary: Containing an Account of the Principal Proper Names mentioned in Ancient Authors and Intended to Elucidate all the Important Points connected with the Geography, History, Biography, Mythology, and Fine Arts of the Greeks and Romans, together with an Account of Coins, Weights, and Measures with Tabular Values of the Same.* New York: Harper and Brothers, 1841.

Apollonius of Rhodes, *Jason and the Golden Fleece*, trans. Richard Hunter. Oxford: Clarendon Press, 1993.

Astell, Ann, and Bonnie Wheeler (eds.), *Joan of Arc and Spirituality.* Basingstoke: Macmillan, 2003.

Auden, W. H., *Collected Shorter Poems 1927–1957.* London: Faber, 2003.

Augustine, *Confessions*, trans. William Watts (1631), 2 vols. Cambridge, Mass.: Harvard University Press, 1912.

Bachelard, Gaston, *Fragments of a Poetics of Fire*, trans. Kenneth Haltman. Dallas, Tex.: Dallas Institute Publications, 1990.

The Poetics of Space, trans. Etienne Gilson. London: The Orion Press, 1964.

Baker, Robert, *The Extravagant.* Notre Dame, Ind.: University of Notre Dame Press, 2005.

Barbot, Mary Elizabeth, 'Emily Dickinson's Parallels', *The New England Quarterly*, 14.4 (1941), pp. 689–96.

Barker, Wendy, *Lunacy of Light: Emily Dickinson and the Experience of Metaphor.* Carbondale, Ill.: Southern Illinois University Press, 1987.

Barnstone, Aliki, *Changing Rapture: Emily Dickinson's Poetic Development.* Lebanon, NH, and London: University Press of New England, 2006.

Benfey, Christopher, 'A Route of Evanescence: Emily Dickinson and Japan', *The Emily Dickinson Journal*, 16.2 (2007), pp. 81–93.

Blake, William, *Blake's Poetry and Designs*, ed. Mary Lynn Johnson and John E. Grant. London: W. W. Norton, 1979.

Bloom, Harold (ed.), *Emily Dickinson.* New York: Chelsea House Publishers, 1985.
  'The Internalisation of Quest Romance', *The Yale Review: A National Quarterly*, 58 (Summer 1969), pp. 526–36.

Boobyer, G. H., *St Mark and the Transfiguration Story.* Edinburgh: T & T Clark, 1942.

Brown, Raymond E., *The Death of the Messiah: From Gethsemane to the Grave*, 2 vols. London: Geoffrey Chapman, 1994.

Browning, Elizabeth Barrett, *The Poems of Elizabeth Barrett Browning.* Boston, Mass.: Crosby and Nichols, 1852.

Buchanan, A. C., *A Place Called Gethsemane.* London: Macmillan, 1927.

Buckingham, Willis J. (ed.), *Emily Dickinson's Reception in the 1890s: A Documentary History.* Pittsburgh, Penn.: University of Pittsburgh Press, 1989.

Buell, Lawrence, *Emerson.* Cambridge, Mass.: Harvard University Press, 2003.

Bulfinch, Thomas, *The Age of Fable: Stories of Gods and Heroes.* Boston, Mass.: Sanborn, Carter and Bazin, 1855.

Bunyan, John, *The Pilgrim's Progress* (1678). Harmondsworth: Penguin, 1965.

Burke, Edmund, *A Philosophical Enquiry into the Origin of our Ideas of the Sublime and Beautiful* (1757). Oxford: Oxford University Press, 1990.

Calvin, Jean, *The Institutes of the Christian Religion*, trans. Henry Beveridge, 2 vols. Edinburgh: T & T Clark, 1895.
  Genesis, ed. Alister McGrath and J. I. Packer. Nottingham: Crossway Books, 2001.

Cameron, Sharon, *Choosing not Choosing: Dickinson's Fascicles.* Chicago: University of Chicago Press, 1992.
  The Corporeal Self: Allegories of the Body in Melville and Hawthorne. Baltimore and London: The Johns Hopkins University Press, 1981.
  Lyric Time: Dickinson and the Limits of Genre. Baltimore and London: The Johns Hopkins University Press, 1979.

Capps, Jack L., *Emily Dickinson's Reading: 1836–1886.* London: Oxford University Press, 1966.

Carlyle, Thomas *Heroes and Hero-Worship* (1841). London: Chapman and Hall, 1897.
  On Heroes, Hero-Worship and the Heroic in History. New York: J. Wiley, 1879 (in the Houghton Library, Harvard, EDR 343).

Casey, Edward, *The Fate of Place: A Philosophical History.* Berkeley, Los Angeles and London: University of California Press, 1997.

Cavell, Stanley, *Emerson's Transcendental Etudes.* Stanford, Calif.: Stanford University Press, 2003.

Channing, William Henry, 'Unitarian Christianity' (1819), in *The Unitarian Controversy 1819–1823*, 2 vols. ed. Bruce Kuklick (London: Garland Publishing, 1987), vol 1, pp. 3–47.

  Religions of China: Address before the Free Religious Association. Boston, 27 May 1870. Boston, Mass.: Press of John Wilson and Son, 1870.

Cleary, Vincent J., 'Emily Dickinson's Classical Education', *English Language Notes*, 18.2 (1980), pp. 119–29.

Cohen, Charles Lloyd, *God's Caress: The Psychology of Puritan Religious Experience*. Oxford: Oxford University Press, 1986.

Coleridge, Samuel Taylor, *Lay Sermons*, ed. R. J. White. London: Routledge, 1972.

  The Literary Remains of Samuel Taylor Coleridge, 4 vols., ed. Henry Nelson Coleridge. London: William Pickering, 1836–9.

Colton, A. M., 'A Sermon on the Power of Habit', *The Old Meeting House and Congregationalist Church in Amherst 1739–1939. Two Hundred Years in View and Review 1739–1939: A record of the Observance of its Two Hundredth Anniversary by the First Congregational Church in Amherst, Massachusetts Nov 4–5th 1939*, comp. Rev. John A. Hawley and Frank Prentice Rand. Amherst, Mass.: The First Congregational Church in Amherst United Church of Christ, 1990.

Connor, Steven, *Dumbstruck: A Cultural History of Ventriloquism*. Oxford: Oxford University Press, 2001.

Cooley, Carolyn Lindley, *The Music of Emily Dickinson's Poems and Letters: A Study of Imagery and Form*. London: McFarland and Co., 2003.

Cotton, John, *Christ the Fountaine of Life: or Sundry Choice Sermons on part of the fift [sic] chapter of the fifst Epistle of St. John*. London: Robert Ibbiton, 1651.

Crumbley, Paul, *Inflections of the Pen: Dash and Voice in Emily Dickinson*. Lexington, Ky.: The University Press of Kentucky, 1997.

Cuddy, Lois A., 'Shelley's Glorious Titan: Reflections on ED's Self-Image and Achievement', *Dickinson Studies, U.S. Poet*, 55.1 (1985), pp. 32–40.

Davies, G. J., 'The Prefigurement of the Ascension in the Third Gospel', *Journal of Theological Studies*, 6.2 (1955), pp. 299–333.

Davis, Thomas M., and Virginia L. (eds.), *Edward Taylor vs. Soloman Stoddard: The Nature of the Lord's Supper*. Boston, Mass.: Twayne Publishers, 1981.

De Arteaga, William L., *Forgotten Power: The Significance of the Lord's Supper in Revival*. Grand Rapids, Mich.: Zondervan Publishing House, 2002.

De Lubac, Henri, *Medieval Exegesis: The Four Senses of Scripture*, vol. 1, trans. Marc Sebanc. Edinburgh: T & T Clark, 1998.

Deforest Widger, Howard, *Carlyle in America: His Reputation and Influence*. Urbana-Champaign, Ill.: Thesis printed by the University of Illinois, 1940.

Dennis, George, *The Cities and Cemeteries of Etruria*, 2 vols. London: John Murray, 1883.

Derrida, Jacques, *The Gift of Death*, trans. David Wills. Chicago and London: University of Chicago Press, 1992.

Diehl, Joanne Feit, *Dickinson and the Romantic Imagination*. Princeton, NJ: Princeton University Press, 1981.

Dobson, Joanne, *Dickinson and the Strategies of Reticence: The Woman Writer in Nineteenth-Century America*. Bloomington and Indianapolis, Ind.: Indiana University Press, 1989.

Doriani, Beth Maclay, *Emily Dickinson: Daughter of Prophecy*. Amherst: University of Massachusetts Press, 1996.

Dressman, Michael R. 'Empress of Calvary: Mystical Marriage in the Poems of Emily Dickinson', *South Atlantic Bulletin*, 42.1 (1977), pp. 39–43.

Eberwein, Jane Donahue, *Dickinson: Strategies of Limitation*. Amherst, Mass.: University of Massachusetts Press, 1985.

'Introducing a Religious Poet: The 1890 Poems of Emily Dickinson', *Christianity and Literature*, 39.3 (1990), pp. 241–61.

Eddins, Dwight, 'Emily Dickinson and Nietzsche: The Rights of Dionysus', *ESQ: A Journal of the American Renaissance*, 27.2 (1981), pp. 96–107.

Edwards, Jonathan, *Letters and Personal Writings*, ed. George S. Claghorn. New Haven and London: Yale University Press, 1998.

Religious Affections (1746), ed. John E. Smith. New Haven and London: Yale University Press, 1959.

'Some Thoughts Concerning the Present Revival of Religion in New England', in *The Great Awakening*, ed. C. C. Goen. New Haven and London: Yale University Press, 1972.

Typological Writings, ed. Wallace Anderson, Mason I. Lowance and David H. Watters. New Haven and London: Yale University Press, 1993.

Emerson, Ralph Waldo, *The Collected Works of Ralph Waldo Emerson*, ed. Joseph Slater, Robert Spiller, Alfred R. Ferguson *et al.*, 6 vols. (Cambridge, Mass.: Harvard University Press, 1971–2003).

Letters and Social Aims. Boston, Mass.: Houghton Mifflin Co., 1903.

Ernst, Katharina, *'Death' in the Poetry of Emily Dickinson*. Heidelberg: Carl Winter, 1992.

Estes, David C., '"Out upon Circumference": Emily Dickinson's Search for Location', *Essays in Literature*, 6.2 (1979), pp. 207–17.

Evans, Stephen C. (ed.), *Exploring Kenotic Christology: The Self-Emptying of God*. Oxford: Oxford University Press, 2006.

Fairbairn, Patrick, *The Typology of Scripture*, 2 vols. Grand Rapids, Mich.: Zondervan Publishing House, 1967.

Farr, Judith, *The Gardens of Emily Dickinson*. Cambridge, Mass., and London: Harvard University Press, 2004.

The Passion of Emily Dickinson. Cambridge, Mass., and London: Harvard University Press, 1994.

Feuerbach, Ludwig, *The Essence of Christianity* (1854), trans. George Eliot. New York: Prometheus Books, 1989.

Fideler, David, *Jesus Christ, Sun of God: Ancient Cosmology and Early Christian Symbolism*. Wheaton: Theosophical Publishing House, 1993.

Finnerty, Páraic, *Emily Dickinson's Shakespeare*. Amherst, Mass.: University of Massachusetts Press, 2006.

Fogle, Richard Harter, *Hawthorne's Imagery: The 'Proper Light and Shadow' in the Major Romances*. Norman, Okla.: University of Oklahoma Press, 1969.

Franklin, R. W., *The Editing of Emily Dickinson: A Reconsideration*. Madison, Wisc.: University of Wisconsin Press, 1967.

Frazer, James, *The Golden Bough*, 2 vols. London: Macmillan, 1890.

Friedenthal, Richard, *Luther*, trans. John Nowell. London: Weidenfeld and Nicolson, 1967.

Freedman, Linda, "'Meadows of Majesty": Baptism as Translation in Emily Dickinson's Poetry', *The Emily Dickinson Journal*, 17.1 (2008), pp. 25–43.

Gaskell, Elizabeth, *Mary Barton*. New York: Penguin, 1977.

Gilbert, Sandra M., and Susan Gubar, *The Madwoman in the Attic: The Woman Writer and the Nineteenth-Century Literary Imagination*. New Haven and London: Yale University Press, 1979.

Gelpi, Albert J., *Emily Dickinson: The Mind of the Poet*. Cambridge, Mass.: Harvard University Press, 1965.

Godbeer, Richard, *The Devil's Dominion: Magic and Religion in Early New England*. Cambridge: Cambridge University Press, 1992.

Grabher, Gudrun, Roland Hagenbuchle and Cristanne Miller (eds.), *The Emily Dickinson Handbook*. Amherst: University of Massachusetts Press, 1998.

Grant, Patrick, *Spiritual Discourse and the Meaning of Persons*. London: Macmillan, 1994.

Hagenbuchle, Roland, and Jaqueline S. Ollier (eds.), *Poetry and the Fine Arts*. Regensburg: Verlag Friedrich Putset, 1989.

Hallen, Cynthia, and Melvin Wilson, *Webplay: Emily Dickinson and Webster's Dictionary*, http://linguistics.byu.edu/faculty/hallenc/EDLexicon/webplay.html

Harde, Roxanne, "'Some are like my own": Emily Dickinson's Christology of Embodiment', *Christianity and Literature 2004*, www.highbeam.com:1–11.

Hassan, Ihab, 'Postmodernism: A Self-Interview', *Philosophy and Literature*, 30.1 (2006), pp. 223–8.

Hawkins, Gary, 'Constructing and Residing in the Paradox of Dickinson's Prismatic Space', *Emily Dickinson Journal*, 9.1 (2002), pp. 49–70.

Hawthorne, Nathaniel, *The Scarlet Letter* (1850). Ware, Herts: Wordsworth, 1992.

Heidegger, Martin, *Being and Time* (1927), trans. John Maquarrie and Edward Robinson. New York: Harper and Row, 1962.

Heil, John Paul, *The Transfiguration of Jesus: Narrative Meaning and Function of Mark 9:2–8, Matt 17:1–8 and Luke 9:28–36*. Rome: Editrice Pontificio Istituto Biblico, 2000.

Heginbotham, Eleanor Elson, *Reading the Fascicles of Emily Dickinson: Dwelling in Possibilities*. Columbus, OH: Ohio State University, 2003.

Helmstadter, Richard J., and Bernard Lightman (eds.), *Victorian Faith in Crisis*. London: Macmillan, 1990.

Herodotus, *The Histories*. London: Penguin, 2003.

Higgins, Rev. J. T., *Gethsemane and Other Discourses*. London: T. Danks, 1885.

Hiltner, Ken, 'Because I, Proserpine, Could Not Stop for Death: Emily Dickinson and the Goddess', *Emily Dickinson Journal*, 10.2 (2001), pp. 22–42.

Holstein, Suzy Clarkson, 'Lighting on the Landscape', *Dickinson Studies, U.S. Poet*, 76.2 (1990), pp. 3–14.

Homans, Margaret, *Women Writers and Poetic Identity*. Princeton, NJ: Princeton University Press, 1980.

Homer, *The Odyssey*, trans. Albert Cook. New York: W. W. Norton and Co., 1974.

Huhn, Pastor K., *Gethsemane: A Glance into the Sanctuary*, trans. M. Gaudian. London: S. W. Partridge and Co., 1901.

Hume, David, *The Philosophical Works of David Hume*. Edinburgh: Port, 1826.

Hurst, L. D., and Wright N. T. (eds.), *The Glory of Christ in the New Testament: Studies in Christology*. Oxford: Clarendon Press, 1987.

Hyde, Lewis, *The Gift: Imagination and the Erotic Life of Property*. New York: Vintage, 1979.

Ickstadt, Heinz, 'Emily Dickinson's Place in Literary History; Or, the Public Function of a Private Poet', *The Emily Dickinson Journal*, 10.1 (2001), pp. 55–69.

Jackson, Thomas (trans.), *Titus Lucretius Carus on the Nature of Things*. Oxford: Oxford University Press, 1929.

Jackson, Virginia, *Dickinson's Misery: A Theory of Lyric Reading*. Princeton, NJ: Princeton University Press, 2005.

James, William, *The Varieties of Religious Experience*, ed. Martin E. Marty. London: Penguin, 1985.

Johnson, Greg, *Emily Dickinson: Perception and the Poet's Quest*. Tuscaloosa, Ala.: The University of Alabama Press, 1985.

Johnson, T. H., *Emily Dickinson: An Interpretative Biography*. Cambridge, Mass.: Harvard University Press, 1955; 1967.

Jones, Rowena Revis, '"A Royal Seal": Emily Dickinson's Rite of Baptism', *Religion and Literature*, 18.3 (1986), pp. 29–51.

Juhasz, Suzanne, *The Undiscovered Continent: Emily Dickinson and the Space of the Mind*. Bloomington, Ind.: Indiana University Press, 1983.

Kant, Immanuel, *Critique of Aesthetic Judgment* (1790), trans. J. C. Meredith. Oxford: Clarendon Press, 1911.

   Observations on the Feeling of the Beautiful and the Sublime (1763), trans. John T. Goldthwait. Berkeley, Los Angeles and Oxford: University of California Press, 1960.

Kantorowicz, Ernst, *The King's Two Bodies: A Study in Mediaeval Political Theology (1957)*. Princeton: Princeton University Press, 1997.

Karlsen, Carol F., *The Devil in the Shape of a Woman: Witchcraft in Colonial New England*. London: W. W. Norton and Co., 1998.

Keats, John, *The Complete Poems*, ed. John Barnard. London: Penguin, 1988.

Kehler, Joel R., 'The House Divided: A Version of American Romantic "Double Consciousness"', *Papers on Language and Literature: A Journal for Scholars and Critics of Language and Literature*, 13.2 (1977), pp. 148–68.

Kenny, Anthony, 'The Transfiguration and the Agony in the Garden', *Catholic Biblical Quarterly*, 19 (1957), pp. 444–52.

Keuss, Jeffrey, *A Poetics of Jesus: The Search for Christ through Writing in the Nineteenth Century*. Aldershot: Ashgate, 2002.

Khan, M. M., 'The Agony of the Final Inch: The Treatment of Pain in Dickinson's Poems', *Dickinson Studies, U.S. Poet*, 47 (1983), pp. 22–34.

Kher, Inder Nath, *The Landscape of Absence: Emily Dickinson's Poetry*. New Haven and London: Yale University Press, 1974.

Kierkegaard, Søren, *Fear and Trembling* (1843), trans. Alastair Hannay. London: Penguin, 2005.

Philosophical Fragments (1844), trans. Howard and Edna Hong. Princeton, NJ: Princeton University Press, 1985.

The Sickness unto Death (1831), trans. Alastair Hannay. London: Penguin, 1989.

Stages on Life's Way (1845), trans. Walter Lowrie. London: Oxford University Press, 1940.

Kilcup, Karen (ed.), *Soft Canons: American Women Writers and Masculine Tradition*. Iowa City, IA: University of Iowa Press, 1999.

Kimnach, Wilson *et al.* (eds.), *The Sermons of Jonathan Edwards: A Reader*. New Haven and London: Yale University Press, 1999.

Kirk, Connie Ann, 'Climates of the Creative Process: Dickinson's Epistolary Journal', in *A Companion to Emily Dickinson*, ed. Martha Nell Smith and Mary Loeffelholz. Oxford: Blackwell, 2008: pp. 334–48.

Knapp, Bettina L., *Emily Dickinson*. New York: Continuum, 1989.

Kuklick, Bruce (ed.), *The Unitarian Controversy 1819–1823*, 2 vols. London: Garland Publishing, 1987.

Leland, Charles G., *Etruscan Roman Remains and the Old Religion*. London: Kegan Paul, 2002.

Lempriere, J., *Classical Dictionary: Containing a Full Account of all the Proper Names mentioned in Ancient Authors with Tables of Coins, Wrights and Measures in Use among the Greeks and Romans*. London: T. Allman, 1847.

Leonard, John, *Naming in Paradise: Milton and the Language of Adam and Eve*. Oxford: Clarendon Press, 1990.

Lewis, Linda M., *The Promethean Politics of Milton, Blake and Shelley*. Columbia, Mo., and London: University of Missouri Press, 1992.

Lieber, Todd M., *Endless Experiments: Essays on the Heroic Experience in American Romanticism*. Columbus, OH: Ohio State University Press, 1973.

Locke, John, *An Essay Concerning Human Understanding*, ed. Peter H. Niddich. Oxford: Oxford University Press, 1975.

The Reasonableness of Christianity, ed. I. T. Ramsay, London: Adam and Charles Black, 1958.

Lopez, Michael, *Emerson and Power: Creative Antagonism in the Nineteenth Century*. DeKalb, Ill.: Northern Illinois University Press, 1996.

Lowance, Mason I., *The Language of Canaan: Metaphor and Symbol in New England from the Puritans to the Transcendentalists*. Cambridge, Mass.: Harvard University Press, 1980.

Ludwig, Allan I., *Graven Images: New England Stonecarving and its Symbols 1650–1815*. London: Wesleyan University Press, 1966.

Lundin, Roger, *Emily Dickinson and the Art of Belief*. Cambridge: Wm. B. Eerdmans Publishing Co., 1998.

Makarushka, Irena S. M., *Religious Imagination and Language in Emerson and Nietzsche*. London: Macmillan, 1994.

Mannon, Melissa, *Gravestones: A Reflection on American Lifestyles* (1991–2001) www.mannon.org/gravestones.

Manning, Susan, 'How Conscious Consciousness Could Grow? Emily Dickinson and William James', in *Soft Canons: American Women Writers and Masculine Tradition*, ed. Karen Kilcup. Iowa City, IA: University of Iowa Press, 1999: pp. 306–33.

The Puritan-Provincial Vision: Scottish and American Literature in the Nineteenth Century. Cambridge: Cambridge University Press, 1990.

Marder, Daniel, *Exiles at Home: A Story of Literature in Nineteenth-Century America*. London: University Press of America, 1984.

Martin, Wendy (ed.), *The Cambridge Companion to Emily Dickinson*. Cambridge: Cambridge University Press, 2002.

Mauss, Marcel, *The Gift* (1950). London: Routledge, 2002.

Mays, James L. (ed.), *Harper's Bible Commentary*. San Francisco: Harper and Row, 1988.

McGiffert, A. C., *Young Emerson Speaks*. Boston, Mass.: Houghton Mifflin Co., 1938.

Mc Gregor, Elisabeth, '"Standing with the Prophets and Martyrs": Emily Dickinson's Scriptural Self-Defence', *Dickinson Studies, U.S. Poet*, 39 (1981), pp. 18–26.

McIntosh, James, *Nimble Believing: Dickinson and the Unknown*. Ann Arbor, Mich.: University of Michigan Press, 2000.

Melville, Herman, *Moby Dick* (1851). London: Penguin, 1992.

Mendilow, Jonathan, 'Shelley's Philosophy of Liberty', *The Journal of Libertarian Studies*, 6.2 (1982), pp. 169–80.

Messmer, Marietta, *A Vice for Voices: Reading Emily Dickinson's Correspondence*. Amherst, Mass.: University of Massachusetts Press, 2001.

Mikics, David, *The Romance of Individualism in Emerson and Nietzsche*. Athens, OH: Ohio University Press, 2003.

Milford, Humphrey (ed.), *The Poetical Works of Elizabeth Barrett Browning with Two Prose Essays*. Oxford: Oxford University Press, 1920.

Miller, Cristanne, *Emily Dickinson: A Poet's Grammar*. Cambridge, Mass.: Harvard University Press, 1987.

Miller, Perry, *Errand into the Wilderness*. Cambridge, Mass.: Harvard University Press, 1956.

The New England Mind: The Seventeenth Century. Cambridge, Mass., and London: Harvard University Press, 1939.

Miller, Ruth, 'Poetry as a Transitional Object', in *Between Reality and Fantasy: Transitional Objects and Phenomena*, ed. Simon A. Grolnik and Leonard Barkin. New York: Aronson, 1978.

Mitchell, Domhnall, 'Emily Dickinson and Class', in *The Cambridge Companion to Emily Dickinson, ed. Wendy Martin*. Cambridge: Cambridge University Press, 2002: pp. 191–215.

Moltmann, Jürgen, *The Crucified God: The Cross of Christ as the Foundation and Criticism of Christian Theology*. London: SCM Press, 1974.

Moore, Hastings, 'Emily Dickinson and the Apophatic Tradition', *Dickinson Studies, U.S. Poet*, 39 (1981), pp. 3–17.

Moses, A. D. A., *Matthew's Transfiguration Story and Jewish–Christian Controversy* Sheffield: Sheffield Academic Press, 1996.

Mudge, Jean McClure, *Emily Dickinson and the Image of Home*. Amherst, Mass.: University of Massachusetts Press, 1975.

New, Elisa, 'Difficult Writing, Difficult God: Emily Dickinson's Poems Beyond Circumference', *Religion and Literature*, 18.3 (1986), pp. 1–29.

The Line's Eye: Poetic Experience, American Sight. Cambridge, Mass.: Harvard University Press, 1998.

The Regenerate Lyric: Theology and Innovation in American Poetry. Cambridge: Cambridge University Press, 1993.

Noble, Marianne, *The Masochistic Pleasures of Sentimental Literature*. Princeton, NJ: Princeton University Press, 2000.

Nygren, Anders, *Agape and Eros*, trans. Phillip S. Watson. London: SPCK, 1982.

O'Hara, Daniel, '"The Designated Light": Irony in Emily Dickinson', *Boundary 2*, 7.3 (1979), pp. 175–98.

Ocáriz, F., L. F. Mateo Seco and J. A. Riestra, *The Mystery of Jesus Christ: A Christology and Soteriology Textbook*. Dublin: Four Courts Press, 1991.

Oliver, Virginia H., *Apocalypse of Green: A Study of Emily Dickinson's Eschatology*. New York: Peter Lang, 1988.

Otto, Rudolph, *The Idea of the Holy: An Inquiry into the Non-Rational Factor in the Idea of the Divine and its Relation to the Rational*, trans. John W. Harvey. London: Oxford University Press, 1928.

Paglia, Camille, *Sexual Personae: Art and Decadence from Nefertiti to Emily Dickinson*. New Haven and London: Yale University Press, 1990.

Phillips, Elizabeth, *Emily Dickinson: Personae and Performance*. Philadelphia and London: Pennsylvania State University Press, 1988.

Plath, Sylvia, *Collected Poems*. London: Faber, 1981.

Plato, *The Republic*, trans. Desmond Lee. London: Penguin, 1987.

Porter, David, *Dickinson: The Modern Idiom*. Cambridge, Mass.: Harvard University Press, 1981.

Reynolds, David S., 'Emily Dickinson and Popular Culture', in *The Cambridge Companion to Emily Dickinson*, ed. Wendy Martin. Cambridge: Cambridge University Press, 2002: pp. 167–91.

Richardson, Robert D. Jr., *Emerson: The Mind on Fire*. Berkeley, Los Angeles and London: University of California Press, 1995.

Ricoeur, Paul, *Essays on Biblical Interpretation*, ed. Lewis S. Mudge. Philadelphia: Fortress Press, 1980.

Robinson, B. P., 'Gethsemane: The Synoptic and the Johannine Viewpoints', *Church Quarterly Review*, 17 (1966), pp. 4–11.

Robinson, John A. T., *The Body: A Study in Pauline Theology*. London: SCM Press, 1952.

Rorty, Richard, *Philosophy and the Mirror of Nature*. Oxford: Blackwell, 1980.

Rose, Edward J., 'The 1839 Wilkinson Edition of Blake's *Songs* in Transcendental America', *Blake Newsletter*, 4.3 (1971), pp. 79–81.

Ruttenburg, Nancy, *Democratic Personality: Popular Voice and the Trial of American Authorship*. Stanford, Calif.: Stanford University Press, 1998.

Sanchez-Eppler, Karen, *Touching Liberty: Abolition, Feminism and the Politics of the Body*. Berkeley, Los Angeles and Oxford: University of California Press, 1993.

Scarry, Elaine, *On Beauty and Being Just*. London: Gerald Duckworth and Co., 2000.

The Body in Pain: The Making and Unmaking of the World. Oxford: Oxford University Press, 1985.

Scholl, Diane Gabrielson, 'From Aaron "Drest" to Dickinson's "Queen": Protestant Typology in Herbert and Dickinson', *The Emily Dickinson Journal*, 3.1 (1994), pp. 1–23.

Sewall, Richard, *The Life of Emily Dickinson*. Cambridge, Mass.: Harvard University Press, 1974.

Shakespeare, William, *The Complete Works*, ed. Stanley Wells and Gary Taylor. Oxford: Clarendon Press, 1988.

Shapiro, James, *Shakespeare and the Jews*. New York: Columbia University Press, 1997.

Shelley, Percy Bysshe, *Prometheus Unbound* (1820), ed. Lawrence John Zillman. Seattle, Wash.: University of Washington Press, 1959.

Shurr, William H., *The Marriage of Emily Dickinson: A Study of the Fascicles*. Lexington, Ky.: The University Press of Kentucky, 1983.

Smith, Martha Nell, *Rowing in Eden: Rereading Emily Dickinson*. Austin, Tex.: University of Texas Press, 1992.

Southwell, Charles, *The Origin, Object and Organization of the Christian Religion*. London: William Friend, [1850s].

St Armand, Barton Levi, *Emily Dickinson and her Culture: The Soul's Society*. Cambridge: Cambridge University Press, 1984.

'Veiled Ladies: Dickinson, Bettine, and Transcendental Mediumship', in *Studies in the American Renaissance*, ed. Joel Myerson. Charlottesville, Va.: University Press of Virginia, 1987.

Stack, George J., *Nietzsche and Emerson: An Elective Affinity*. Athens, OH: Ohio University Press, 1992.

Staten, Henry, *Eros in Mourning*. Baltimore and London: The Johns Hopkins University Press, 1995.

Stonum, Gary Lee, *The Dickinson Sublime*. Madison, Wisc., and London: The University of Wisconsin Press, 1990.

Stout, Janis P., *The Journey Narrative in American Literature: Patterns and Departures*. London: Greenwood Press, 1983.

Swyderski, Ann, 'Dickinson and 'that Foreign Lady – ', *Symbiosis: A Journal of Anglo-American Literary Relations*, 4.1 (2000), pp. 51–65.

‘Dickinson's Enchantment: The Barrett Browning Fascicles', *Symbiosis: A Journal of Anglo-American Literary Relations*, 7.1 (2003), pp. 76–98.

Taylor, Carol Anne, 'Kierkegaard and the Ironic Voices of Emily Dickinson', *Journal of English and Germanic Philology*, 77.4 (1978), pp. 569–81.

Taylor, John, *Icon Painting*. Oxford: Phaidon, 1979.

Tennyson, Alfred Lord, *In Memoriam* (1850). London: W. W. Norton and Co., 2004.

Thoreau, Henry David, *Walden* (1854). Oxford: Oxford University Press, 1997.

Thrall, M. E., 'Elijah and Moses in Mark's Account of the Transfiguration', *New Testament Studies*, 16 (1969–70), pp. 305–17.

Todd, John Emerson, *Emily Dickinson's Use of the Persona*. The Hague: Mouton, 1973.

Trelawney, E. J., *Recollections of the Last Days of Shelley and Byron*. Boston, Mass.: Ticknor and Fields, 1859.

Tucker, Jean, 'A Journey through the Archives of the First Church', *The First Vacation Papers Humorous and Other, Collected for Publication by his Brother G. Q. Colton*. New York: Worthington Co., 1890.

Uno, Hiroko, 'Emily Dickinson's Encounter with the East: Chinese Museum in Boston', *The Emily Dickinson Journal*, 17.1 (2008), pp. 43–67.

Virgil, *The Aeneid*, trans. C. Day Lewis, ed. Jasper Griffin. Oxford: Oxford University Press, 1952.

Wadsworth, Charles, *A Sermon preached in the Arch Street Presbyterian Church, Philadelphia, on Thanksgiving Day, November 25, 1852*. Philadelphia: Moran and Sickels, 1852.

Walker, Williston, *A History of the Christian Church*, 3rd edn. Edinburgh: T & T Clark, 1976.

Wallace, Ronald S., *Calvin's Doctrine of the Word and Sacrament*. Edinburgh: Scottish Academic Press, 1995.

Walsh, Liam G., *The Sacraments of Initiation*. London: Geoffrey Chapman, 1988.

Wand, J. W. C., *Transfiguration*. London: The Faith Press, 1967.

Weber, Hans Reudi, *The Cross: Tradition and Interpretation*. London: SPCK, 1979.

Webster, Noah, *An American Dictionary of the English Language; First Edition in Octavo, Containing the Whole Vocabulary of the Quarto, with Corrections, Improvements and Several Thousand Additional Words to which is Prefaced an Introductory Dissertation on the Origin, History and Connection of the Languages of Western Asia and Europe, with an Explanation of the Principles on which Languages are Formed*, 2 vols. New Haven: Published by the Author, 1841.

Weisbuch, Robert, *Emily Dickinson's Poetry*. Chicago and London: University of Chicago Press, 1972.

Weiskel, Thomas, *The Romantic Sublime*. Baltimore and London: The Johns Hopkins University Press, 1976.

Werner, Marta L., *Emily Dickinson's Open Folios: Scenes of Reading, Surfaces of Writing*. Ann Arbor, Mich.: University of Michigan Press, 1995.

Whitman, Walt, *Complete Poems and Prose of Walt Whitman*. Philadelphia: Ferguson Bros & Co., 1881.

Wilson, Douglas B., 'Euripides' Alcestis and the Ending of Shakespeare's *The Winter's Tale*', *Iowa State Journal of Research*, 58.3 (1984), pp. 345–55.

Wolff, Cynthia Griffin, *Emily Dickinson*. Cambridge, Mass.: Perseus, 1988.

Wolosky, Shira, *Emily Dickinson: A Voice of War*. New Haven and London: Yale University Press, 1984.

'The Metaphysics of Language in Emily Dickinson (As Translated by Paul Celan)', in *Trajectories of Mysticism in Theory and Literature*, ed. Philip Leonard. London: Macmillan, 2000: pp. 25–46.

Wright, Conrad, *The Liberal Christians: Essays on American Unitarian History*. Boston, Mass.: Beacon Press, 1970.

Wright, L. M., *Jesus the Pagan Sun God*. Swindon: Fairview Books, 1996.

Wright, N. T., *The Resurrection of the Son of God*. London: SPCK, 2003.

Wynne, Vincent W., 'Abraham's Gift: A Psychoanalytic Christology', *Journal of the American Academy of Religion*, 73.3 (2005), pp. 759–81.

Yarnold, Edward, *The Second Gift: A Study of Grace*. Slough: St Paul's Publication, 1974.

Index

Letters are referenced by number and poems by first line.

Lightning Source UK Ltd.
Milton Keynes UK
UKOW06n0742191017
311256UK00009B/201/P